Lecture Notes in Artificial Intelligence   8268

Subseries of Lecture Notes in Computer Science

LNAI Series Editors

Randy Goebel
  University of Alberta, Edmonton, Canada
Yuzuru Tanaka
  Hokkaido University, Sapporo, Japan
Wolfgang Wahlster
  DFKI and Saarland University, Saarbrücken, Ge

LNAI Founding Series Editor

Joerg Siekmann
  DFKI and Saarland University, Saarbrücken, Germany

David Riaño   Richard Lenz
Silvia Miksch   Mor Peleg   Manfred Reichert
Annette ten Teije (Eds.)

Process Support and Knowledge Representation in Health Care

AIME 2013 Joint Workshop, KR4HC 2013/ProHealth 2013
Murcia, Spain, June 1, 2013
Revised Selected Papers

 Springer

Volume Editors

David Riaño
Universitat Rovira i Virgili, Tarragona, Spain
E-mail: david.riano@urv.net

Richard Lenz
University of Erlangen-Nuremberg, Erlangen, Germany
E-mail: richard.lenz@cs.fau.de

Silvia Miksch
Vienna University of Technology, Austria
E-mail: miksch@ifs.tuwien.ac.at

Mor Peleg
University of Haifa, Israel
E-mail: morpeleg@is.haifa.ac.il

Manfred Reichert
Ulm University, Germany
E-mail: manfred.reichert@uni-ulm.de

Annette ten Teije
VU University Amsterdam, The Netherlands
E-mail: annette@cs.vu.nl

ISSN 0302-9743   e-ISSN 1611-3349
ISBN 978-3-319-03915-2   e-ISBN 978-3-319-03916-9
DOI 10.1007/978-3-319-03916-9
Springer Cham Heidelberg New York Dordrecht London

Library of Congress Control Number: 2013955017

CR Subject Classification (1998): I.2, J.3, H.4, H.5, H.2-3, C.2, D.2, J.1

LNCS Sublibrary: SL 7 – Artificial Intelligence

Typesetting: Camera-ready by author, data conversion by Scientific Publishing Services, Chennai, India

Printed on acid-free paper

Springer is part of Springer Science+Business Media (www.springer.com)

Preface

Healthcare organizations are facing the challenge of delivering high quality services to their patients at affordable costs. These challenges become more prominent with the growth in the aging population, the prevalence of chronic diseases, and the rise of healthcare costs. High degree of specialization of medical disciplines, huge amounts of medical knowledge and patient data to be consulted in order to provide evidence-based recommendations, and the need for personalized healthcare are widespread trends in this information-intensive domain. The emerging situation necessitates computer-based support for the management of healthcare processes and knowledge as well as to help clinical decision-making.

For a second time, this workshop brings together researchers from two communities who address these challenges from two different perspectives. The knowledge-representation for healthcare community, which is part of the larger medical informatics community, has been focusing on knowledge representation and reasoning to support knowledge management and clinical decision-making. This community has been developing representation methods, technologies, and tools for integrating all the important elements that health care providers work with: Electronic Medical Records (EMRs) and healthcare information systems, clinical practice guidelines, and standardized medical vocabularies. The process-oriented information systems in healthcare community, which is part of the larger business process management (BPM) community, has been studying ways to adopt BPM technology in order to provide effective solutions for healthcare process management. BPM technology has been successfully used in other sectors for establishing process-aware enterprise information systems (vs. collections of stand-alone systems for different departments in the organization). Adopting BPM technology in the healthcare sector is starting to address some of the unique characteristics of healthcare processes, including their high degree of flexibility, the integration with EMRs and shared semantics of healthcare domain concepts, and the need for tight cooperation and communication among medical care teams.

In 2012, a joint workshop was organized bringing together healthcare knowledge representation as dealt with in previous KR4HC workshops, and healthcare process support as addressed in previous ProHealth workshops, with considerable success. Participants in the joint workshop could explore the potential and the limitations of the two approaches for supporting healthcare knowledge and process management and clinical decision-making. The workshop also provided a forum wherein challenges, paradigms, and tools for optimized knowledge-based clinical process support could be debated. All the organizers and participants of the workshop agreed on the high profit of the event which encouraged us to organize a second edition of the joint workshop in 2013.

Under the same objectives of this first workshop, the new joint workshop aimed to increase the interactions between researchers and practitioners from these different, yet similar fields to improve the understanding of domain specific requirements, methods and theories, tools and techniques, and the gaps between IT support and healthcare processes yet to be closed. This forum also provided an opportunity to explore how the approaches from the two communities could be better integrated.

Providing computer-based support in healthcare is a topic that has been picking up speed for more than two decades. We are witnessing a plethora of different workshops devoted to various topics involving computer applications for healthcare. In the last years, our goal has been to try to join forces with other communities in order to learn from each other, advance science, and create a stronger and larger community. The history of the two workshops, KR4HC and ProHealth, demonstrates the efforts we have made in that direction so far.

The first KR4HC workshop, held in conjunction with the 12th Artificial Intelligence in Medicine conference (AIME 2009), brought together members of two existing communities: the clinical guidelines and protocols community, who held a line of four workshops (European Workshop on Computerized Guidelines and Protocols (CPG 2000, CPG 2004); AI Techniques in Health Care: Evidence-based Guidelines and Protocols 2006; Computer-based Clinical Guidelines and Protocols 2008) and a related community who held a series of three workshops devoted to the formalization, organization, and deployment of procedural knowledge in healthcare (CBMS 2007 Special Track on Machine Learning and Management of Health Care Procedural Knowledge 2007; From Medical Knowledge to Global Health Care 2007; Knowledge Management for Health Care Procedures 2008). Since then, two more KR4HC workshops have been held, in conjunction with the ECAI 2010 and the AIME 2011 conferences.

The first ProHealth workshop took place in the context of the 5th International Conference on Business Process Management (BPM) in 2007. The next three ProHealth Workshops were also held in conjunction with BPM conferences (BPM 2008, BPM 2009, and BPM 2011). The aim of ProHealth has been to bring together researchers from the BPM and the Medical Informatics communities. As the workshop was associated with the BPM conference that had never been attended by researchers from the Medical Informatics community, we had included Medical Informatics researchers as keynote speakers of the workshop, members of the Program Committee, and to our delight, saw a number of researchers from the Medical Informatics community actively participating in ProHealth workshops. Following the keynote talk given by Manfred Reichert from the BPM community at the Artificial Intelligence in Medicine 2011 (AIME 2011) conference, where KR4HC was held, the organizers of ProHealth and KR4HC workshops showed their interest to hold their workshops in conjunction as part of the BPM 2012 conference, which marked a landmark in the collaboration between the two communities. Now, we are continuing the efforts that started then with a second joint workshop on Knowledge Representation for Healthcare and Process-Oriented Information Systems in Healthcare (KR4HC/ProHealth).

The KR4HC/ProHealth 2013 workshop focused on IT support of high-quality healthcare processes. It addressed topics including semantic interoperability in healthcare, modeling clinical guidelines, knowledge-based techniques for handling clinical data, and content aware healthcare services and guidance.

The workshop received 19 papers from Italy (4), The Netherlands (4), Israel (3), Austria (2), Canada (2), Spain (2), Germany (1), and Norway (1). Papers had to clearly establish their research contribution as well as their relation to healthcare processes. Ten full papers were selected to be presented in the workshop according to their relevance, quality, and originality. These papers appear in this volume together with a paper by the keynote speaker, Prof. Stefan Schulz from the Institut für Medizinische Informatik, Statistik und Dokumentation, at Medizinische Universität Graz, Austria.

In his keynote paper "How Ontologies can Improve Semantic Interoperability", Prof. Schulz discussed some experiences on how semantic interoperability has been addressed through the use of standard terminologies and information models and the efforts of the Network of Excellence SemanticHealthNet to construct a generalized methodology for semantic enhancement of health care resources. Semantic enhancement consists of the annotations of those resources with OWL axioms in order to provide a semantic interpretation and also to provide interoperability among healthcare IT systems and resources. In the paper entitled "SemanticCT: A Semantically-Enabled System for Clinical Trials", the authors Z. Huang, A. ten Teije, and F. van Harmelen introduce the system SemanticCT that allows semantic integration of data for clinical trials and provides several services such as semantic search for clinical trials and patient data, finding trials for a patient, and finding patients for a trial.

Three additional papers were presented on modeling clinical practice guidelines. The paper "Identifying Patient-Action Sentences Using a Heuristic-Based Information Extraction Method", by R. Wenzina, and K. Kaiser, proposes a rule-based combination of linguistic and semantic information in order to automate the detection of condition-action textual sentences in clinical practice guidelines. This work is relevant, for example, in computerizing clinical guidelines. Secondly, the paper "Supporting Computer-Interpretable Guidelines' Modeling by Automatically Classifying Clinical Actions" by A.L. Minard, and K. Kaiser provides a comparison of several rule-based and machine learning methods to categorize the clinical actions appearing in clinical guidelines. Based on support vector machine technology, the current best supervised classification process becomes a promise to reduce the workload of modeling clinical guidelines. In the third paper, "Discovering Probabilistic Structures of Healthcare Processes", A. Hommersom, S. Verwer, and P. J. F. Lucas face the problem of capturing the uncertainty of medical protocols and disease evolutions as an automata learning process. The method proposed is tested for patients with transient ischemic attack in The Netherlands, considering patients with myocardial infarction separately from patients not diagnosed with myocardial infarction.

The next three papers focus on knowledge-based techniques for handling clinical data. In their paper "Implementation of a System for Intelligent

Summarization of Longitudinal Clinical Records", A. Goldstein and Y. Shahar describe the inner working of CliniText, a software system conceived to provide verbal summaries of electronic patient records in order to help healthcare professionals to focus on the relevant issues. In the paper, the work is mainly tested on clinical numeric data registered in the electronic record of patients with cardiac problems. In "Knowledge-Based Patient Data Generation", Z. Huang, F. van Harmelen, A. ten Teije, and K. Dentler address the challenge of synthesizing large scale patient data under a knowledge-based approach. The synthesis of realistic data is achieved by the incorporation of a knowledge-base in the domain of application that can be extracted from biomedical publications or web resources. The synthesis of data has been tested in the breast cancer domain and the data exploited by the SemanticCT tool in order to check patient eligibility for clinical trials. The paper "An Ontology-Driven Personalization Framework for Designing Theory-Driven Self-Management Interventions", by S. S. R. Abidi and S. Abidi, presents a patient-centered framework to help individuals to manage themselves their chronic diseases. An ontology is presented for modeling social cognition theory (SCT) in terms of educational issues and strategies, assessment and care personalization. This ontology was tested to provide support in a self-management program for cardiac conditions.

The last three papers focus on context-aware services and guidance. In the paper entitled "Dynamic Homecare Service Provisioning: A Field Test and its Results", by A. Zarghami, M. Zarifi, M. van Sinderen, and R. Wieringa, a platform for dynamic homecare service provisioning is proposed and validated in a field test. The paper is mainly centered in the set-up of the experiments and the analysis of the results in terms of platform adaptivity, tailorability, and evolvability. In the paper "iALARM: An Intelligent Alert Language for Activation, Response, and Monitoring of Medical Alerts" by D. Klimov and Y. Shahar, the two-tier architecture iALARM is introduced. This architecture is designed for the management of clinical alerts that are expressed in a formal language which is able to capture the target population, a declarative part describing the triggering pattern, and a procedural part defining the way the alarm must be raised. M. Iannaccone, M. Esposito, and G. De Pietro, discuss "GLM-CDS: A Standards-Based Verifiable Guideline Model for Decision Support in Clinical Applications". The set of already existing languages and systems for computer-interpretable guidelines representation and exploitation is extended in this paper with a new model, the GuideLine Model for Clinical Decision Support (GLM-CDS). The different components of GLM-CDS are discussed: the control-flow model, the information model, the terminological model, and the computer-interpretable encoding system. An example of application of the model to hypertension is provided.

To conclude, we would like to thank the invited speaker, Prof. Stefan Schulz, as well as the members of the Program Committee and the reviewers for their efforts to help us select the papers. They aided us to compile a high-quality program for the KR4HC/ProHealth 2013 workshop and a second later review for the papers to appear in this book. We would also like to acknowledge the splendid support of the local organization and the AIME 2013 workshop chairs, and the forty-three participants that registered and attended the workshop.

September 2013

David Riaño
Richard Lenz
Silvia Miksch
Mor Peleg
Manfred Reichert
Annette ten Teije

Organization

The joint international workshop KR4HC/ProHealth brought together the sixth edition of the "Workshop of Process-Oriented Information Systems in Health Care" and the fifth edition of the "Workshop on Knowledge Representation for Health Care". The edition of this book with the invited keynote and a selection of the best papers of that event was organized by David Riaño (Universitat Rovira i Virgili, Tarragona, Spain), Richard Lenz (University of Erlangen and Nuremberg, Germany), Silvia Miksch (Vienna University of Technology, Austria), Mor Peleg (University of Haifa, Israel), Manfred Reichert (University of Ulm, Germany), and Annette ten Teije (VU University Amsterdam, The Netherlands).

Program Committee

Syed Sibte Raza Abidi	Dalhousie University, Canada
Roberta Annicchiarico	Santa Lucia Hospital, Italy
Luca Anselma	Università di Torino, Italy
Joseph Barjis	TU Delft, The Netherlands
Oliver Bott	University of Applied Sciences and Art at Hanover, Germany
Fabio Campana	CAD RMB, Italy
Paul De Clercq	Medecs BV, The Netherlands
John Fox	Oxford University, UK
Arturo González-Ferrer	University of Haifa, Israel
Adela Grando	University of Edinburgh, UK
Robert A. Greenes	Harvard University, USA
Femida Gwadry-Sridhar	University of Western Ontario, Canada
Tamás Hauer	University of the West of England, UK
David Isern	Universitat Rovira i Virgili, Spain
Stefan Jablonski	Universität Bayreuth, Germany
Katharina Kaiser	Vienna University of Technology, Austria
Patty Kostkova	City University London, UK
Vassilis Koutkias	Aristotle University of Thessaloniki, Greece
Peter Lucas	University Nijmegen, The Netherlands
Wendy MacCaull	St. Francis Xavier University, Canada
Ronny Mans	Technical University of Eindhoven, The Netherlands
Mar Marcos	Universitat Jaume I, Spain
Stefani Montani	Università del Piemonte Orientale, Italy

Table of Contents

How Ontologies Can Improve Semantic Interoperability in Health Care

Stefan Schulz* and Catalina Martínez-Costa

Institute for Medical Informatics, Statistics and Documentation,
Medical University of Graz, Austria
{stefan.schulz,catalina.martinez}@medunigraz.at

Abstract. The main rationale of biomedical terminologies and formalized clinical information models is to provide semantic standards to improve the exchange of meaningful clinical information. Whereas terminologies should express context-independent meanings of domain terms, information models are built to represent the situational and epistemic contexts in which domain terms are used. In practice, semantic interoperability is encumbered by a plurality of different encodings of the same piece of clinical information. The same meaning can be represented by single codes in different terminologies, pre- and postcoordinated expressions in the same terminology, as well as by different combinations of (partly overlapping) terminologies and information models.
Formal ontologies can support the automatically recognition and processing of such heterogeneous but isosemantic expressions. In the SemanticHealthNet Network of Excellence a semantic framework is being built which addresses the goal of semantic interoperability by proposing a generalized methodology of transforming existing resources into "semantically enhanced" ones. The semantic enhancements consist in annotations as OWL axioms which commit to an upper-level ontology that provides categories, relations, and constraints for both domain entities and informational entities. Prospects and the challenges of this approach – particularly human and computational limitations – are discussed.

Keywords: Formal Ontology, Medical Terminologies, Health Care Standards.

1 Introduction

Semantic Interoperability had been defined in 2000 as "...*integrating resources that were developed using different vocabularies and different perspectives on the data. To achieve semantic interoperability, systems must be able to exchange data in such a way that the precise meaning of the data is readily accessible and the data itself can be translated by any system into a form that it understands*" [1]. Thirteen years after, the lack of semantic interoperability is, more than ever, a painful obstacle to a more rational, effective, secure, and cost-efficient data and information management in health care and biomedical research. The above citation distinguishes between

---

* Corresponding author.

D. Riaño et al. (Eds.): KR4HC 2013/ProHealth 2013, LNAI 8268, pp. 1–10, 2013.
© Springer International Publishing Switzerland 2013

vocabularies and perspectives, thus highlighting the deep-rooted division between ontology ("what there is") [2] and epistemology ("what we can know") [3]. On the level of current health informatics standards, this is mirrored by two genres of semantic resources proposed for recording health data:

- Vocabularies, i.e. artefacts that describe and systematize meanings of terms, with the common distinctions between terminologies (which provide standardized meanings), thesauri (which introduce semantic relations between (groups of) terms), ontologies (which provide formulations of the properties and relations of domain entities [4], as denoted by domain terms), and classifications (which introduce exhaustive partitions for statistical purposes).
- Information models, which are representational artefacts that provide standardized structure (section, entry, cluster, etc.) and context (diagnosis, past history, medication order) for data acquired for a given purpose.

Typical vocabularies are the MeSH thesaurus [5], the OBO foundry ontologies [6], SNOMED CT [7], and classification systems like ICD-10 [8]. Typical information models are the ones provided by the openEHR [9] specification and the standards EN13606 [10] and HL7 [11].

To cite an example, the clinical expression "*Suspected Heart failure caused by ischemic heart disease*" would then have two components, the terminology component "*Heart failure caused by ischemic heart disease*", which is a term, which – ontologically – denotes all individual heart failure conditions caused by ischemic heart disease, and the epistemic component "*Suspected*", which expresses that the clinician has – according to the diagnostic results collected for a particular patient – a certain belief but no certainty that the patient under scrutiny hosts a medical condition of a certain type.

According to the vocabulary/information model distinction, each component should be expressed by the respective representational artefact, and the binding between both parts should be done in a uniform way. However, what we observe in practice rarely follows this paradigm. Clinical terminologies often assign a single code to complex phrases such "*Suspected Heart failure caused by ischemic heart disease*" (SNOMED CT) or "*Tuberculosis of larynx, trachea and bronchus, without mention of bacteriological or histological confirmation*" (ICD-10). In other cases a post-coordination syntax is used, such as in SNOMED CT:
84114007 | *heart failure* |: 408729009 | *finding context* |: 415684004 | *suspected* |: 42752001 | *due to* |: 414545008 | *ischaemic heart disease* |.

Fig. 1 demonstrates the different flavours of representing clinical information from the perspective of the end user. There are good reasons to tailor data acquisition forms to the users' needs and to the terminologies they are familiar with. But how can such different rendering of the same information content be reduced to an interoperable semantic representation?

Fig. 1. Heterogeneous representations of the same clinical content

This problem is addressed by the project SemanticHealthNet [12], proposing an engineering approach based on formal ontologies, using the description logics [13] language OWL-DL [14] as standardized by the Semantic Web community. Supported by easy-to-use editing tools and reasoning engines, OWL is a well-established language in biomedical ontology research and practice. SemanticHealthNet aims at developing, on a European level, a scalable and sustainable organisational and governance process for the semantic interoperability of clinical and biomedical information. The goal is to ensure that EHR systems are optimised for patient care, public health and clinical research across healthcare systems and institutions. SemanticHealthNet focuses on a cardiovascular use case, upon which the capture of the needs for evidence-based, patient-centred integrated care and for public health is based, capitalizing on existing European consensus in the management of chronic heart failure and cardiovascular prevention. Experts in EHR architectures, clinical data structures, terminologies and ontology take part of the project and tailor and pilot their best-of-breed resources in response to the needs articulated by clinicians.

2   Methods

For the purpose of interoperable descriptions within SemanticHealthNet we aim at formally describing the meaning of Health Record information entities. Each (atomic) information entity is semantically annotated, using one or more OWL DL expressions which follow predefined representational patterns. The content of these annotations addresses epistemic information (viz. whether the information is confirmed or speculative, whether it has been reported by the patient or by a caregiver, or whether it refers to the current or a past situation) and it is equally linked to clinical expressions such as the codes or combination of codes in terminologies like SNOMED CT.

Our approach to ontology follows a series of principles (cf. [15]):

- Ontologies are formal-mathematical systems that precisely describe (classes of) entities of a domain as they exist in reality [4]. This requires that the modeller always has to analyse which entities really exist. The question "what exists?" is crucial [2]. For instance, in our above example what certainly exists is the informational entity, which expresses a physician's state of knowledge related to a given type of disease. However, the existence of this disease in the reality of the patient under treatment is not guaranteed when it is referred to as "suspected". (Even the attribution "confirmed" to a diagnostic statement does not preclude a certain risk of diagnostic error).

- Each representational unit in an ontology has a strict ontological commitment supported by pairwise disjoint and exhaustive upper-level categories (process, material object, quality, information entity...); a closed set of basic relations such as 'is part of', 'has participant', 'is bearer of'; constraining axioms such as that a process can only have processes as parts but not as participants.
- There is a strict bipartition between classes and individuals; what is a class and an individual is given by the domain and not at the discretion of the modeller, given that the upper level ontology provides precise elucidations of what each category means.
- Full class definitions are aimed at, as far as possible, following the Aristotelian genus / differentia principle [16].
- Naming conventions are followed, aiming at choosing self-explaining and non-ambiguous natural language identifiers [17].
- Complexity is reduced, as much as possible, by identifying reusable ontology design patterns [18].

We have chosen the upper level ontology BioTopLite [19], which provides general classes, relations (object properties), and constraints, using the description logics dialect OWL-DL [14]. Under the BioTopLite category *Information object* all (structural) information models are represented, whereas the SNOMED CT classes are placed under other BioTopLite categories like *Condition*, *Quality*, etc.

The representational challenge is two-fold. First, we have to analyse the exact meaning of the "binding" between representational artefacts and entities in a medical ontology. Second, we have to create patterns for the different distributions of content between information models and ontologies. These patterns should allow the formation of semantically equivalent (isosemantic) expressions, to be ascertained by machine reasoning. As shown in Fig. 2, information entities of clinical models will be annotated (i.e. semantically enhanced) with OWL-DL expressions conforming to certain predefined patterns, based on the proposed ontological infrastructure. These patterns are added to clinical models during their creation, in order to be filled with patient data given an appropriate software tool support. As a result, each model will have a set of annotations, which will be further processed by description logics reasoners. Finally, a query system will allow performing homogeneous queries to retrieve patient data from heterogeneously represented datasets.

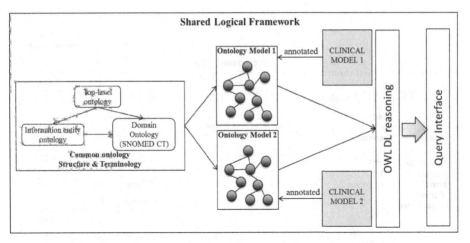

Fig. 2. Shared logical framework proposed in SemanticHealthNet

3   Results

A view of an ontology as a formal account of "what exists" reaches its boundaries when it is expected to represent statements about what does not exist, or about what only exists to a certain degree of likelihood. We reiterate that the latter abounds in medicine, where diagnoses derive from the results of clinical, lab, and imaging findings, which, synoptically, make the presence of a certain disorder very likely, but nevertheless carry a certain degree of uncertainty.

A recorded statement "Dr X suspects that Y suffers from heart failure" is, strictly spoken, a second-order statement. The subject-matter of Dr X's utterance is a sentence for which the truth-value remains undefined (the meaning of the verb "suspects", insinuates certain likelihood for a positive truth value).

As there is no way in OWL-DL to express such statements, we have suggested an approximation, the validity of which is, however, still subject to investigations. Let **d** be a diagnostic statement instance and S a clinical situation type referred to:

> **d** rdf:type '*Diagnostic statement*' and
>   **'has information quality'** some *Suspected* and
>   **'is about situation'** only *S*

The use of the value restriction ('only' in Manchester Syntax) reduces the type of the clinical situation to S. However, it does not require that S is instantiated, which would be the case with the connector 'some'.

The information instance **d**, as such is characterized as a member of the class '*Information entity*', which is further specified by the attribute class *Suspected*.

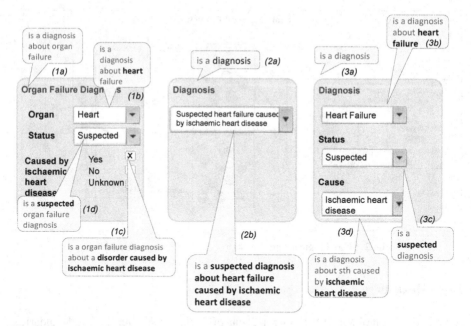

Fig. 3. Three isosemantic representations (see Fig. 1), with free-text annotations attached, each of which with a pointer to a corresponding OWL-DL representation (1a- 3d) in the text

Fig. 3 enhances Fig. 1 by semi-formal free text annotations. Both fixed and variable elements (in bold) are referred to in the annotations, and each one can be translated into an OWL-DL axiom. Each form corresponds to one information entity instance, viz. **d1** (left), **d2** (center), and **d3** (right), and is defined by the conjunction of its annotations. Following the axioms for each of the three forms are provided.

d1 rdf:type *'Diagnostic statement'* and **'is about situation'** only *'Organ failure'*   (1a)

d1 rdf:type *'Diagnostic statement'* and **'is about situation'** only *'Heart failure'*   (1b)

d1 rdf:type *'Diagnostic statement'* and **'is about situation'** only (*'Disorder'*   (1c)
and **'caused by'** some *'Ischaemic heart disease'*)

d1 rdf:type *'Diagnostic statement'* and **'is about situation'** only *'Organ failure'*   (1d)
and **'has information quality'** some *'Suspected'*

d2 rdf:type *'Diagnostic statement'*   (2a)

d2 rdf:type *'Diagnostic statement'* and **'is about situation'** only (*'Heart failure'*   (2b)
and **'caused by'** some *'Ischaemic heart disease'*)
and **'has information quality'** some *'Suspected'*

d3 rdf:type *'Diagnostic statement'*   (3a)

d3 rdf:type *'Diagnostic statement'* and **'is about situation'** only *'Heart failure'*   (3b)

d3 rdf:type *'Diagnostic statement'*
      and **'has information quality'** some *'Suspected'*   (3c)

d3 rdf:type *'Diagnostic statement'* and **'is about situation'** only (*'Disorder'*
      and **'caused by'** some *'Ischaemic heart disease'*)   (3d)

The above axioms have been defined by following a predefined pattern for representing a clinical diagnosis statement:

'Diagnostic statement' **subClassOf**
   'Information Entity'
      and **'has information quality'** some *'CertaintyAttributeC'*
      and **'outcome of'** some *'DiagnosticProcedureD'*
      and **'is about situation'** only *'Clinical SituationX'*

The expressions that end with a single capital letter represent variable parts, which can be filled in with specific clinical data (e.g. *'Suspected'* for *'CertaintyAttributeC'*, or the expression *'Heart failure'* and **'caused by'** some *'Ischaemic heart disease'* for *'ClinicalSituationX'*).

In a first study, we have identified the following seven patterns described in Table 1. They can be further specialised, as it is the case of the above one, used to represent a diagnostic statement and a specialisation of the pattern PT.1 shown in the table below.

Table 1. Initial set of patterns identified

Pattern ID	Pattern description
PT.1	Information about clinical situation with condition present
PT.2	Information about clinical situation with condition absent
PT.3	Information about quality
PT.4	Information about past clinical situation
PT.5	Information about no past clinical situation
PT.6	Plan to perform a process
PT.7	Clinical process

The use of patterns and their representation in OWL DL allows using DL reasoning to compare different distributions of content between information models and ontologies, in order to test whether they are semantically equivalent. For instance, a DL reasoner will infer that the three sample forms in Fig. 3, together with the values selected, refer to the diagnosis of heart failure caused by ischemic heart disease, independently of their representation as a pre-coordinated expression in SNOMED CT or by means of heterogeneous combination of information model structures. This means that the following DL query example will retrieve the three information entity instances **d1**, **d2** and **d3**:

'Diagnostic statement' and **'is about situation'** only (*'Heart failure'*
and **'caused by'** some *'Ischaemic heart disease'*)
and **'has information quality'** some *'Suspected'*

4 Conclusions

Semantic interoperability of clinical information remains a largely unresolved issue. Both vocabularies and information models have been developed as semantic representations of structured clinical information. When bound together, syntactically diverse representations emerge, from which semantic equivalence can hardly be inferred. A solution proposed in the EU Network of Excellence SemanticHealthNet is based on formal ontologies using the description logics language OWL-DL. The basic idea is to add semantic annotations to atomic information entities. These annotations are OWL DL expressions which describe both informational and clinical entities, and which are rooted in the upper level ontology BioTopLite. The binding of both kinds of entities would, ideally, be achieved by a second-order expressivity, which, however is not supported by the language. This restriction is currently being circumvented by using OWL value restrictions.

The annotations follow a set of predefined patterns, which aim at explicitly stating what is represented by each representational artefact (i.e. vocabulary/information model). As they are described using a DL-based language, formal reasoning can be used to infer semantic equivalence even for quite different distributions of content between information models and ontologies, as well as different degrees of (pre/post)-coordination.

The SemanticHealthNet approach uses semantic artefacts as they exist and as they are used in practice. This descriptive approach is different from several attempts to pursue semantic interoperability by providing strict guidance how clinical information should be represented, which often turned out to be impracticable. An example of this is TermInfo [20], which attempts to solve the overlapping between the SNOMED CT and LOINC terminologies, and the HL7 information models. Other projects and initiatives that follow a more prescriptive approach are CIMI [21], CEM [22], LRA [23] or DCMs [24]. Although SemanticHealthNet values such standardization efforts, it works on the less optimistic hypothesis that current as well as future systems that represent clinical information will continue using different EHR models (proprietary or based on some standard), and that the cost of implementing a map to a "canonical" model that supports semantic interoperability will be too high. Instead, SemanticHealthNet proposes a semantic layer, which provides a consistent semantic representation of clinical information, but which is independent of a given information model standard and could even comply with information extracted from clinical narratives by advanced language technologies.

Nevertheless, we are aware of two kinds of significant bottlenecks, which will require special attention. First, human factors matter insofar as the semantic annotations of information model components and values require considerable intellectual effort.

We postulate that the use of semantic patterns can mitigate this effort, as it presents a simplified representation for the user from which OWL expressions are automatically generated. The task would therefore boil down to the selection of the patterns to be used by clinical models. Ideally this could be supported by appropriate clinical model editing tools.

Second, reasoning performance has to be controlled. OWL DL entailment is known to be complete for NEXPTIME, which limits its scalability. However, preliminary tests in SemanticHealthNet, using OWL-DL design patterns for the SNOMED CT context model [25] on medium-size ontology modules have shown favourable runtime performance. Besides, DL reasoning does not perform well with a big amount of instance data, which would make SPARQL [26] the query language of choice. However, SPARQL does not support most of OWL entailments, which means that it lacks reasoning capabilities which are essential in our approach. Other alternatives and query languages, e.g. combinations of SPARQL with OWL have to be further investigated.

Summing up, SemanticHealthNet is breaking new ground by consequently using Semantic Web techniques, above all description logics, as an intermediate representation for both ontological and epistemic aspects of the electronic health record. The main goal is to address the needs for an improved interoperability of clinical data, which is an important prerequisite for clinical data management and research support in the beginning era of data-intensive personalized medicine. Still in an experimental phase, SemanticHealthNet is currently focussing on the representation of a heart failure summary. Although it could be shown that semantic interoperability can be supported, the technological uptake of this approach will require a series of challenges (human, computational) to be met, as well as a consensus process within a heterogeneous group of stakeholders.

Acknowledgements. This work has been funded by the SemanticHealthNet Network of Excellence within the EU 7th Framework Program, Call: FP7-ICT- 2011-7, agreement 288408. http://www.semantichealthnet.eu/

References

1. Heflin, J., Hendler, J.: Semantic Interoperability on the Web (2000), http://www.cs.umd.edu/projects/plus/SHOE/pubs/extreme2000.pdf (last accessed July 17, 2013)
2. Quine, W.V.: On what there is. In: Gibson, R. (ed.) Quintessence-Basic Readings from the Philosophy of W. V. Quine. Belknap Press, Cambridge (2004)
3. Bodenreider, O., Smith, B., Burgun, A.: The Ontology - Epistemology Divide: A Case Study in Medical Terminology. In: Proceedings of FOIS 2004, pp. 185–195. IOS Press, Amsterdam (2004)
4. Hofweber, T.: Logic and Ontology. In: Zalta, E.N. (ed.) The Stanford Encyclopedia of Philosophy, 2013th edn. (Spring 2013), http://plato.stanford.edu/archives/spr2013/entries/logic-ontology/ (last accessed July 17, 2013)
5. United States National Library of Medicine (NLM). Medical Subject Headings, MeSH (2013), http://www.nlm.nih.gov/mesh (last accessed July 17, 2013)

6. Smith, B., Ashburner, M., Rosse, C., Bard, J., Bug, W., Ceusters, W., Goldberg, L.J., Eilbeck, K., Ireland, A., Mungall, C.J.: OBI Consortium. In: Leontis, N., Rocca-Serra, P., Ruttenberg, A., Sansone, S.A., Scheuermann, R.H., Shah, N., Whetzel, P.L., Lewis, S. (eds.) The OBO Foundry: Coordinated Evolution of Ontologies to Support Biomedical Data Integration. Nature Biotechnology, vol. 25(11), pp. 1251–1255 (November 2007)
7. Systematized Nomenclature of Medicine - Clinical Terms, SNOMED CT (2008), http://www.ihtsdo.org/snomed-ct (last accessed July 17, 2013)
8. World Health Organization (WHO). International Classification of Diseases (ICD) (2013), http://www.who.int/classifications/icd (last accessed July 17, 2013)
9. OpenEHR. An open domain-driven platform for developing flexible e-health systems, http://www.openehr.org (last accessed July 17, 2013)
10. En13606 Association, http://www.en13606.org/ (last accessed July 17, 2013)
11. Health Level Seven International, http://www.hl7.org/ (last accessed July 17, 2013)
12. SemanticHealthNet Network of Excellence, http://www.semantichealthnet.eu/ (last accessed July 17, 2013)
13. Baader, F., Calvanese, D., McGuinness, D.L., Nardi, D., Patel-Schneider, P.F.: The Description Logic Handbook. Theory, Implementation, and Applications, 2nd edn. Cambridge University Press, Cambridge (2007)
14. W3C OWL working group. OWL 2 Web Ontology Language, Document Overview. W3C Recommendation (December 11, 2012), http://www.w3.org/TR/owl2-overview/ (last accessed July 17, 2013)
15. Schulz, S., Jansen, L.: Formal ontologies in biomedical knowledge representation. Yearbook of Medical Informatics (2013)
16. Cohen, S.M.: Aristotle's metaphysics. Stanford Encyclopedia of Philosophy (2012), http://plato.stanford.edu/entries/aristotle-metaphysics/ (last accessed July 17, 2013)
17. Schober, D., Smith, B., Lewis, S.E., Kusnierczyk, W., Lomax, J., Mungall, C., Taylor, C.F., Rocca-Serra, P., Sansone, S.A.: Survey-based naming conventions for use in OBO Foundry ontology development. BMC Bioinformatics 10, 125 (2009)
18. Seddig-Raufie, D., Jansen, L., Schober, D., Boeker, M., Grewe, N., Schulz, S.: Proposed actions are no actions: re-modeling an ontology design pattern with a realist top-level ontology. J. Biomed. Semantics 3(suppl. 2), S2 (2012)
19. Schulz, S., Boeker, M.: BioTopLite: An Upper Level Ontology for the Life Sciences. In: Evolution, Design and Application. Workshop on Ontologies and Data in Life Sciences, Koblenz, Germany, September 19-20 (2013)
20. TermInfo Project, http://www.hl7.org/special/committees/terminfo/ (last accessed July 17, 2013)
21. Clinical Information Modeling Initiative (CIMI), http://informatics.mayo.edu/CIMI/ (last accessed July 17, 2013)
22. Clinical Element Model (CEM), http://informatics.mayo.edu/sharp/ (last accessed July 17, 2013)
23. Logical Record Architecture (LRA), http://www.connectingforhealth.nhs.uk/systemsandservices/data/lra (last accessed July 17, 2013)
24. Detailed Clinical Models (DCMs), http://www.detailedclinicalmodels.nl/ (last accessed July 17, 2013)
25. Martínez Costa, C., Schulz, S.: Ontology-based reinterpretation of the SNOMED CT context model. In: Fourth International Conference in Biomedical Ontologies (ICBO 2013), Montreal, Canada, July 6-9 (2013)
26. SPARQL Query Language For RDF. W3C Recommendation (January 15, 2008), http://www.w3.org/TR/rdf-sparql-query/ (last accessed July 17, 2013)

SemanticCT: A Semantically-Enabled System for Clinical Trials

Zhisheng Huang, Annette ten Teije, and Frank van Harmelen

Department of Computer Science,
VU University Amsterdam, The Netherlands
{huang,annette,Frank.van.Harmelen}@cs.vu.nl

Abstract. In this paper, we propose an approach of semantically enabled systems for clinical trials. The goals are not only to achieve the interoperability by semantic integration of heterogeneous data in clinical trials, but also to facilitate automatic reasoning and data processing services for decision support systems in various settings of clinical trials. We have implemented the proposed approach in a system called *SemanticCT*. SemanticCT is built on the top of LarKC (Large Knowledge Collider), a platform for scalable semantic data processing. SemanticCT has been integrated with large-scale trial data and patient data, and provided various automatic services for clinical trials, which include automatic patient recruitment service (i.e., identifying eligible patients for a trial) and trial finding service (i.e., finding suitable trials for a patient).

1 Introduction

Clinical trials provide tests which generate safety and efficacy data for health interventions. Clinical trials usually involve large-scale and heterogeneous data. The lack of integration and of semantic interoperability among the systems of clinical trials and the systems of patient data, i.e. electronic health record (EHRs) and clinical medical records (CMRs), is the main source of inefficiency of clinical trial systems. Thus, many procedures in clinical trials, such as patient recruitment (i.e., identifying eligible patients for a trial) and trial finding (i.e., finding suitable trials for a patient), have been considered to be laborious.

Enhancing clinical trial systems with semantic technology to achieve the semantic interoperability of large-scale and heterogeneous data would improve the performance of clinical trials significantly. Those semantically-enabled systems would achieve efficient and effective reasoning and data processing services in various settings of clinical trials systems.

In this paper, we propose an approach of semantically enabled systems for clinical trials. The proposed approach has been implemented in the system called *SemanticCT*[1]. The system provides semantic integration of various data in clinical trials. The system is designed to be a semantically enabled system of decision support for various scenarios in medical applications. SemanticCT has been semantically integrated with various data, which include various trial documents

---

[1] http://wasp.cs.vu.nl/sct

D. Riaño et al. (Eds.): KR4HC 2013/ProHealth 2013, LNAI 8268, pp. 11–25, 2013.
© Springer International Publishing Switzerland 2013

with semantically annotated eligibility criteria and large amount of patient data with structured EHR and clinical medical records. Well-known medical terminologies and ontologies, such as SNOMED, LOINC, etc., have been used for the semantic interoperability.

SemanticCT is built on the top of LarKC (Large Knowledge Collider), a platform for scalable semantic data processing[2]. With the built-in reasoning support for large-scale RDF/OWL data of LarKC, SemanticCT is able to provide various reasoning and data processing services for clinical trials, which include faster identification of eligible patients for recruitment service and efficient identification of eligible trials for patients.

The contribution of this paper is: (1) a framework that enables semantic technologies for medical tasks related to the domain of clinical trials. (2) a proof of concept of the framework by SemanticCT with a focus on three tasks: (i) semantic search for clinical trials and patient data,(ii) trial finding for patients, (iii) identifying patients for a trial.

This paper is organized as follows: Section 2 presents the general ideas of semantically enabled systems for clinical trials. In section 3 we focus on three tasks in the clinical trial domain: search in clinical trials and patient data, trial finding for patients and identifying eligible patients for trials. Section 4 describes a formalization of eligibility criteria of clinical trials. Section 5 proposes the architecture of SemanticCT and describes various services and interfaces of the system. Section 6 discusses the related work and make the conclusions.

2   Approach

The goal of SemanticCT is to exploit semantic techniques in the domain of medical trials such that several tasks like trial finding and identifying eligible patients for trials can be supported. In this section we describe the semantic data integration and the platform. Notice that we use existing semantic technologies, available medical ontologies, data sources, and semantic annotaters.

2.1   Semantic Data Integration

Semantic data integration of various data in clinical trials is a basic step to build a semantically enabled system for clinical trials. Many existing trial data are usually represented as XML data with the standard fields. For example, the clinical trial service in the U.S. National Institutes of Health[3] provides the structured CDISC 20 fields of XML-encoded trial data. We can convert those XML data into standard semantic data, like RDF NTriple data with the annotations of medical ontologies or terminologies, like SNOMED, LOINC, MESH and others. Those ontologies can be used individually, or in a group with the ontology alignments which are provided by the BioPortal ontology service[4] or

---

[2] http://www.larkc.eu

[3] http://www.clinicaltrials.gov

[4] http://bioportal.bioontology.org/

other alignment tools. LinkedCT[5] provides large-scale semantic data of clinical trials with the standard formats of Linked Open Data in the Semantic Web.

The semantic annotations of clinical trials can be obtained by using many semantic annotation tools/systems, which have been developed by the community of the Semantic Web. BioPortal and MetaMap[6] provide satisfying services for semantic annotations with biomedical ontologies. Those annotation data are also represented as XML ones. Similarly it is easy to use XSLT to convert those XML encoded data into RDF NTriple ones. This means that for semantic interoperability we can exploit the available mappings among ontologies or to load an own allignment as RDF NTriples.

Some EHR prototype systems have been developed to support some kinds of semantics-enriched patient data. Those patient data can be accessed via the servers provided by those systems. However, real patient data are usually protected and not allowed for public access, because of the legal issue and privacy reason. We have developed a knowledge-based patient data generator which can synthesize required patient data for the purpose of tests by using some domain knowledge to control the data generation and make the generated data look like realistic ones[6].

In the paper we take three tasks into account: search in clinical trials or patient records, trial finding for patients, and identifying eligible patients for trials. For our feasibility tests we use clinical trials of breast cancer and we integrated the following data in SemanticCT:

Clinical Trials. We got the XML-encoded data of 4665 clinical trials of breast cancer from the official NCT website www.clinicaltrials.gov, and used XSLT to convert the XML-encoded data into RDF NTriple data, which consists of 1,200,565 triples and 335, 507 entities.

Medical Ontologies. We got the latest release of SNOMED terminologies and converted them into RDF NTriple data. The concepts and definitions of converted SNOMED consists of 4,048,457 triples, which correspond with 2,046,810 entities.

Semantic Annotations of Clinical Trials. We used the semantic annotation server of BioPortal to obtain the XML-encoded semantic annotations of the 4665 clinical trials with the medical terminologies/ontologies such as SNOMED, LOINC, HL7, MESH, RxNorm, and EVS. We converted the semantic annotation data into RDF NTriple. The total data size is about 3.0 GB. For the experiment, we load the semantic annotation data with the SNOMED concepts only. This part of data consists of 106,334 triples (454MB data).

Patient Data. We used APDG (Advanced Patient Data Generator), a knowledge-based patient data generator, to create 10,000 patient data of breast cancer, which cover the main properties of female breast cancer patients, like demographic data (e.g., gender and age), diagnosis, TNM stage (T for primary tumor, N for regional lymph nodes, and M for distant metastasis), hormone

---

[5] http://linkedct.org/
[6] http://metamap.nlm.nih.gov/

receptor status, e.g., the status of ER (Estrogen Receptor), PR (Progesterone Receptor), and HER2 (Human Epidermal Growth Factor Receptor 2), etc. We have collected the domain knowledge from medical literature (like PubMed) and web pages (like those from Wikipedia) and encoded those domain knowledge to control the generation of patient data and make the generated patient data look like realistic ones[6]. The generated patient data set consists of 660,000 triples.

Thus, the total loaded RDF NTriple data are over 6 million triples. It is sufficient for a demonstration prototype which runs at an ordinary laptop (dual core and 4GB memory) with extremely good performance. Most SPARQL queries in SemanticCT can be finished within one second. Thus, the time performance is not a big issue. What we concern mainly is whether such an approach can be used for supporting clinical trial tasks by developing a trial finding service and a patient recruitment service.

2.2 Semantic Platform

There have been several well-developed triple stores which can be used to serve as a semantic platform to build SPARQL endpoints for the services of querying over large-scale semantic data. Well-known triple stores are OWLIM[7] and Virtuoso[8]. Those triple stores usually support for basic RDFS reasoning over semantic data.

LarKC is a platform for scalable semantic data processing. OWLIM is used to be the basic data layer of LarKC. LarKC fulfills the needs in sectors that are dependent on massive heterogeneous information sources such as telecommunication services, biomedical research, and drug-discovery[4]. The platform has a pluggable architecture in which it is possible to exploit techniques and heuristics from diverse areas such as databases, machine learning, cognitive science, the Semantic Web, and others. LarKC provides a number of pluggable components: retrieval, abstraction, selection, reasoning and deciding. In LarKC, massive, distributed and necessarily incomplete reasoning is performed over web-scale knowledge sources[9]. One of our clinical trial task requires a new reasoning component (see section 4) which can be plugged in the LarKC platform.

3 Tasks in Clinical Trial Domain

There are a large number of tasks in the domain of clinical trials. In this paper we focus on the tasks search, trial finding for patients and identifying eligible patients for trials with the main question in mind whether the approach of semantically enabled system for clinical trials can support those knowledge intensive tasks.

3.1 Search

SemanticCT provides various search services over large-scale integrated data: clinical trials, medical ontologies and patient data (see section 2.1).

---

[7] http://www.ontotext.com/owlim
[8] http://virtuoso.openlinksw.com/

The semantic integration is realised by several available medical ontologies and mappings between those ontologies from BioPortal. We also provide the service for browsing semantically annotated eligibility criteria of trials, search services for patient data browsing and specific patient finding, such as, show all triple-negative breast cancer patients. These search facilities are all realized by enabling semantic technologies into the domain of clinical trials.

3.2 Trial Finding for Patients

The trial finding service is one which searches for suitable trials for a given patient. Namely, based on the patient data, the system will check the requirement of clinical trials with the patient data to see whether or not the trial can be considered as a candidate trial for further deliberation by the patient and the clinician to make the decision. Some requirements (such as gender and age) have been structured in the original XML data. Some of those requirements are stated in the eligibility criteria (i.e., inclusion criteria or exclusion criteria), which are represented in natural language text. There are different approaches to deal with the information in text. We can either use SPARQL queries with regular expressions over eligibility criteria, or SPARQL queries directly over semantic annotations of eligibility criteria, or formalize the text by using some kind of formalization to make the structured eligibility criteria.

Given a patient data, it seems to be ideal to check if all the properties of a patient meets the requirements of a trial. However, we have found that it is not necessary, because checking with a few properties are sufficient to reduce significant amount of candidate trials and result in a small amount of trials for further deliberation.

For the experiment, we select just a small set of checking items, which consists of some structured fields, such as demographic data (gender and age), and some unstructured data (i.e., those in the text of eligibility criteria) such as stage, menopausal status, and hormone receptor status. The latter can be checked by using regular expressions with filters in SPARQL queries. Of course, we are interested in the trials which are currently recruiting, rather than those which have been completed. Thus, the initial SPARQL query of trial finding for a female patient aged 40 at stage 2 can be represented as follows:

```
PREFIX ...
select distinct ?ctid ?summary ?criteria
where { ?ct rdf:type sct:ClinicalTrial.
?ct sct:NCTID ?ctid.
?ct sct:EligibilityGender 'Female'.
?ct sct:OverallStatus "Recruiting".
?ct sct:EligibilityMinAge ?minage.
?ct sct:EligibilityMaxAge ?maxage.
?ct sct:BriefSummary ?summary.
?ct sct:EligibilityCriteriaTextblock ?criteria.
FILTER(?minage <= '40 Years'&& ?maxage >= '40 Years').
FILTER regex(str(?criteria), 'stage 2').}
```

In the query above, the regex 'stage 2' is used to match the stage in the eligibility criteria. The way of text matching is not sufficient to find all the targeted information. We can extend the regular expressions to cover various expressions which talk about the stage in natural language text. It is quite clear that we cannot exhaust all the expressions which talk about the stage in natural language text. Furthermore, the query cannot make a distinction between the text appears in inclusion criteria and that in exclusion criteria, unless we introduce more complex regular expressions which can detect the beginning and the ending of those criteria.

We add checking on more properties of patients, like menopausal status and hormone receptor status. That would reduce more candidate trials. Such reduction is very useful for clinicians. Figure 6 summarizes the results of trial finding of 4667 breast cancer trials with those selected properties for 11 randomly selected tests. Actually each test represents a type of patients with their corresponding properties. From the figure, we know that the selection of trials based on age and stage give already a large reduction (on average 20 trials remains), adding menopausal status reduces a bit more (on average 19 trials remains), adding HR status reduces again a little more (on average 15 trials remains). With this rather limited set of patient properties (namely age, stage, menopausal status and HR status) the maximal number of candidate trials is 28 (patient 6) and the minimal number of candidate trials is 3 (patient 10). We have also detected the problem that some item checking by regular expressions cannot deal with negation information correctly, in particular, for those appear in exclusion criteria. For example, for checking on 'hormone receptor status', four trials have been mistakenly identified (one in patient test 1,8,9,11).

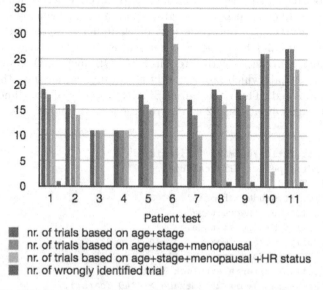

Fig. 1. Trial Finding for Patient by SPARQL Queries with Regular Expression

Table 1. Selection of number of trials on average for trial finding for patients by SPARQL Queries with Regular Expressions

	Nr. of trials	% of trials	Min	Max
total breast cancer trials:	4667	100%		
selection on Age+Stage:	20	0.42%	11	32
selection on Age+Stage+MenoPausal Status:	19	0.40%	11	32
selection on Age+Stage+MenoPausal Status+HR status:	15	0.32%	3	28

This feasibility test shows us that SPARQL queries with regular expressions are useful and promising to select trials for a specific patient.

3.3   Identifying Eligible Patients for Trials

Another task is to provide faster identification service of eligible patients for clinical trials. That requires the formalization of eligibility criteria, so that matching patient data with formalized eligibility criteria for automatic identification of clinical trials for patients. In [5] we propose a rule-based formalization for eligibility criteria, which is briefly discussed in the next section 4.

We have picked up 10 clinical trials randomly and formalized their eligibility criteria by using the rule-based formalization. We have tested the system for automatically identifying eligible patients for those selected trials. The system is able to find minimally 241 patients and maximally 750 patients out of the 10,000 patients for each trial, within less five seconds, for the system which is running on an ordinary laptop (dual core and 4GB memory)[5]. This formalization is also useful for trial finding service, because it can provide exactly matching on the data, without relying on exhaustive regular expression patterns. This feasibility test shows us that rule-based formalization of eligibility criteria for identifying eligible patients for trials is doable in an effective and efficient way. Clearly the next step is to set-up an experiment with real patient data and validation of the results with a clinician.

4   Rule-Based Reasoning

For reasoning over various semantic data for clinical trials, SPARQL queries are not always powerful and flexible enough to specify complex requirements of eligibility criteria. In the experiments with automatic identification of eligible patients, we have observed that SPARQL queries with regular expressions are not always sufficient, for instance, for checking eligibility criteria.

For example, in order to check if an eligibility criteria require a patient of the stage 2 breast cancer, we have to use a regular expression to cover various expressions which talk about the stage in natural language text, like this:

```
FILTER regex(str(?criteria),
'stage 2|stage II |stage 0, 1, 2|stage I, II|stage IIa|stage IIb')
```

As we have discussed before, it is quite clear that we cannot exhaust all the expressions which talk about the stage in natural language text. Therefore, that would result in some eligibility criteria uncheckable at the run time (i.e., querying time). We have developed a rule-based formalization of eligibility criteria for clinical trials[5], so that eligibility criteria in natural language text can be processed offline, i.e., when their formalizations are generated.

Compared with existing formalizations, the rule-based formalization is more efficient and effective, because of the declarative form, easy maintenance, reusability and expressivity[5].

There exist various rule languages which can be used for the formalization of eligibility criteria. In the researches of artificial intelligence, logic programming languages, like Prolog, are well known and popular rule-based languages. Several rule-based languages, like SWRL [9] and RIF[10], have been proposed for the semantics-enable rule-based language. In biomedical domain, the Arden syntax [11] has been developed to formalize rule-like medical knowledge. However, compared with logic programming language Prolog, both SWRL, RIF and the Arden syntax have very limited functionalities for data processing.

In SemanticCT, the rule-based formalization is developed based on the logic programming language Prolog. We select the SWI-Prolog[12] as the basic language for the rule-based formalization of eligibility criteria, because of its Semantic Web support and powerful processing facilities [8].

We formalize the knowledge rules of the specification of eligibility criteria of clinical trials with respect to the following different levels of knowledge: trial-specific knowledge, domain-specific knowledge, and common knowledge.

Trial-Specific Knowledge. Trial-specific knowledge are those rules which specify the concrete details of the eligibility criteria of a specific clinical trial. Those criteria are different from a trial to another trial.

Given a patient ID, we suppose that we can obtain its patient data through the common knowledge of the interface with SPARQL endpoints and its internal data storage. Thus, in order to check if a patient meets an inclusion criterion, we can check if its patient data meet the criterion.

Furthermore, we would not expect to check all the criteria with respect to the patient data, because some of those required data may be missing in the patient data. We introduce a special predicate getNotYetCheckedItems to collect those criteria which have not yet been formalized for the trial.

For example, the inclusion criteria in the trial NCT00002720 can be formalized as follows:

```
meetInclusionCriteria(_PatientID, PatientData, CT,
            NotYetCheckedItems):-
                CT = 'nct00002720',
                breast_cancer_stage(PatientData, '1'),
```

---

[9] http://www.w3.org/Submission/SWRL/
[10] http://www.w3.org/TR/rif-overview/
[11] http://www.hl7.org/special/Committees/arden/index.cfm
[12] http://www.swi-prolog.org/

```
invasive_breast_cancer(PatientData),
er_positive(PatientData),
known_pr_status(PatientData),
age_between(PatientData, 65, 80),
postmenopausal(PatientData),
getNotYetCheckedItems(CT, NotYetCheckedItems).
```

Which states that the inclusion criteria include: i) Histologically proven stage I, invasive breast cancer, ii) Hormone receptor status: Estrogen receptor positive and Progesterone receptor positive or negative, iii) Age: 65 to 80, and iv) Menopausal status: Postmenopausal.

Domain-Specific Knowledge. Those trial-specific rules above may involve some knowledge which are domain relevant, i.e., the domain knowledge, which are trial independent. We formalize those part of knowledge which are relevant with domain knowledge in the libraries of domain-specific knowledge. For example, for clinical trials of breast cancer, we formalize the knowledge of breast cancer in the knowledge bases of breast cancer, a domain-specific library of rules.

An example of this type of knowledge is a patient of breast cancer is triple negative if the patient has estrogon receptor negative, progesterone receptor negative and protein HER2 negative status. It can be formalized in Prolog as follows:

```
triple_negative(Patient):- er_negative(Patient),
                           pr_negative(Patient),
                           her2_negative(Patient).
```

We consider patient data as a set of property-value pairs. A general format of patient data, called the PrologCMR format, is designed to be a list of property-value pairs. This general format of patient data is flexible to represent the data from different formats of CMRs, because we can design a CMR-specific interface to obtain the corresponding data via different data servers, which can be a SPARQL endpoint, internal data storage server, or a database server[5]. Then, we can convert the patient data into one in the PrologCMR format. We introduce the general predicate getItem(PatientData, Property, Value) to get the value of the property from the patient data.

For example, these receptor status can be straightforward formalized as follows:

```
er_positive(PatientData):- getItem(PatientData, er, ER),
                           ER = 'positive'.
```

Common Knowledge. The specification of the eligibility criteria may involve some knowledge which are domain independent, like the knowledge for temporal reasoning and the knowledge for manipulating semantic data and interacting with data servers, e.g. how to obtain the data from SPARQL endpoints. We formalize the knowledge in several rule libraries, which can be reusable for different applications.

Example of this type of knowledge is temporal reasoning with constructs like last-month.

```
lastmonth(LastMonth):- today(Today),
              Today = date(_Year, ThisMonth, _Date),
              ThisMonth > 1, LastMonth is ThisMonth - 1.

lastmonth(LastMonth):- today(Today),
              Today = date(_Year, ThisMonth, _Date),
              ThisMonth is 1, LastMonth is 12.
```

Based on the SWI-Prolog's Web libraries, we can develop the interface with SPARQL endpoints to obtain semantic data (e.g. semantics-enable patient data and medical ontologies) for the rule-based formulation of eligibility criteria.

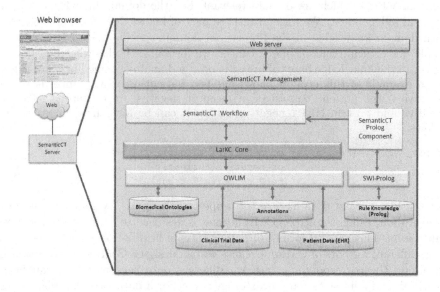

Fig. 2. The architecture of SemanticCT

This reasoning component is developed as a LarKC component for the task of identifying eligible patients for trials. The rule-based reasoning component is also useful for trial finding service, because it can provide exactly matching on the data, without relying on exhaustive regular expression patterns. In the future we want to use this component for trial finding for patients. This requires that all eligibility criteria of the trials are modeled in this rule-based approach.

5   System

5.1   Architecture

The architecture of SemanticCT is shown in Figure 2. SemanticCT Management plays a central role of the system. It launches a web server which serves as the application interface of SemanticCT, so that the users can use a web browser to access the system locally (i.e., from the localhost) or remotely (i.e., via the Web). SemanticCT Management manages SPARQL endpoints which are built as SemanticCT workflows for several tasks like semantic search, patient recruitment, trial feasibility. A generic reasoning plug-in in LarKC provides the basic reasoning service over large-scale semantic data, like RDF/RDFS/OWL data. SemanticCT Management interacts with the SemanticCT Prolog component which provides the rule-based reasoning[5,3].

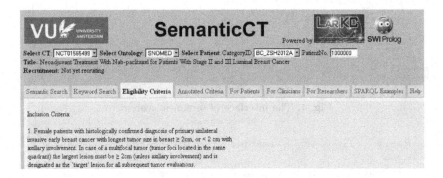

Fig. 3. The GUI of SemanticCT

LarKC, which consists of the LarKC core for plug-in and workflow management and the LarKC data layer, serves as the infrastructure of SemanticCT for semantic data management. The LarKC data layer manages the semantic data repositories of SemanticCT. Those semantic data repositories consist of i) biomedical terminologies or ontologies, such as SNOMED CT, LOINC, MeSH, RxNorm, etc., ii) semantic data of clinical trials, like those from LinkedCT, or semantic data which are converted from the original XML-encoded data of clinical trials, iii) semantic annotation data of trials, which are generated from the biomedical semantic annotation servers, and iv) patient data, which can be the semantic data obtained from EHR systems, or created by the knowledge-based patient data generator[6]. Those semantic data repositories can be located locally or distributively.

5.2   Interface and Service

For the demonstration prototype of SemanticCT, we merge the interfaces for various groups of users into a unique one on a Web browser, without considering their data protection issues, like access authority and password checking. A screenshot of the interface of the demonstration prototype SemanticCT is shown in Figure 3. Notice the several tabs that are available for various services and different types of users and discussed below.

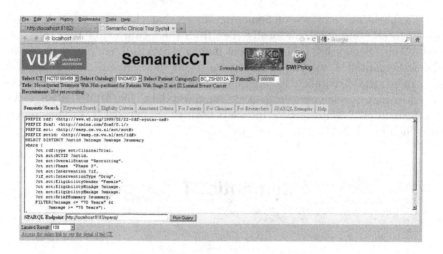

Fig. 4. The interface of semantic search

Semantic Search | Keyword Search | Eligibility Criteria | **Annotated Criteria** | For Patients | For Clinicians | For Researchers | SPARQL Examples | Help

Inclusion Criteria:

1. Female patients with histologically confirmed diagnosis of primary unilateral invasive early breast cancer with longest tumor size in breast >= 2cm, or < 2 cm with axillary involvement. In case of a multifocal tumor (tumor foci located in the same quadrant) the largest lesion must be >= 2cm (unless axillary involvement) and is designated as the 'target' lesion for all subsequent tumor evaluations.

2. The breast tumors must be ER positive: more than 1% of stained tumor cells by IHC, and HER2 negative: 0, or 1+ score by IHC, or 2+ with FISH/CISH negative for HER2 amplification (defined as a ratio of HER-2neu copies to chromosome 17 centromere (CEP17) signals < 1.8), according to the local laboratory).

Fig. 5. Semantic Annotation

- Semantic search: Figure 4 shows the interface of the semantic search, with a SPARQL example which searches for all recruiting phase 3 trials for female patients with the age between 70 and 75. We provide a set of SPARQL query templates, so that the users can select some of them and change some parameters of the templates to make their own queries (see SPARQL examples)
- Keyword search: We provide the ordinary search by using keywords to search over the eligibility criteria, or summaries of clinical trials. The extended keyword search provides complex keyword searches with the Boolean operators.
- Eligibility criteria: the eligibility criteria of the trial are shown.
- Annotated criteria: the service for browsing semantically annotated eligibility criteria of trials, see Figure 5.
- For patients: One of the main services in SemanticCT is the trial finding service. Currently, we provide the trial finding service by using SPARQL queries with regular expressions. The interface of patient services is shown in Figure 6. Notice that the SPARQL query is not visible for the user, but behind the button "show the CTs for this patient".

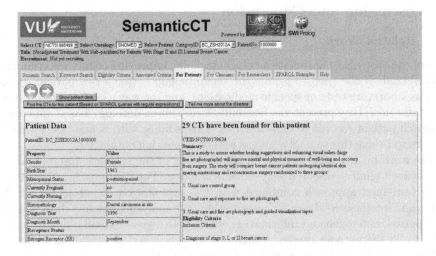

Fig. 6. Patient Service view and Trial Finding

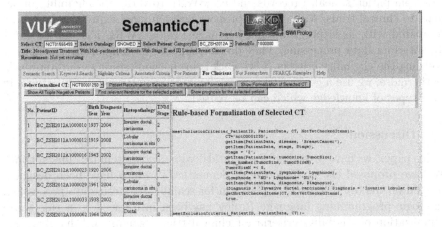

Fig. 7. Clinician services view and Rule-based formalization for Eligible Patient Identification

- For clinicians: SemanticCT provides several services for clinicians (see Figure 7). Those services include i) patient data browsing, ii) specific patient finding, such as, show all triple-negative breast cancer patients, and iii) patient recruitment for the selected clinical trial. The interface of clinician service for patient recruitment is shown in Figure 7. Notice that patient recruitment service is based on the rule-based formalization of the eligibility criteria.
- For Researchers: Semantic search for patient recruitment is one of the main services here.

Notice as well that the user can select an ontology from a list. In Figure 3 SNOMED is selected.

6   Discussion and Conclusion

6.1   Related Work

One of the obstacle to automate a clinical task like improving cohort selection for clinical trials is the need to bridge the semantic gap between raw patient data, such as laboratory tests or specific medications, and the way a clinician interprets this data. In [7] they presented a feasibility study for an ontology-based approach to match patient records to clinical trials. This is inline with SemanticCT which enables to bridge this semantic gap as well by exploiting ontologies.

The work in [1] is also focused on the enabling of the semantic interoperability between clinical research and clinical practice. Their approach is based on a SOA-oriented approach combined with the exploitation of ontologies which forms an "intelligence" layer for interpreting and analyzing existing data, which is dispersed, heterogeneous information, which is to a great extend publicly available. In [2] the authors present a method, entirely based on standard semantic web technologies and tool, that allows the automatic recruitment of a patient to the available clinical trials. They use a domain specific ontology to represent data from patients' health records and use SWRL to verify the eligibility of patients to clinical trials. Although we propose an even more expressive language. Compared with logic programming language Prolog SWRL has limited functionalities for data processing. They do also support for temporal reasoning for modeling the eligibility criteria. This work is in the same spirit as our approach. Furthermore, we use a general framework for specifying the eligibility criteria in three types of knowledge which can be reused.

6.2   Discussion

In this paper, we have presented a semantically-enabled system for clinical trials. We have proposed the architecture of SemanticCT, which have been designed to build on the top of LarKC, a platform for scalable semantic data processing. The logic programming language Prolog has been introduced to a rule-based formulization of eligibility criteria for clinical trials. SemanticCT has been semantically integrated with large-scale and heterogeneous data.

We have conducted several experiments for reasoning and data processing services over SemanticCT. The experiment of trial finding service shows that SPARQL queries with regular expressions are useful to deal with the information which can be easily obtained by the processing (like menopausal status and hormone receptor status). The experiment of the rule-based formalization shows that it is efficient and effective approach for faster identifying eligible patients. What we have implemented and tested is just a prototype of SemanticCT. Thus, it provides only a basic step for developing semantically enabled systems for clinical trials.

6.3   Future Work

There are many interesting issues for future work of SemanticCT, which include trial finding by using rule-based reasoning, more comprehensive workflow processing for decision support procedure, deeper reasoning with biomedical ontologies, personalized information services for patients, clinicians, and researchers, etc. We are going to provide more extended services for clinicians, which include finding relevant and latest literature like those from PubMed for the selected patient, and showing prognosis for selected patients. The existing implemented prognosis service in SemanticCT is quite simple, for it shows only the 5 year survival rate, based on the TNM stage of patients. A comprehensive prognosis service would be able to make analysis of all the relevant patient data to finding most-relevant clinical evidence for the prognosis analysis. We will continue the development of SemanticCT and deploy it in real application scenarios.

Acknowledgments. This work is partially supported by the European Commission under the 7th framework programme EURECA Project (FP7-ICT-2011-7, Grant 288048).

References

1. Andronikou, V., Karanastasis, E., Chondrogiannis, E., Tserpes, K., Varvarigou, T.A.: Semantically-enabled intelligent patient recruitment in clinical trials. In: Proceedings of International Conference on P2P, Parallel, Grid, Cloud and Internet Computing, pp. 326–331 (2010)
2. Besana, P., Cuggia, M., Zekri, O., Bourde, A., Burgun, A.: Using semantic web technologies for clinical trial recruitment. In: International Semantic Web Conference, pp. 34–49 (2010)
3. Bucur, A., ten Teije, A., van Harmelen, F., Tagni, G., Kondylakis, H., van Leeuwen, J., Schepper, K.D., Huang, Z.: Formalization of eligibility conditions of CT and a patient recruitment method, D6.1. Technical report, EURECA Project (2012)
4. Fensel, D., van Harmelen, F., Andersson, B., Brennan, P., Cunningham, H., Della Valle, E., Fischer, F., Huang, Z., Kiryakov, A., Lee, T., School, L., Tresp, V., Wesner, S., Witbrock, M., Zhong, N.: Towards LarKC: a platform for web-scale reasoning. In: Proceedings of the IEEE International Conference on Semantic Computing (ICSC 2008). IEEE Computer Society Press, CA (2008)
5. Huang, Z., ten Teije, A., van Harmelen, F.: Rule-based formalization of eligibility criteria for clinical trials. In: Peek, N., Marín Morales, R., Peleg, M. (eds.) AIME 2013. LNCS, vol. 7885, pp. 38–47. Springer, Heidelberg (2013)
6. Huang, Z., van Harmelen, F., ten Teije, A., Dentler, K.: Knowledge-based patient data generation. In: Lenz, R., Mikszh, S., Peleg, M., Reichert, M., ten Teije, D.R.A. (eds.) ICAPR 2001. LNCS (LNAI), Springer (2013)
7. Patel, C., Cimino, J., Dolby, J., Fokoue, A., Kalyanpur, A., Kershenbaum, A., Ma, L., Schonberg, E., Srinivas, K.: Matching patient records to clinical trials using ontologies. In: Aberer, K., Choi, K.-S., Noy, N., Allemang, D., Lee, K.-I., Nixon, L.J.B., Golbeck, J., Mika, P., Maynard, D., Mizoguchi, R., Schreiber, G., Cudré-Mauroux, P. (eds.) ASWC 2007 and ISWC 2007. LNCS, vol. 4825, pp. 816–829. Springer, Heidelberg (2007)
8. Wielemaker, J., Huang, Z., van der Meij, L.: SWI-Prolog and the web. Journal of Theory and Practice of Logic Programming (3), 363–392 (2008)
9. Witbrock, M., Fortuna, B., Bradesko, L., Kerrigan, M., Bishop, B., van Harmelen, F., ten Teije, A., Oren, E., Momtchev, V., Tenschert, A., Cheptsov, A., Roller, S., Gallizo, G.: D5.3.1 - requirements analysis and report on lessons learned during prototyping. Larkc project deliverable (June 2009)

Identifying *Condition-Action* Sentences Using a Heuristic-Based Information Extraction Method

Reinhardt Wenzina and Katharina Kaiser

Institute of Software Technology and Interactive Systems
Vienna University of Technology
Favoritenstrasse 9-11, 1040 Vienna, Austria

Abstract. Translating clinical practice guidelines into a computer-interpretable format is a challenging and laborious task. In this project we focus on supporting the early steps of the modeling process by automatically identifying conditional activities in guideline documents in order to model them automatically in further consequence. Therefore, we developed a rule-based, heuristic method that combines domain-independent information extraction rules and semantic pattern rules. The classification also uses a weighting coefficient to verify the relevance of the sentence in the context of other information aspects, such as effects, intentions, etc. Our evaluation results show that even with a small set of training data, we achieved a recall of 75 % and a precision of 88 %. This outcome shows that this method supports the modeling task and eases the translation of CPGs into a semi-formal model.

Keywords: computer-interpretable clinical guidelines, medical guideline formalization, Many-Headed Bridge (MHB), UMLS, Information Extraction (IE).

1 Introduction

Clinical Practice Guidelines (CPGs) are defined as "systematically developed statements to assist practitioners and patient decisions about appropriate healthcare for specific circumstances" [6]. They include recommendations describing appropriate care for the management of patients with a specific clinical condition. An important part of CPG contents refers to the procedures to perform, often formulated together with specific conditions that have to hold in order to execute an activity.

CPGs are published as textual guidelines, but in order to deploy them in some kind of computerized tool (e.g., a reminder system or a more complex decision-support system) they have to be represented in specialized languages (see [15,7] for a comparison and overview). Although different authoring/editing tools are often associated with these languages, authoring is a labor-intensive task that requires comprehensive knowledge in medical as well as computer science.

There have been several approaches to ease the modeling process, amongst others by introducing intermediate representations that provide more semi-structured and less formal formats. One of them is MHB, the Many-Headed Bridge

D. Riaño et al. (Eds.): KR4HC 2013/ProHealth 2013, LNAI 8268, pp. 26–38, 2013.

[21], that tries to bridge the gap between the guideline text and its corresponding formalized model. It falls in the category of document-centric approaches [22] and is devised to produce a non-executable XML document with the relevant CPG fragments, starting from the original text. The knowledge of a CPG is thereby represented in a series of chunks that correspond to a certain bit of information in the CPG (e.g., a sentence, part of a sentence, more than one sentence). The information in a chunk is structured in various dimensions, e.g., control flow, data flow. To additionally support the modeling task for non-IT experts, MHB was further developed and split into MHB-F (free-text version) and MHB-S (semantically enriched version) [19]. MHB-F now provides a very simplified structure to make the modeling even for non-IT experts feasible and to leave modeling details to knowledge engineers in a later step.

In order to ease the laborious modeling, parts of the task should be automated by applying information extraction methods. In this work we will focus on the identification of *condition-action* sentences that form a prominent aspect of the process flow in CPGs. The discovery of such combinations is not a trivial one. On the one hand, *condition-action* sentences are rarely of the form '*if* condition *then* action', but require more sophisticated identification methods. On the other hand, conditions may refer to effects, intentions, or events and not activities, and these combinations have to be sorted out by our method. Table 1 shows a few example sentences in regard to their MHB-F aspects.

Table 1. Examples of sentences and their categorization in MHB-F

sentence	MHB-F aspect
An episiotomy should be performed if there is a clinical need such as instrumental birth or suspected fetal compromise.	decision based activity
Women with pain but no cervical changes should be re-examined after two hours.	decision based activity
Women should be informed that in the second stage they should be guided by their own urge to push.	clinical activity
The partogram should be used once labour is established.	background information
Administration of inhaled steroids at or above 400 mcg a day of BDP or equivalent may be associated with systemic side-effects .	effect

Legend: activity , condition , effect , explanation

In order to identify *condition-action* sentences we propose a rule-based method using a combination of linguistic and semantic information. Furthermore, we introduce a weighting coefficient called *relevance rate (rr)* that shows whether a sentence is relevant for modeling.

The following section gives a short overview on the usage of information extraction methods as well as knowledge-based approaches for guideline modeling. Our method is explained in Section 3 and subsequently evaluated and discussed in Sections 4 and 5.

2   Background and Related Work

Guideline developers edit CPGs in a free-text format. In order to transform the medical knowledge described in a guideline into execution models a translation process is required. Moser and Miksch [14] detected prototypical patterns in free-text guidelines to bridge this gap. Serban et al. [18] proposed an ontology-driven extraction of linguistic patterns to pre-process a CPG in order to retrieve control knowledge. The evaluation showed that the modeling as well as the authoring process of guidelines was supported. Language engineering methods were used in SeReMed [5] to detect diagnoses or procedures in medical documents. The method was successfully applied to X-ray reports. These documents however, show a standardized structure and therefore are easier to handle by knowledge engineering methods than CPGs. Taboada et al. [23] identified relationships between diagnoses and therapy entities in free-text documents by matching the core information units of a sentence with a collection of predefined relationships but the quality of this matching was not rated. To implement a rule based approach to recognize medical entities the MeTAE (Medical Texts Annotation and Exploration) platform was used by Abacha and Zweigenbaum [1]. Additionally, semantic relations between each pair of these entities were identified by means of MetaMap [2]. Consequently, relations between a problem (e.g., disease) and a corresponding treatment were found. The method was applied to selected articles and abstracts of PubMed but not to CPGs. In [8] a heuristic-based approach using information extraction methods independent of the final guideline representation language was defined. This method was implemented and applied to several guidelines containing a high amount of semi-structured text. The adoption of this methodology on *'living-guidelines'* [9] showed promising results. A set of semantic patterns representing activities based on semantic relations was generated by Kaiser et al. [10] to identify medical activities in CPGs. Its effectiveness was proved by a study which showed that a large part of control flow related aspects could be identified. The relation between the activity and a corresponding condition, however, was not part of the method but is an important requirement for the future automatic translation of a guideline.

3   Methods

Condition-based medical activities are expressed in clinical practice guidelines in various ways and mostly found in single sentences. These sentences affect the clinical pathway and therefore are relevant to the computer-interpretable model of the guideline. In order to classify such a sentence as relevant, we based our approach on the following hypothesis:

1. A sentence owns a certain domain independent linguistic structure, and
2. contains recurrent domain dependent semantic key patterns.

We propose a rule-based, heuristic method using linguistic and semantic patterns to classify sentences in CPGs as relevant for describing conditional activities in order to move towards an automatic translation of such sentences into MHB in a following future step (an example is shown in Figure 1). Therefore, we analyzed a CPG document to develop a general linguistic pattern set and a semantic pattern set based on UMLS Semantic Types. These pattern sets then form the basis for the subsequent classification by calculating the *relevance rate (rr)*.

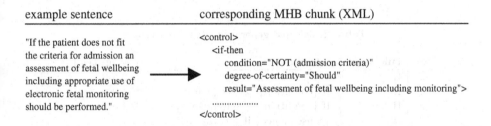

example sentence	corresponding MHB chunk (XML)

"If the patient does not fit the criteria for admission an assessment of fetal wellbeing including appropriate use of electronic fetal monitoring should be performed."	\<control\>
	  \<if-then
	    condition="NOT (admission criteria)"
	    degree-of-certainty="Should"
	    result="Assessment of fetal wellbeing including monitoring"\>
	  ....
	\</control\>

Fig. 1. A condition-action sentence represented as MHB-chunk

3.1   Knowledge Sources and Tools

The Unified Medical Language System (UMLS) [11] combines selected health and biomedical vocabularies to facilitate the standardized exchange of medical data between computer systems. It offers three different components:

1. The Metathesaurus which is an aggregation of medical terms and codes of different vocabularies (e.g., MeSH, SNOMED CT, etc.).
2. The Semantic Network which reduces the complexity of the Metathesaurus by assigning semantic types to the concepts of the Metathesaurus in order to group and define relationships among them.
3. The SPECIALIST Lexicon and Lexical Tools which provide natural language processing tools.

The open source framework for text engineering GATE (Version 6) [4] allows the combination of different text engineering components to develop reusable applications. The following components were used in our method:

- ANNIE: A set of information extraction (IE) components, distributed within the GATE system and relying on finite state algorithms and the JAPE language [3].
- OpenNLPChunker supports the detection of phrases within a parsed text.
- MetaMap Annotator: A tagger that maps biomedical texts to the UMLS Metathesaurus and discovers Metathesaurus concepts and their semantic types [2].

3.2   Manual Development of the General Linguistic Pattern Set

For the development of the general linguistic pattern set we used a chapter from an Asthma guideline developed by SIGN [17], where *chapter 4: pharmacological management* had been modeled in the semi-structured modeling language MHB-F [21] by a guideline modeling expert. We analyzed this chapter with regard to the control flow aspects and started generating an initial linguistic pattern set based on trigger words (12 occurrences for 'if' and 4 occurrences for 'should').

Table 2. Selected general linguistic patterns

#	rule type	pattern	weight(w)
1	IF	* [Ii]f *	0.5
2	IF	If {condition} {consequence}.	1.0
3	IF	If {condition}, {consequence}.	1.0
4	IF	{consequence} if {condition}.	1.0
5	IF	If {condition} then {consequence}.	1.0
6	SHOULD	* should have *	0.5
7	SHOULD	* should be *	0.5
...	..	...	...

In order to identify the semantic clauses of a sentence (these are the parts describing the *condition* and the *consequence*), the patterns had to be grouped into 6 different patterns for 'if' and 4 different patterns for 'should' (some straightforward patterns are listed in Table 2). Condition and consequence are distinguished according to the sentence's syntax, punctuation and its sequence of phrases. Two complex examples including conditions spread over multiple phrases are shown in Figure 2.

We assigned a weighting factor to every pattern of the set - the value 0.5 to show that only a trigger word was found and 1.0 to express that also the semantic clauses were identified. These constants can be adapted for new rule types in the future.

If there is a response to LABA , but control remains poor , continue with the LABA and increase the dose of inhaled steroid to ...

In children under five years , higher doses may be required if there are problems in obtaining consistent drug delivery.

Legend: condition ,   consequence

Fig. 2. Sentences with multi-part conditions

3.3   Generation of the Domain-Dependent Semantic Pattern Set

Amongst the general syntactic patterns we also used semantic patterns based on the UMLS Semantic Network. Therefore, we used the MetaMap plugin within the GATE framework to automatically identify medical concepts in our text and assign them to their corresponding UMLS concepts and semantic types (represented by four-letter abbreviations - e.g., 'popg' stands for 'Population Group'). By this way it was possible to find out the sequence of semantic types in the clauses of the sentences (see Figure 3).

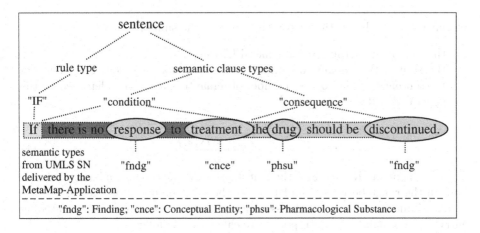

Fig. 3. Semantic abstraction of a sentence

Finally, the complete semantic abstraction of a sentence including rule type, semantic clause type and sequence of semantic types was added to the semantic pattern pool (see Table 3). A total of 32 entries was automatically generated.

Table 3. Structure of the semantic pattern pool (selected samples)

rule type	semantic clause type	sequence of semantic types
IF	condition	[fndg][cnce]
IF	consequence	[phsu][fndg]
IF	consequence	[idcn][qlco][resa][ftcn][ftcn]
SHOULD	condition	[aggp][podg][dsyn]
SHOULD	consequence	[qnco][tmco][resa][orch, phsu][idcn]
SHOULD	condition	[podg][qlco][ftcn][orgf][qlco][gngm][phsu]

3.4 Calculation of the Relevance Rate

The relevance rate rr is a measure to find out whether a sentence contains a condition-action combination. Furthermore, it shall classify a sentence as crucial for the clinical pathway in contrast to other information aspects like intentions or explanations which are modeled in MHB-F in a different way. To find this semantic difference the syntax of the sentences as well as their containing medical semantic types must be respected. In order to calculate the relevance rate for a selected sentence its semantic abstraction has to be generated and compared with every entry in the semantic pattern pool. If the rule type and the semantic clause type are matching, the similarity of the sequences of the semantic types is calculated by using the Dice coefficient [12]. The highest value is selected for further calculation.

In general, the value of the relevance rate rr is the sum of

- the weight(w) of the applied general IE rule, and
- the sum of the maximum similarity value (s_i) for each semantic clause of the sentence divided by the number of semantic clauses (n) identified by the general IE rules.

$$rr = w + \frac{\sum_{i=1}^{n} \max\{s_i\}}{n} \qquad (1)$$

The weight of the IE rule and the arithmetic average of the similarity values - both in the range between 0 and 1 - have the same influence on the rr.

The similarity value s_i of the semantic clause of a sentence and a matching entry in the semantic pattern pool were calculated as follows:

- If the semantic clause contains only one semantic type it is compared to those entries of the semantic pattern pool that also show only one semantic type (to receive a better accuracy). In the case that both types are equal the value for s_i is set to 1.0, otherwise
- both sequences of semantic types are interpreted as a string each and two sets of 4-letter string bigrams are composed out of them. Subsequently, these two sets are used for the calculation of the Dice coefficient.

Example:
Given are the sequence of semantic types of a new semantic clause S and the sequence of semantic types of a matching entry of the semantic pattern pool P.

S: [fndg] [orgf] [qlco] [gngm] [phsu] and P: [strd] [gngm] [phsu] [ortf].

The resulting 4-letter string bigrams are:

$S = \{$ "*fndgorgf*", "*orgfqlco*", "*qlcogngm*", "*gngmphsu*"$\}$
$P = \{$ "*strdgngm*", "*gngmphsu*", "*phsuortf*"$\}$.

The Dice coefficent is defined as twice the shared information over the sum of cardinalities:

$$s_i = \frac{2n_t}{n_s + n_p} \tag{2}$$

where n_t corresponds to the number of bigrams found in both sets, n_s is the number of bigrams in S, and n_p the number of bigrams in P. So the result of this example is $s = \frac{2*1}{4+3} = \frac{2}{7}$.

The general interpretation of the rr is shown in Table 4.

Table 4. Interpretation of the relevance rate

value	interpretation
$rr = 0.5$	only a trigger word or word combination were found; no semantic clause could be identified
$rr = 1.0$	an appropriate general IE pattern was found and semantic clauses could be identified
$1.0 < rr <= 2.0$	additionally, a semantic similarity between the sequences of the semantic types was detected

4   Evaluation

The guidelines *Management of active low-risk labour - Admission for Birth* [16] (chapters 1, 2.1, 2.2, and 2.3) and *CBO Treatment of Breast Cancer* (chapter 3) were applied to evaluate the method. These guidelines were intentionally selected, because they cover a completely different medical application area in contrast to the Asthma guideline and furthermore an MHB[1] [21] model already existed, used as a "golden standard".

The IE rules for the domain independent patterns and the generation of the semantic patterns were implemented with GATE - the processing resources for the calculation of the relevance rate are shown in Figure 4. The IE rules were applied to the guidelines and the identified sentences were annotated with the

---

[1] MHB is the former version of MHB-F.

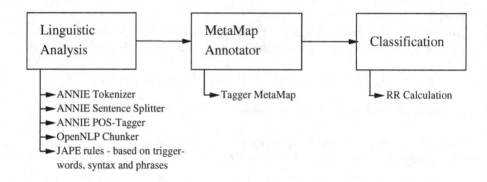

Fig. 4. Processing resources used in GATE

semantic types retrieved from the UMLS via the MetaMap plugin. 50 sentences were found which complied to the IE rules. Twenty out of the 50 sentences had been modeled in MHB as control flow related aspects (activities based on special medical conditions) and therefore their rr was expected to be higher than 1. The other 30 sentences represented information about intentions and explanations in MHB with an expected rr lower or equal 1. The evaluation results are shown in Table 5 differentiated by the rule types.

Table 5. Evaluation results I ($rr > 1$: tp and fp; $rr \leq 1$: fn and tn)

			type: IF		type: SHOULD		total	
Gold Standard	tp	fn	14	3	1	2	15	5
	fp	tn	1	2	1	26	2	28

tp = true positive; fn = false negative; fp = false positive; tn = true negative

With the described method it was possible to identify 15 sentences which correctly contained control flow related aspects. Only two sentences got an incorrect rr higher than 1. They were not correctly rated, because they did not describe condition-based activities. Other 5 sentences got an rr lower than 1 although their rr should have been higher as they contained condition-based activities. Thus, the method had a recall of 75% and a precision of 88% (see Table 6). The negative predictive value of 79% was higher than the recall value and showed that 28 sentences had been correctly classified.

Generally, the results proved that the rules of type "if" showed much better results for the precision (93%) and the recall (82%) than the ones of type "should". Nevertheless, the negative predictive value for the latter type showed a rate of 93%.

The analyzed guidelines contained 7 sentences with control flow related information but they were not classified because their patterns did not exist in the Asthma guideline. Consequently, no corresponding general linguistic IE rule existed in the pattern pool. An extension of the general linguistic pattern set with

Table 6. Evaluation results II

Guideline	type: IF			type: SHOULD			total		
	REC	PRE	NPV	REC	PRE	NPV	REC	PRE	NPV
Breast Cancer	100%	67%	100%	-	-	100%	100%	67%	100%
Adm. for Birth	80%	100%	0%	33%	50%	88%	72%	93%	75%
total	82%	93%	40%	33%	50%	93%	75%	88%	85%

REC   the number of correctly identified sentences over the number of the modeled sentences in the golden standard (=recall)

PRE   the number of correctly identified sentences over the entire number of identified sentences (=precision)

NPV   the number of correctly not identified sentences over the number of not modeled sentences in the golden standard (=negative predictive value)

Table 7. Selected sentences with an $rr \leq 1.0$

sentence	rr	reason
If, notwithstanding these procedures cervical dilatation doesn't progress, consider cesarean section after 2-3 hours of regular and painful contraction with no cervical changes.	0.5	Sentences with such a linguistic structure did not exist in the Asthma guideline → no IE rule was implemented to identify semantic clauses
If dilatation progress is not regular (<1 cm/hour in nulliparous, <1,5 cm/hours in parous) consider: - amniotomy; - oxytocin administration.	0.5	A list of resulting activities was not found in the Asthma guideline → no IE rule was implemented to identify semantic clauses
In case of abnormal FHR, monitoring should be continuous.	1.0	The sentence was wrongly categorized with a rule for 'should' because no rules for "in case of" were implemented → no semantic similarity within the semantic pool pattern was found
After umbilical cord clamping, if the second stage of labour has been physiological, the baby is given to the mother and covered.	1.0	The semantic clauses were found, but no semantic similarity occured

rules for the trigger words "when", "could" and "in case of" should be taken into consideration. Additionally, 1 condition based activity could not be found, because the semantic information was distributed over more than one sentence. In Table 7 selected examples are shown with a relevance rate lower or equal than 1.0 together with the corresponding reasons.

Even though only a small amount of training data (16 sentences) was available from the Asthma guideline, our method identified condition-based activities for control flow related aspects in a guideline document. Furthermore, it showed that the combination of domain independent information extraction rules and an automatically created semantic pattern pool leads to valuable results.

5   Conclusions and Further Work

The aim of this paper was to develop a method to identify condition-action sentences. By defining a set of linguistic patterns we split up sentences semantically - from one selected training guideline - into their clauses showing the condition and the consequence. We used the UMLS Semantic Network [13] to find out which types of medical concepts were applied in these clauses. The outcome was a semantic abstraction of every training sentence which then was stored in a semantic pattern pool. This pool facilitated the classification of new sentences regarding to their relevance to the corresponding MHB-F model expressed by the measure relevance rate (rr).

Modeling experts benefit from the method in two ways:

1. Condition-based activities in free-text guidelines, which must be modeled in MHB-F, are identified and rated.
2. These sentences are automatically split into the condition and the resulting activity.

An integration of the presented method into modeling tools will ease the work of all parties involved.

Ongoing steps will be (1) the implementation of additional information extraction rules to expand the general linguistic pattern set in order to improve the hit rate; (2) the extension of the semantic pattern pool with additional training data in order to increase the significance of the relevance rate; (3) the application of the method in the context of *'living-guidelines'* [20]; (4) an investigation, whether this method can support the modeling of processes also in other application areas by substituting the UMLS SN by other domain dependent thesauri; (5) the refinement of information extraction rules to make a step towards an automatic translation of condition-based activities of free-text guidelines into the modeling language MHB-F; and (6) the development of case studies to evidence the effectiveness of the method in real-world scenarios. If it is possible to tap the full potential of the presented method, the implementation of CPGs will be fostered tremendously.

Acknowledgement. This research was carried out as part of project no. TRP71-N23 funded by the Austrian Science Fund (FWF).

References

1. Abacha, A.B., Zweigenbaum, P.: Automatic extraction of semantic relations between medical entities: a rule based approach. Journal of Biomedical Semantics 2(suppl. 5), S4+ (2011)
2. Aronson, A.R., Lang, F.M.M.: An overview of MetaMap: historical perspective and recent advances. Journal of the American Medical Informatics Association: JAMIA 17(3), 229–236 (2010)

3. Cunningham, H., Maynard, D., Bontcheva, K., Tablan, V.: GATE: A framework and graphical development environment for robust NLP tools and applications. In: Proceedings of the 40th Anniversary Meeting of the Association for Computational Linguistics (2002)

4. Cunningham, H., Maynard, D., Bontcheva, K., Tablan, V., Aswani, N., Roberts, I., Gorrell, G., Funk, A., Roberts, A., Damljanovic, D., Heitz, T., Greenwood, M.A., Saggion, H., Petrak, J., Li, Y., Peters, W.: Text Processing with GATE (Version 6). University of Sheffield Department of Computer Science (2011), http://tinyurl.com/gatebook

5. Denecke, K.: Semantic structuring of and information extraction from medical documents using the UMLS. Methods of Information in Medicine 47(5), 425–434 (2008)

6. Field, M.J., Lohr, K.N. (eds.): Clinical Practice Guidelines: Directions for a New Program. National Academies Press, Institute of Medicine, Washington, DC (1990)

7. Isern, D., Moreno, A.: Computer-based execution of clinical guidelines: A review. International Journal of Medical Informatics 77(12), 787–808 (2008)

8. Kaiser, K., Akkaya, C., Miksch, S.: How can information extraction ease formalizing treatment processes in clinical practice guidelines? A method and its evaluation. Artificial Intelligence in Medicine 39(2), 151–163 (2007)

9. Kaiser, K., Miksch, S.: Versioning computer-interpretable guidelines: Semiautomatic modeling of 'Living Guidelines' using an information extraction method. Artificial Intelligence in Medicine 46(1), 55–66 (2009)

10. Kaiser, K., Seyfang, A., Miksch, S.: Identifying treatment activities for modelling computer-interpretable clinical practice guidelines. In: Riaño, D., ten Teije, A., Miksch, S., Peleg, M. (eds.) KR4HC 2010. LNCS, vol. 6512, pp. 114–125. Springer, Heidelberg (2011)

11. Lindberg, D., Humphreys, B., McCray, A.: The Unified Medical Language System. Methods of Information in Medicine 32(4), 281–291 (1993)

12. Manning, C.D., Schütze, H.: Foundations of statistical natural language processing. MIT Press, Cambridge (1999)

13. McCray, A.: UMLS Semantic Network. In: Proc. of the 13th Annual Symposium on Computer Applications in Medical Care (SCAMC), pp. 503–507 (1989)

14. Moser, M., Miksch, S.: Improving clinical guideline implementation through prototypical design patterns. In: Miksch, S., Hunter, J., Keravnou, E.T. (eds.) AIME 2005. LNCS (LNAI), vol. 3581, pp. 126–130. Springer, Heidelberg (2005)

15. Peleg, M., Tu, S., Bury, J., Ciccarese, P., Fox, J., Greenes, R., Hall, R., Johnson, P.D., Jones, N., Kumar, A., Miksch, S., Quaglini, S., Seyfang, A., Shortliffe, E.H., Stefanelli, M.: Comparing Computer-Interpretable Guideline Models: A Case-Study Approach. The Journal of the American Medical Informatics Association (JAMIA) 10(1), 52–68 (2003)

16. Remine: Documentation of formalized guidelines (2010), http://www.remine-project.eu/

17. Scottish Intercollegiate Guidelines Network (SIGN): British Guideline on the Management of Asthma. A national clinical guideline. Scottish Intercollegiate Guidelines Network (SIGN) (May 2011)

18. Serban, R., ten Teije, A., van Harmelen, F., Marcos, M., Polo-Conde, C.: Extraction and use of linguistic patterns for modelling medical guidelines. Artif. Intell. Med. 39(2), 137–149 (2007)

19. Seyfang, A., Kaiser, K.: MHB-F Specification (2011)

20. Seyfang, A., Martínez-Salvador, B., Serban, R., Wittenberg, J., Miksch, S., Marcos, M., ten Teije, A., Rosenbrand, K.: Maintaining formal models of living guidelines efficiently. In: Bellazzi, R., Abu-Hanna, A., Hunter, J. (eds.) AIME 2007. LNCS (LNAI), vol. 4594, pp. 441–445. Springer, Heidelberg (2007)
21. Seyfang, A., Miksch, S., Marcos, M., Wittenberg, J., Polo-Conde, C., Rosenbrand, K.: Bridging the gap between informal and formal guideline representations. In: Brewka, G., Coradeschi, S., Perini, A., Traverso, P. (eds.) European Conference on Artificial Intelligence (ECAI 2006), vol. 141, pp. 447–451. IOS Press, Riva del Garda (2006)
22. Sonnenberg, F.A., Hagerty, C.G.: Computer-interpretable clinical practice guidelines. where are we and where are we going? Yearb Med. Inform., 145–158 (2006)
23. Taboada, M., Meizoso, M., Riaño, D., Alonso, A., Martínez, D.: From natural language descriptions in clinical guidelines to relationships in an ontology. In: Riaño, D., ten Teije, A., Miksch, S., Peleg, M. (eds.) KR4HC 2009. LNCS, vol. 5943, pp. 26–37. Springer, Heidelberg (2010)

Supporting Computer-interpretable Guidelines' Modeling by Automatically Classifying Clinical Actions

Anne-Lyse Minard and Katharina Kaiser

Institute of Software Technology and Interactive Systems
Vienna University of Technology
Favoritenstrasse 9-11, 1040 Vienna, Austria
firstname.lastname@tuwien.ac.at

Abstract. Modeling computer-interpretable clinical practice guidelines is a complex and tedious task that has been of interest for several attempts to automate parts of this process. When modeling guidelines one of the tasks is to specify common actions in everyday's practical medicine (e.g., drug prescription, observation) in order to link them with clinical information systems (e.g., an order-entry system). In this paper we compare a rule-based and a machine-learning method to classify activities according to the *Clinical Actions Palette* used in the Hybrid-Asbru ontology. We use syntactic and semantic features, such as the Semantic Types of the UMLS to classify the activities. Furthermore, we extend our methods by using 2-step classification and combining machine learning and rule-based approaches. Results show that machine learning performs better than the rule-based method on the classification task. They also show that the 2-step classification method improves the categorization of activities.

Keywords: Clinical Practice Guidelines, Hybrid-Asbru, Common Clinical Actions, Natural Language Processing, Classification.

1 Introduction

Clinical practice guidelines (CGPs) are important means to provide state-of-the-art medical care in diagnosis and treatment of patients and therefore improve the quality in health care and reduce costs [9]. Computer-interpretable CPGs (CIGs) have been shown to improve the adherence to these guidelines and support the medical personnel by providing patient-specific recommendations at point of care [23]. In order to enable efficient linking of the CIGs on clinical information systems (e.g., order-entry systems), it is necessary to explicitly represent common clinical actions, such as drug prescriptions or physical examinations. Several approaches have been made to classify such clinical actions, for instance, the Unified Service Action Model (USAM) of HL7 RIM [24], the Action Palette by Essaihi et al. [8], or the *Clinical Actions Palette* used in the *Hybrid-Asbru* [27] CIG formalism.

Modeling CIGs is a complex and tedious task that involves the cooperation of both knowledge engineers and medical experts. Automating parts of the modeling process reduces the workload and information extraction techniques are a valuable means for that (e.g., [13]). In order to automatically model procedural parts of the CPGs for a computerized execution, actions need to be specified according to their highest level of detail.

D. Riaño et al. (Eds.): KR4HC 2013/ProHealth 2013, LNAI 8268, pp. 39–52, 2013.

We address the challenge of classifying clinical activities according to the *Clinical Actions Palette* in a way that enables specification of actions in Hybrid-Asbru. Our techniques can be used for supporting or to some extent replacing extracting actions, which is currently accomplished manually by knowledge engineers together with medical experts. Such an automatic classification can then be integrated in a CIG authoring tool to reduce the workload of the modellers. Automatically generated model fragments always need to be manually validated by human experts. However, this validation should be less laborious than a manual classification.

One difficulty we are faced with is to distinguish between two confusable classes, such as *drug-administration* and *drug-prescription* by using sentence elements. In some cases it is difficult even for a human annotator to assign the correct class. Thus, we propose not only sole rule-based or machine learning methods, but also a two-step classification approach, where these methods can be combined.

This paper is organized as follows. In Section 2 we present the context of our work and we make a brief overview of similar works and techniques. A description of the materials and methods is given in Section 3 and then in Section 4 an evaluation of the proposed methods is presented and discussed. Finally, in Section 5 we present our conclusions.

2   Background and Related Work

Asbru [25] is a formalism that represents CIGs as a hierarchy of time-oriented skeletal plans. However, it does not include explicit constructs for expressing common clinical actions such as drug prescription or physical examination. Although these actions are frequently used in everyday's clinical practice the textual nature of the knowledge role can limit its interpretation by the execution engine (e.g., to extract the precise dose of a drug in a drug-prescription action or the name of the laboratory test in an observation).

Hybrid-Asbru is an extension of Asbru which was expanded to include, amongst others, the *Clinical Actions Palette* to explicitly express common clinical actions such as drug prescriptions or physical examinations.

Currently, the actions palette includes the following actions: (1) anamnesis – used to specify querying patients for relevant history; (2) physical-examination – used to specify the performance of various physical examinations to the patient (e.g., measuring heart rate); (3) observation – used to specify an observation like an order of a laboratory test (e.g., WBC count); (4) procedure – used to specify some clinical procedure by a clinician; (5) drug-administration – used to specify the administration of a drug and its details (e.g., route) to a patient by a care-provider; (6) drug-prescription – used to specify a prescription of a drug and its details (e.g., dose) to a patient by a clinician; (7) referral – indicates a referral of a patient to a specialist in a particular medical domain (e.g., endocrinologist); and (8) notification – used to specify advising or educating a patient.

We are focusing on labeling activities according to this *Clinical Actions Palette*. We consider this task as a multi-class classification task where the aim is to categorize a segment of a sentence that describes an action into one of the 8 classes. We work on the segment-level due to the fact that a sentence can contain multiple activities of different types.

Some Natural Language Processing tasks are based on sentence classification, such as text structuring, opinion mining, or sentiment analysis (see [22] for a summary of systems developed for the i2b2 challenge 2011 on sentiment analysis of suicide notes). Khoo et al. [16] evaluated the performance of three classification algorithms (Naive Bayes, Decision Trees, and SVM) for sentence classification in e-mails. By using bag-of-words features, they showed that SVM outperforms the other classification algorithms. McKnight and Srinivasan [21] structured MedLINE abstracts in *Introduction, Method, Result,* and *Conclusion* sections. They chose SVM and linear classifiers using a large corpus with structured abstracts. There are also approaches using Conditional Random Fields (CRF), as they enable sequential modeling (i.e., taking into account the labeling of adjacent instances and features) [17,5]. In most cases, the set of features contains bag-of-words features, UMLS concepts or semantic types, features related to the position of the sentence, and sequential features (features from adjacent sentences). In our task there are no discourse dependencies between activities, so the use of CRF is not relevant. To deal with close classes, Chung and Coiera [5] proposed a two-step classification method. From five classes, two of them were very close. In the first step, they gathered the two close classes and classified sentences in the resulting four classes. Using a SVM classifier they learned then to distinguish between the two close classes. This two-step method obtained better results than the initial 5-class classification.

Few works were done on sentence classification in CPGs, for example to detect sentences that contain activities [14] or to classify some kind of activities depending whether they contain a clinical rule, a treatment recommendation, etc. [26]. Bouffier and Poibeau [3] developed a set of rules to detect activity and condition segments in French CPGs. To the best of our knowledge, there are no works which aim to classify activities in CPGs.

3 Materials and Methods

Classifying activities involves representing them by semantic, lexical, syntactic, etc. information in order to find similarities between activities and other activities already categorized. We present in this section our corpus, how we represent information, and the methods employed for the classification.

3.1 Corpus

In order to be able to develop and test our method we built a corpus consisting of eight CPGs. They cover different specialities, such as Cardiology (3), Endocrinology (2), Oncology (2), Pulmonology (1), and were developed by six different institutions (i.e., NICE[1], ACOG[2], CBO[3], SIGN[4], ADA[5], AHA[6]). The guidelines were selected to

---

[1] National Institute for Health and Clinical Excellence; http://www.nice.org.uk
[2] The American Congress of Obstetricians and Gynecologists; http://www.acog.org
[3] Dutch Institute for Healthcare Improvement; http://www.cbo.nl
[4] Scottish Intercollegiate Guidelines Network; http://www.sign.ac.uk
[5] American Diabetes Association; http://www.diabetes.org
[6] American Heart Association; http://www.heart.org

show whether we can develop a reliable method that is applicable on different medical specialities having varied types of activities as well as on similar guideline topics from different institutions to have a variation in the document structure and language.

We work on activity classification and not on activity extraction, so we use semi-structured texts as input, i.e., texts have been manually annotated with *activity* markups. For the development and the evaluation of our methods, we manually annotated activities in the eight guidelines and classified them according to the *Clinical Actions Palette*. Our corpus contained 348 annotated activities. In Table 1, we indicate the number of activities for each activity type.

Table 1. Number of activities of each type in the corpus

Activity Type	Number
anamnesis	6
drug-administration	42
drug-prescription	99
notification	46
observation	41
physical-examination	37
procedure	52
referral	25
total	348

In sentence (1) we give an example of a sentence containing an activity, which is assigned the type *drug-prescription*. Sentence (2) shows an example of a recommendation indicating that an action must not be activated. This kind of activity has not been annotated because only the activities that can be executed are interesting for the modeling of the CPGs.

(1)

(2)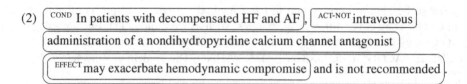

3.2   Text Pre-processing

Before the classification task starts, we preprocess the text to obtain semantic and syntactic information from sentences. We used GATE [7], an open source free software for text processing, which provides a set of text engineering tools from which we used the ANNIE tokenizer, sentence splitter, and gazetteer [6], the openNLP[7] POS tagger and chunker, and the MetaMap [2] plugin. In addition, we also developed some handwritten extraction rules and implemented them with JAPE[8]. Figure 1 presents the architecture of the text pre-processing system. The description of some of these modules is following.

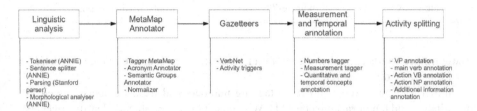

Fig. 1. Pipeline for pre-processing CPGs

GATE's MetaMap plugin maps text with concepts of the UMLS Metathesaurus [19]. We extended it by detecting acronyms and annotating them with their according UMLS concepts. Each UMLS concept is also assigned its *semantic group*, a coarser classification of the semantic types, defined by [20].

We then analyzed two CPGs (Atrial Fibrillation [10] and Gestational Diabetes [1]) according to their activities and the classes they are assigned to. Special emphasis was put on verbs and on other trigger words that could be used to identify the type of activity. We used the ANNIE gazetteer to annotate the verbs and the trigger words in the documents. A gazetteer consists of lists of entities (or more generally of words) which are used to find occurrences of these entities in text. We choose that the matching is done on word lemmas [9].

We used VerbNet [18] to classify verbs according to the VerbNet classes. There are 101 top-level classes and 270 first-level classes that include verbs that are syntactically and semantically close. From the top-level classes we manually selected 15 classes that deemed relevant for identifying different classes of activities according to our analysis (see Table 2 for examples). We have kept verbs that express an activity in our domain, such as verbs of the "removing" and "measure" classes. But we have also retained classes of verbs used to make a recommendation, such as the "communication" class.

We also observed that there are common words in each kind of activity. For example, in the *notification* activity there are words such as "advice", "inform", etc. We built a list with these activity triggers and used a gazetteer to annotate them in the corpus.

---

[7] http://opennlp.apache.org

[8] JAPE (Java Annotation Patterns Engine) provides finite state transduction over annotations based on regular expressions.

[9] The lemma of a word is its canonical form. For example, the lemma of a noun will correspond to its singular form (the lemma of "symptoms" is "symptom") and the lemma of a verb will often correspond to its infinitive form (the lemma of "achieved" is "achieve").

Table 2. Examples of verbs in relevant VerbNet classes (in the second column, the first number is the number of the class, and the second one the number of the sub-class)

Top-level classes	First-level classes	Verbs
Verbs of Assessment	assessment-34.1	analyze, evaluate, review
	estimate-34.2	approximate, count, assess
Indicate verbs	indicate-78	imply, predict, expose

These trigger words are categorized in four classes: *trigger_inform*, *trigger_treat*, *trigger_examine*, and *trigger_refer*.

Furthermore, we used plugins for tagging numbers and measurements as well as quantitative and temporal concepts [11]. With the latter we are able to identify concepts such as age, duration, frequency, and measurement.

3.3 Feature Representation

Using lexical features means to be domain-dependent and to have a well-represented training corpus. For example, in diabetes CPGs the UMLS concept "hypoglycaemic therapy" will be a marker for a *drug-prescription* activity, but not in oncology CPGs. We chose to use mainly semantic and syntactic features to obtain a classification model more general and less guideline-dependent. We defined the following features that are extracted from the activity sentence segment:

- Semantic types and semantic groups of UMLS concepts;
- VerbNet classes of verbs;
- The presence of a measurement indication;
- The main verb of the sentence, if it is in the activity sentence segment (i.e., the root node in the dependency graph);
- Triggers of the activity (word and class).

The features extracted, as described in the previous subsection, also contain some noise or are even missing. For example, MetaMap does not recognize all concepts in the text (e.g., because of their particular form, abbreviations, etc.) or assigns wrong semantic types. Also POS tagging or chunking are sources of errors. We did not evaluate the feature extraction process in general, but tried to optimize its output [15] and chose to deal with noise and silence of features.

The features are binary-features that are set to either 0 or 1, depending on whether they are present in the activity sentence segment or not. In total, there are 157 features.

3.4 Rule-Based Method

We manually developed extraction rules for each of the eight classes. The rules are based on the features described above. Thereby, features are combined and can also be explicitly excluded for a certain activity type. Table 3 shows the number of rules for each activity type and some examples. The example for *drug-administration* means that if a UMLS concept of semantic type "Spatial concept" (spco), a UMLS concept of semantic group "Chemicals and drugs" (CHEM), and the trigger word "administration" appears in the activity clause, it is assigned the "drug-administration" class.

Table 3. Number of rules for each activity type and some examples. Weights of the rules are indicated in brackets

Activity type	# rules	Example
anamnesis	1	
drug-administration	6	`IF ST=spco and SG=CHEM and tg=administration` (0.8)
drug-prescription	10	
notification	3	`IF tg_class!=trigger_refer and tg=advise` (0.3)
observation	8	`IF ST=lbtr and tg=check` (0.6)
physical-examination	12	
procedure	8	
referral	5	

Legend: ST=semantic type (w=0.3), SG=semantic group (w=0.2), tg=trigger word (w=0.3), tg_class=trigger class (w=0.2), lbtr= Laboratory or Test results.

Each feature in the rule has a weight used to select the correct class in case of multi-label instance. For example, an activity can be classified both in "drug-administration" and "procedure" classes, the matched rule with the higher weight (i.e., the sum of the weights of each feature) will be selected. The features are weighted differently. For instance, the weight for a semantic type feature will be 0.3 while the weight of a VerbNet feature will be set at 0.2. The weights were adjusted by applying rules on the development corpus. The weight for an absent feature (i.e. a feature included in the rule that must be absent of the sentence segment) is null.

The rule base was developed using a molecular approach: we started with developing a set of highly reliable rules and gradually extended our rule base to cover also less frequent patterns. Here, we had also to take care to avoid over-generation of rules by concurrently optimizing recall and precision. In this way, completeness of the rules is not achieved, but the rule set is optimized with regard to precision and recall to also work on new and unseen input.

3.5   Machine-Learning Method

Next, we used a supervised machine learning approach which uses the features described in subsection 3.3. Supervised machine learning is a technique that automatically learns a model to classify data from a reference corpus in which data has already been classified. The model can then be applied on new data. We have tested different classifiers through the WEKA suite [12], and obtained the best results with a SVM (Support Vector Machine) based classifier called LibSVM [4]. Moreover, SVM-based classifiers are often used for classification tasks in Natural Language Processing domain and is given good results. The SVM method uses an input vectorial representation of data and functions for finding the optimal separation among data. It supports multi-class classification and uses a "one-against-one" approach, i.e., a model is built for each pair of classes and a vote on decision values allows one to obtain one label for each instance. We used LibSVM with a linear kernel and the default parameters.

3.6   Combination of Classifiers and Rules

In order to improve our "single-step" methods we proposed further methods using combinations of the methods mentioned above (see Figure 2 for the alternative approaches). During our experiments we observed that some classes are confusable. We proposed 2-step methods to improve the classification in these confusable classes: first instances are classified in upper-level classes and then for each upper-level class, they are classified in sub-classes. By combining close classes together, we are able to minimize classification errors in the first step and specialize our classification in the subsequent step.

For example, we observed that the "drug-prescription" (see sentence (3) for an example) and "drug-administration" (see sentence (4)) classes are confusable (e.g. they share semantic properties, such as the words used for expressing an action or the semantic types of the main concepts).

(3) **A single oral bolus dose of propafenone or flecainide ("pill-in-the-pocket") can be administered** to terminate persistent AF outside the hospital [...]

(4) **Unfractionated heparin may be administered either by continuous intravenous infusion in a dose sufficient** [...]

Thus, we combined the close classes together into 3 upper-level classes *treatment or procedure* ("drug-administration", "drug-prescription", and "procedure"), *examination* ("observation" and "physical-examination"), and *other activities* ("referral", "anamnesis", and "notification"). So in a first step, activities are classified in these upper-level classes and in a second step, they are then classified in the final activity class. We developed two different methods for this two-step classification:

SVM-SVM Classification. We used a SVM classifier to learn to classify activities in the 3 upper-level classes. Then three classifiers were trained to distinguish the sub-classes. The different classifiers use different features. For example, features which represent verbs are more useful for the class "referral" and "notification" than for classes "drug-administration" and "drug-prescription", and the measurement features are useful for the upper-level classification rather than for distinguishing between "drug-administration" and "drug-prescription".

SVM-rule-Based Classification. This method uses the same classifier for the upper-level classes than the previous method. For distinguishing among the sub-classes, the rule-based method is used. Rules described in subsection 3.4 are applied on the instances classified in the upper-level classes. For example, on the instances classified in the *examination* upper-level class we apply rules of the "observation" and "physical-examination" sub-classes. Thus, in the second step less rules need to be applied on one activity, which reduces the error rate.

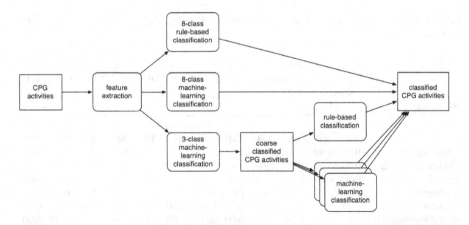

Fig. 2. Classification approaches. After extracting features we applied a rule-based approach (see top) or a SVM-based machine learning approach (below) for classifying activities in one step. At the bottom the 2-step approaches are represented with the SVM-based coarse classification in the first step and then either a rule-based classification or three different SVM-based classifiers.

4   Evaluation

For the evaluation of our method, we chose a cross-learning evaluation, i.e., the classifier is trained with 5 CPGs and the two CPGs used for the development and tested on the remaining CPG. By this way we evaluated the system on 6 CPGs using a different training set each time. For the evaluation we employ the classic measures: recall (1), precision (2), F-measure (3), and accuracy (4). The upper-bound of these 4 measures is 1.00. A perfect accuracy means that the system has correctly classified all the positive instances. The F-measure takes into account positive and negative instances, whereas the accuracy evaluates only the classification of positive instances.

$$Recall = \frac{\text{number of activities correctly classified}}{\text{number of activities to classify}} \qquad (1)$$

$$Precision = \frac{\text{number of activities correctly classified}}{\text{number of classified activities}} \qquad (2)$$

$$F\text{-}measure = \frac{2 \cdot (\text{precision} \cdot \text{recall})}{(\text{precision} + \text{recall})} \qquad (3)$$

$$Accuracy = \frac{\text{total number of activities correctly classified}}{\text{total number of activities}} \qquad (4)$$

We also use macro-recall, macro-precision, and macro-F-measure, which correspond to the average of recall, precision, and F-measure respectively of each class.

In Table 4 the results obtained from both the machine learning method (ML) and the rule-based method (RB) are presented. In the first part, the F-measure obtained for each class is shown for both methods. Then macro-recall, macro-precision, macro-F-measure, and accuracy is given for both methods on the 6 corpora. Bold numbers in

Table 4. Results of the 8-class classification with machine learning (ML) and rule based (RB) methods

	Diabetes type II (ADA)		Pre-eclampsia (ACOG)		Asthma (SIGN)		Breast Cancer (CBO)		Chronic HF (NICE)		Breast Cancer (NICE)	
# activities	33		24		42		7		42		47	
	F-measure											
	ML	RB	ML	RB	ML	RB	ML	RB	ML	RB	ML	RB
observation	0.29	0.40	0.40	0.00	0.67	0.75	-	-	0.33	0.00	0.22	0.00
physical-examination	0.60	0.67	0.75	0.67	-	-	-	-	0.75	0.36	-	-
referral	0.00	0.00	-	-	1.00	1.00	-	-	0.17	0.53	0.67	0.00
anamnesis	-	-	-	-	0.00	0.00	-	-	-	-	0.00	0.00
notification	0.33	0.40	-	-	0.00	0.00	0.80	0.00	0.18	0.00	0.63	0.00
drug-administration	-	-	0.00	0.67	0.00	0.00	1.00	1.00	-	-	0.00	0.00
drug-prescription	0.50	0.00	0.94	0.57	0.78	0.72	1.00	0.67	0.87	0.75	0.31	0.15
procedure	0.38	0.14	0.55	0.60	0.00	0.44	1.00	0.50	0.20	0.31	0.48	0.30
Macro-recall	0.45	0.41	0.58	0.48	0.39	0.54	0.92	0.50	0.52	0.31	0.47	0.05
Macro-precision	0.40	0.24	0.50	0.58	0.43	0.45	1.00	0.63	0.48	0.40	0.43	0.20
Macro-F-measure	**0.35**	0.27	**0.53**	0.50	0.41	**0.49**	**0.95**	0.54	**0.36**	0.28	**0.33**	0.06
Accuracy	**0.39**	0.33	**0.67**	0.54	0.60	**0.62**	**0.86**	0.43	**0.50**	0.48	**0.36**	0.11

macro-F-measure and accuracy indicate the better performing method comparing ML and RB methods.

The ML method performs better for the classification of activities in 5 of the 6 CPGs. In most cases the classification in the *drug-prescription* and *physical-examination* is good whereas for the other classes the results depend on the corpus. No activities are categorized in the *anamnesis* class neither by the classifier nor by the rules because there are not enough examples of this class in the training corpus (six instances overall). The overall accuracy[10] on the 6 corpora is 0.50 for the ML method and 0.40 for the RB method. So with the ML method half of the activities are correctly classified. The results are significantly different (with a confidence level of more than 95% with the Mc Nemar's test).

Table 5 shows the results of the 2-step classification methods. In the upper part F-measures of the first step for each of the 3 upper-level classes are given, whereas in the lower part we present the final results obtained after the second classification applying ML or RB methods. Bold numbers in macro F-measure and accuracy show for which corpus and with which method the performance are better with the 2-step classification compared to the 1-step classification (Table 4).

The results for the first-step classification are quite promising. We have an overall F-measure[11] of about 0.82 and an overall accuracy of 0.80 (so 80% of the activities are correctly classified). For the second step we obtain an overall accuracy of 0.54 with the

---

[10] The overall accuracy is the sum of all the activities correctly classified through the 6 corpora divided by the number of activities.

[11] The overall F-measure is the average of F-measures obtained from each corpus.

Table 5. Results of the 2-step classification. In bold the improvements of the 2-step method in comparison to the 1-step method are presented.

	Diabetes type II (ADA)		Pre- eclampsia (ACOG)		Asthma (SIGN)		Breast Can- cer (CBO)		Chronic HF (NICE)		Breast Can- cer (NICE)	
First-step					**F-measure**							
Treatment/procedure	0.76		0.90		0.88		1.00		0.81		0.81	
Examination	0.80		0.82		0.73		-		0.76		0.67	
Other activities	0.60		-		0.80		1.00		0.85		0.67	
Macro-F-measure	0.72		0.86		0.80		1.00		0.81		0.71	
Second-step	**ML**	**RB**	**ML**	**RB**	**ML**	**RB**	**ML**	**RB**	**ML**	**RB**	**ML**	**RB**
Macro-recall	0.49	0.27	0.61	0.52	0.40	0.53	0.92	0.88	0.55	0.31	0.50	0.05
Macro-precision	0.41	0.17	0.53	0.58	0.43	0.42	1.00	0.83	0.49	0.33	0.41	0.22
Macro-F-measure	**0.39**	0.18	**0.56**	0.51	0.41	0.45	0.95	0.79	**0.40**	0.29	**0.38**	0.08
Accuracy	**0.45**	0.24	**0.71**	0.54	0.60	0.60	0.86	0.71	**0.52**	0.45	**0.40**	0.13

ML method and 0.39 with the RB method. By using an SVM classifier in the second step the classification is slightly better than with the 1-step methods. The results obtained with the 1-step RB method and the 2-step ML method are significantly different (with a confidence level of 99% with the Mc Nemar's test). However the difference observed between the 1-step ML method and the 2-step ML method is not significant.

Errors Analysis. Analyzing our results we observed different types of errors:

- Features representing an activity were not present in the training corpus: in sentence (5), the verb *discuss* has not been learned from the corpus.
- Wrong or imprecise UMLS semantic type: in example (6), *intramuscular* is linked to the general semantic type *Functional Concept* (rather than to *Spatial Concept*).
- External knowledge is needed to distinguish between two close classes, such as *drug-prescription* and *drug-administration*, e.g., to know if a drug must allways be administered by a physician or could be prescribed.
- Activity annotations may also include other knowledge roles, such as conditions (see sentence (7)), other activities, effects, intentions, etc. This results in a lot of noise in the extracted features.

(5) [Their risks and benefits should be **discussed** with the patient]   and   their   side-effects carefully monitored.

(6) [Consider whether **intramuscular (IM)** hydrocortisone is required].

(7) [...] [consider referring **patients with inadequately controlled asthma,** **especially children**, to specialist care].

To resolve these errors improvements have to be made. First we must increase the size of the training corpus to have a better representation of activity expressions. Then the completion of the trigger list by adding more synonyms could be beneficial to offset the size of the training corpus. Moreover, relating our system to external knowledge like a domain-ontology can enable the system to distinguish between close classes. Finally, a normalization of the sentence to have only information relevant for the activity represented might be beneficial.

5 Conclusion

We have presented a comparison of methods to categorize activities in CPGs according to the *Clinical Actions Palette*. We show that a 2-step method using SVM classifiers is better than a 1-step classification approach using rules or machine learning. Our aim was to deal with a small training corpus by using mainly non-lexical features and also to find a way to classify in confusable classes. For the second issue, involving external resources will be necessary, because the use of rules or a 2-step classification method is not sufficient.

Such a classification of clinical activities can be integrated into a CIG authoring system, but still requires manual validation by human experts. However, an automatic classification will reduce the workload and its validation will still be less burden than a completely manual modeling. Furthermore, in a next step elements and attributes specifying the activity and required for the modeling can be automatically extracted and larger guideline fragments can be generated.

In the future, we plan to improve our classification by extending our training corpus and to extract relevant information from activity segments (e.g., removing some adverbials). We will also work on the detection of relations between activities (e.g., to identify that a drug-prescription activity "Inhaled steroids should be considered for patients with ..." is linked to an adjustment of dose "... and increase the dose of inhaled steroid to 800 mcg/day (adults) ...". Finally, it will be interesting to work on the detection of abort and complete conditions, because these might be formulated similar to activities ("If there is no response to inhaled long-acting beta2 agonist, stop the LABA ...").

Acknowledgements. This research was carried out as part of project no. TRP71-N23 funded by the Austrian Science Fund (FWF) and of the MobiGuide project partially funded by the European Commission under the 7th Framework Program, grant #287811.

References

1. American Diabetes Association: Standards of medical care in diabetes–2011. Diabetes Care 34(suppl. 1), S11–S61 (2011)
2. Aronson, A.R., Lang, F.M.: An overview of metamap: historical perspective and recent advances. J. Am. Med. Inform. Assoc. 17, 229–236 (2010)
3. Bouffier, A., Poibeau, T.: Analyzing the Scope of Conditions in Texts: A Discourse-Based Approach. In: Proceedings of the 11th Conference of the Pacific Association for Computational Linguistics, Sapporo, France (2009)

4. Chang, C.C., Lin, C.J.: LIBSVM: A library for support vector machines. ACM Transactions on Intelligent Systems and Technology 2, 27:1–27:27 (2011)

5. Chung, G.Y., Coiera, E.: A study of structured clinical abstracts and the semantic classification of sentences. In: Proc. of the BioNLP Workshop 2007: Biological, Translational, and Clinical Language Processing (BioNLP 2007). Association for Computational Linguistics (ACL), Stroudsburg (2007)

6. Cunningham, H., Maynard, D., Bontcheva, K., Tablan, V.: GATE: A Framework and Graphical Development Environment for Robust NLP Tools and Applications. In: Proceedings of the 40th Anniversary Meeting of the ACL (ACL 2002) (2002)

7. Cunningham, H., Maynard, D., Bontcheva, K., Tablan, V., Aswani, N., Roberts, I., Gorrell, G., Funk, A., Roberts, A., Damljanovic, D., Heitz, T., Greenwood, M.A., Saggion, H., Petrak, J., Li, Y., Peters, W.: Text Processing with GATE (Version 6) (2011)

8. Essaihi, A., Michel, G., Shiffman, R.N.: Comprehensive categorization of guideline recommendations: Creating an action palette for implementers. In: AMIA 2003 Symposium Proceedings, pp. 220–224. AMIA (2003)

9. Field, M.J., Lohr, K.N. (eds.): Clinical Practice Guidelines: Directions for a New Program. National Academies Press, Institute of Medicine, Washington, DC (1990)

10. Fuster, V., Rydén, L.E., Cannom, D.S., et al.: ACCF/AHA/HRS Focused Updates Incorporated Into the ACC/AHA/ESC 2006 Guidelines for the Management of Patients With Atrial Fibrillation: A Report of the American College of Cardiology Foundation/American Heart Association Task Force on Practice Guidelines. Circulation 123(10), e269–e367 (2011)

11. Gooch, P.: A modular, open-source information extraction framework for identifying clinical concepts and processes of care in clinical narratives. Ph.D. thesis, Centre for Health Informatics, School of Informatics, City University London (2012)

12. Hall, M., Frank, E., Holmes, G., Pfahringer, B., Reutemann, P., Witten, I.H.: The weka data mining software: an update. SIGKDD Explor. Newsl. 11(1), 10–18 (2009)

13. Kaiser, K., Akkaya, C., Miksch, S.: How can information extraction ease formalizing treatment processes in clinical practice guidelines? A method and its evaluation. Artificial Intelligence in Medicine 39(2), 151–163 (2007)

14. Kaiser, K., Seyfang, A., Miksch, S.: Identifying treatment activities for modelling computer-interpretable clinical practice guidelines. In: Riaño, D., ten Teije, A., Miksch, S., Peleg, M. (eds.) KR4HC 2010. LNCS, vol. 6512, pp. 114–125. Springer, Heidelberg (2011)

15. Kang, N., van Mulligen, E.M., Kors, J.A.: Comparing and combining chunkers of biomedical text. Journal of Biomedical Informatics 44(2), 354–360 (2011)

16. Khoo, A., Marom, Y., Albrecht, D.: Experiments with sentence classification. In: Proccedings of the 2006 Australasian Language Technology Workshop (ALTW 2006), pp. 18–25 (2006)

17. Kim, S.N., Martinez, D., Cavedon, L., Yencken, L.: Automatic classification of sentences to support evidence based medicine. BMC Bioinformatics 12(suppl. 2), S5 (2011)

18. Kipper, K., Korhonen, A., Ryant, N., Palmer, M.A.: A large-scale classification of English verbs. Language Resources and Evaluation 42(1), 21–40 (2008)

19. Lindberg, D., Humphreys, B.L., McCray, A.T.: The unified medical language system. Methods of Information in Medicine 32(4), 281–291 (1993)

20. McCray, A.: An upper-level ontology for the biomedical domain. Comp. Funct. Genomics 4(1), 80–84 (2003)

21. McKnight, L., Srinivasan, P.: Categorization of sentence types in medical abstracts. In: Proc. of the AMIA Annual Symposium, pp. 440–444 (2003)

22. Pestian, J.P., Matykiewicz, P., Linn-Gust, M., South, B., Uzuner, O., Wiebe, J., Cohen, K.B., Hurdle, J., Brew, C.: Sentiment analysis of suicide notes: A shared task. Biomedical Informatics Insights 5, 3–16 (2012)

23. Quaglini, S.: Compliance with clinical practice guidelines. In: ten Teije, A., Miksch, S., Lucas, P.J. (eds.) Computer-based Medical Guidelines and Protocols: A Primer and Current Trends, Studies in Health Technology and Informatics, ch. 9, vol. 139, pp. 160–179. IOS Press (2008)

24. Schadow, G., Russler, D.C., Mead, C.N., McDonald, C.J.: Integrating medical information and knowledge in the HL7 RIM. In: Proceedings of the AMIA Annual Symposium, pp. 764–748 (January 2000)

25. Shahar, Y., Miksch, S., Johnson, P.: The Asgaard project: A task-specific framework for the application and critiquing of time-oriented clinical guidelines. Artificial Intelligence in Medicine 14, 29–51 (1998)

26. Song, M., Kim, S., Park, D., Lee, Y.: A multi-classifier based guideline sentence classification system. Healthc. Inform. Res. 17(4), 224–231 (2011)

27. Young, O., Shahar, Y., Liel, Y., Lunenfeld, E., Bar, G., Shalom, E., Martins, S.B., Vaszar, L.T., Marom, T., Goldstein, M.K.: Runtime application of Hybrid-Asbru clinical guidelines. Journal of Biomedical Informatics 40, 507–526 (2007)

Discovering Probabilistic Structures of Healthcare Processes

Arjen Hommersom, Sicco Verwer, and Peter J.F. Lucas

Institute for Computing and Information Sciences
Radboud University Nijmegen, The Netherlands
{arjenh,s.verwer,peterl}@cs.ru.nl

Abstract. Medical protocols and guidelines can be looked upon as concurrent programs, where the patient's state dynamically changes over time. Methods based on verification and model-checking developed in the past have been shown to offer insight into the correctness of guidelines and protocols by adopting a logical point of view. However, there is uncertainty involved both in the management of the disease and the way the disease will develop, and, therefore, a probabilistic view on medical protocols seems more appropriate. Representations using Bayesian networks capture that uncertainty, but usually concern a single patient group and do not capture the dynamic nature of care. In this paper, we propose a new method inspired by automata learning to represent and identify patient groups for obtaining insight into the care that patients have received. We evaluate this approach using data obtained from general practitioners and identify significant differences in patients who were diagnosed with a transient ischemic attack. Finally, we discuss the implications of such a computational method for the analysis of medical protocols and guidelines.

Keywords: Clinical guidelines, temporal knowledge representations, knowledge extraction from healthcare databases.

1 Introduction

Much of the existing clinical knowledge that is concerned with quality of care is summarised in medical protocols and guidelines that describe standards of healthcare. From a computational point of view they can be looked upon as concurrent programs. Methods to investigate properties of protocols and guidelines, based on semi-automatic verification and model-checking, have been developed in the past (e.g. [1–3]). These methods take a logical point of view on protocols and guidelines and only offer insight into their formal correctness. A complementary view on healthcare is to look at the care that is actually given. This will reveal correspondences, usually called *compliance* [4], as well as differences with a given guideline, allowing one to obtain insight into where caregivers deliberately or accidentally departed from a guideline, and where they simply followed the guideline. Probabilistic models, such as Bayesian networks, allow one to

D. Riaño et al. (Eds.): KR4HC 2013/ProHealth 2013, LNAI 8268, pp. 53–67, 2013.
© Springer International Publishing Switzerland 2013

capture, in principle, the necessary structural information from recorded data in such way that the structures can be related to the logical structure of a guideline. Probabilistic approaches are in particular suitable for revealing the probabilistic nature of care processes, clarifying in essence how frequent particular care paths are taken. However, so far most of the research around care processes ignored probabilistic relational information. As a consequence, it is not completely clear which methodology for probabilistic methods can be successful used for this purpose, and what information they can actually reveal. In this paper we propose novel methods that can be used as a basis for such a methodology.

With the widespread introduction of information systems in healthcare during the last decade, there are now very big healthcare datasets available that enable developing such views on the structure of the given care. Examples of such datasets are those from NIVEL[1], a Dutch institutes with which we collaborate; they collect data of all patients of a large number of representative general practices in the Netherlands. For various diseases, the patients in this dataset have been treated according to guidelines. For example, for patients who were diagnosed with a transient ischemic attack, TIA for short, Dutch general practitioners generally follow a guideline developed by the NHG (Dutch General Practitioners society)[2]. However, guidelines are mostly concerned with single diseases, despite the fact that the majority of patients have multiple diseases (e.g. two-third of patients older than 65 years have two or more diseases at the same time). To get insight into the relationship between the guidelines and the actual care, which is described in healthcare data, computational learning methods can be of help.

In this paper, we take the first steps toward developing a technique for discovering probabilistic structures in healthcare data. The main idea behind the methodology is to combine ideas from Bayesian network learning with methods from learning automata. In particular, we will focus in this paper on one of the key ingredients of learning automata, which is the identification of *states*. The contribution of this technique is that the probabilistic representation that is learned provides insight into the different subgroups of patients. For example, we may identify patient groups with a different risk profile or patients groups that are treated significantly different from other patient groups. The underlying hypothesis is that these differences will be relevant in the care of the patient, and therefore should have a connection to the guideline.

This paper is organised as follows. In the next section, we discuss the background of computer-based protocols, Bayesian networks and automata learning. Then, in Section 3, the principal ideas underlying the work are discussed and we introduce a new method for learning subgroups of patients by the identification of states. In Section 4, this new learning method is applied to a dataset consisting of patients diagnosed with a TIA and we discuss some possible implications for clinical guidelines. In Section 5, we discuss some related work and in Section 6, we conclude.

---

[1] http://www.nivel.nl

[2] http://nhg.artsennet.nl/kenniscentrum/k_richtlijnen/
k_nhgstandaarden/Samenvattingskaartje-NHGStandaard/M45_svk.htm (in Dutch)

2 Background: Protocols and Learning

In this section, we will discuss computer-based protocols and guidelines. After this, we introduce Bayesian networks and briefly introduce background on learning automata, which inspired the work presented in this paper.

2.1 Computer-Based Protocols and Guidelines

Medical guidelines and protocols, medical protocols for short, are the main, prescriptive instrument of healthcare to promote quality of care [5]. Many countries have a special institute – e.g., the National Institute of Clinical Excellence (NICE) for the UK – that in collaboration with healthcare professionals, often clinical specialists and epidemiologists, and relevant patient organisations work on the production of such protocols.

Nowadays, there are also computer-based representations of medical protocols and this research has made considerable progress in the last decade [6]. A popular way to describe protocol modelling is through the paradigm of 'task-network models'. A task consists of a number of steps, each step having a specific function or goal [6–8]. Examples of languages that support task models, and which have been evolving since the 1990s, include PRO*forma* [9], Asbru [10], EON [11], and GLIF3 [8]. The network-of-task approach allows modelling the plan-like execution of protocols, which can also be modelled using logical methods (e.g. [12]). Computer-based versions of medical protocols allow adding support for their maintenance and updating without going through the entire text again as is still standard practice in protocol development.

2.2 Bayesian Networks

Bayesian networks are powerful graphical representations that represent conditional independence assumptions [13], i.e., information about whether or not sets of random variables influence other sets of variables under the assumption that other variables have been observed for a problem at hand. There is a considerable body of work (e.g. [14, 15]), indicating that Bayesian networks offer a natural and intuitive formalism for constructing clinically relevant models.

Formally, a *Bayesian network* is a tuple $B = (G, X, P)$, with $G = (V, E)$ a directed acyclic graph (DAG), $X = \{X_v \mid v \in V\}$ a set of random variables indexed by V, and P a joint probability distribution of the random variables in X. P is represented as a Bayesian network with respect to the graph G if P can be written as a product of the probability of each random variable, conditional on their parents:

$$P(X_1, \ldots, X_n) = \prod_{v \in V} P(X_v \mid X_{\mathrm{pa}(v)})$$

where $\mathrm{pa}(v)$ is the set of parents of v. In the following, we will assume that each variable is binary with values *true* and *false*. We will write x_i for $X_i = true$ and $\neg x_i$ for $X_i = false$.

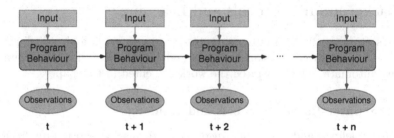

Fig. 1. Abstract temporal process, with the form of a Markov Process, driven by the execution of a program. Note that probabilistic graphical models support decomposing the program state by means of a graphical independence structure.

Bayesian networks allow modelling evolution of stochastic processes as a function of time; various types of so-called temporal Bayesian networks, also called dynamic Bayesian networks, have been proposed for this purpose [16]. A simple example of a temporal Bayesian network describing the state change of a program based on its execution is shown in Fig. 1. Use of techniques from temporal Bayesian networks offer interesting possibilities for studying program behaviour in detail. In particular, these allow exploring run-time behaviour of a given protocol by showing the interactions at different points in time.

Bayesian networks can also be learnt from data, which encompasses both learning the graph structure of the model and its associated parameters [17]. A major problem is that the search space of network structures (directed acyclic graphs) is extremely large [18] even if one takes into account that many different networks represent the same conditional independence information [19], i.e., are *Markov equivalent*. There are different ways to learn a Bayesian network from data using search-based, dependency-analytic and hybrid approaches, and the results obtained by these methods are generally good. Finally, there are methods available to learn temporal Bayesian networks from data [20].

2.3   Identification of Automata

Another research area that is of immediate relevance to this paper is known as *automaton identification*, which concerns itself with constructing (learning) state machine models automatically from execution traces [21]. Since state machines are key models for the design and analysis of computer systems [22], the problem of learning finite state machines from data enjoys a lot of interest from the software engineering and formal methods communities. They use learned automaton models for providing insight into complex software systems and test their properties using model checking and testing techniques. In the literature, this approach has been used for learning and analysing models for different types of complex software systems such as web-services [23], the biometric passport [24], and java programs [25].

Formally, automaton identification can be seen as a grammatical inference [26] problem in which the traces are modelled as the words of a language, and the

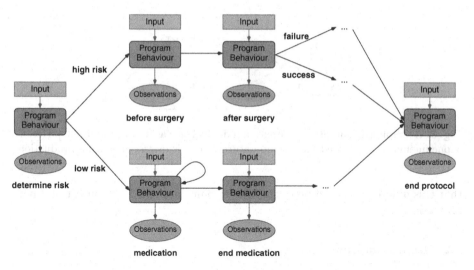

Fig. 2. An automaton representation of a medical protocol. The model contains guards that makes the future execution dependent on the value of a certain variable. In addition there is recursion that can loop back to already visited states. Every state contains a Bayesian network model for the properties of patients that visit those states, at the time(s) they visit them.

goal is to find a model for this language. The most commonly used language model is the deterministic finite state automaton (DFA) [27]. Hence, its learning (identification) problem is one of the best studied problems in grammatical inference, and many algorithms have been developed for this purpose.

3 Methods

3.1 General Idea

It is surprising that learning Bayesian networks from program state data has never been tried since it is well known that Hidden Markov Models (HMMs, a type of temporal Bayesian network) and probabilistic automata are equivalent in terms of the distributions they can represent [28]. The standard method of adding behavioural abstractions to HMMs is to generalise the relations within a state to be an arbitrary Bayesian network [29], ending up with a model such as Fig. 1. Technically, there is no reason why this standard generalisation cannot be applied to an automaton model instead of an HMM, ending up with a model such as Fig. 2.

In this paper, we investigate how to identify the *states*, which is the key ingredient to learn automata. For example, the question is if we can identify that certain patient groups should be treated differently, e.g., low or high risk patient groups. If this is the case, then this (*i*) provides information about compliance in case the patients are treated according to some protocol, or (*ii*) indicates

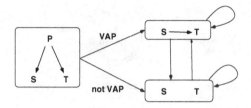

Fig. 3. A simplified example of contextual independence as it appeared in [31]. Here P is pneumonia, T is elevated body temperature, and S is increased sputum production.

that this difference should be taken into account into the development of a new protocol.

3.2   Representation

The state can be seen a particular configuration of characteristics that hold for a patient group. In this first paper on learning automata of Bayesian networks, we take the most simple case: we condition on a single characteristic of the patient. This is essentially a multinet representation [30]. Suppose, for example, we have a joint distribution $P(X_V)$ over all variables X_V represented by a Bayesian network $B = (G, X, P)$. By the chain rule, taking into account the independences represented by the graph, we can pick a single $v \in V$ and write:

$$P(X_V) = P(X_{V\setminus\{v\}} \mid X_v)P(X_v)$$

Let $X^* = X_{V\setminus\{v\}}$, then, assuming all variables are binary, consider the two conditional distributions:

$$P^{x_v}(X^*) = P(X^* \mid x_v)$$
$$P^{\neg x_v}(X^*) = P(X^* \mid \neg x_v)$$

and the distribution $P(X_v)$. Clearly, the distribution $P(X_v)$ is easy to represent by a single number $P(x_v)$ as $P(\neg x_v) = 1 - P(x_v)$. The distributions P^{x_v} and $P^{\neg x_v}$, on the other hand, can be represented by Bayesian networks B^{x_v} and $B^{\neg x_v}$. Obviously, the triple $\langle B^{x_v}, B^{\neg x_v}, P(x_v)\rangle$, which we call a *split Bayesian network* can represent exactly the same distribution as the original Bayesian network B. However, this more extended representation may indicate different relationships between variables in the populations where x_v or $\neg x_v$ hold, and thus, can provide more insight than B alone. It is not difficult to see that this can be done recursively by further conditioning on other characteristics.

Consider for example Fig. 3, showing a simplified example of relationships in patients with ventilator-associated pneumonia (VAP). When patients arrive at the ICU, they may already have pneumonia (P), which (indirectly) connects sputum production (S) with an elevated body temperature (T). Pneumonia diagnosed after they arrive at the ICU is classified as VAP. Only for the patients with VAP, there is a relationship between S and T. While the model on the left-hand-side would be an appropriate model for all patients at the ICU, the two models allow for a richer representation of the relevant knowledge.

3.3 Learning Models

Typically, a split model is, while often more insightful, also a more complex model. In this paper, we propose two statistically motivated ways to determine whether these more complex models should be chosen over a Bayesian network representation.

A search-and-score-based method for learning Bayesian network uses a scoring function to measure the goodness of fit of a structure to the data. This score typically approximates the probability of the structure given the data and represents a trade-off between how well the network fits the data and how complex the network is. There are several ways to search for the optimal networks, e.g., a tabu search is often used. There are also various scoring functions for Bayesian networks. For example, in our experience, the Akaike information criterion (AIC) score works well for learning models from epidemiological datasets.

The AIC score of a split network can be derived as follows. Suppose have a dataset D and B a candidate Bayesian network with distribution P, let $L = \Pr(D \mid B) = \prod_{r \in D} P(r \mid B)$ be called the *likelihood* of the Bayesian network, where $r \in D$ is a record in dataset D, and the probability distribution of the Bayesian network B, P, is used to compute Pr using the common assumption that the records are independent and identically distributed. Furthermore, let k be the number of parameters in the network, where $k = \sum_{v \in V} 2^{|pa(v)|}$, if the network contains only binary variables. Then the AIC score is defined as:

$$\text{AIC} = 2k - 2\log L$$

Note that models with the lowest AIC are selected, i.e., with the highest likelihood and lowest number of parameters. Furthermore, suppose we split on X_v, let D^{x_v} be the data records $D^{x_v} \subseteq D$ where x_v holds, and $D^{\neg x_v} = D \setminus D^{x_v}$. Let $L^{x_v} = P^{x_v}(D^{x_v} \setminus \{x_v\})P(x_v)$ and $L^{\neg x_v} = P^{\neg x_v}(D^{\neg x_v} \setminus \{\neg x_v\})P(\neg x_v)$. Given a split model $M = \langle B^{x_v}, B^{\neg x_v}, P(x_v) \rangle$, it follows that the likelihood is the product of L^{x_v} and $L^{\neg x_v}$. The number of of parameters is the number of parameters used to represent the Bayesian networks, plus one to represent $P(x_v)$. This yields:

$$\text{AIC} = 2(k^{x_v} + k^{\neg x_v} + 1) - 2\log(L^{x_v} \times L^{\neg x_v}) = \text{AIC}^{x_v} + \text{AIC}^{\neg x_v} + 2$$

Of course, several other methods can be used to determine splits, such as the BIC or BDE score which are often used in Bayesian network learning.

Besides the score-based methods, automata learning uses hypothesis testing to determine whether a split should occur, in particular we will use a likelihood-ratio test. In that case, we consider a test statistic, which looks similar to the AIC:

$$D = -2\log \frac{L}{L^{x_v} \times L^{\neg x_v}} = 2(\log L^{x_v} + \log L^{\neg x_v} - \log L)$$

D is distributed according to a chi-squared distribution with $k^{x_v} + k^{\neg x_v} + 1 - k$ degrees of freedom. A significance test can thus be used to decide whether to split on a certain variable.

4   Experiments

Below we discuss our first experimental results, indicating that the proposed methodology is promising.

4.1   Data

The data used for analysis were obtained from the Netherlands Information Network of General Practice (LINH). All Dutch inhabitants are obligatory registered with a general practice, and the LINH registry contains information of routinely recorded data from about all patients of approximately 90 general practices. Longitudinal data of approximately one and half million patient years, covering the decade 2002-2011, were considered. From this data, we selected patients who were diagnosed with a transient ischemic attack (TIA) during this time-frame.

From this data, we selected a number of variables. This included the gender of the patient, a number of cardiovascular diseases (atherosclerosis, angina pectoris, stroke, cerebral infarction, hypertension, and heart failure), relevant classes of drugs that may be prescribed (antihypertensives, antilipemics, antithrombics, and antidiabetics), and a number of possible consequences of cardiovascular diseases (atrial fibrillation, orthostatic hypotension, and ankle edema).

4.2   Learning of Networks

For the patients diagnosed with TIA we first learnt a Bayesian network from the available data, consisting of 600 patients who suffered a TIA. The resulting graph is shown in Fig. 4. The thickness of the arcs indicate the significance of the relationships, which was obtained by bootstrapping. The graph shows the statistical (in)dependences amongst variables. While this graph provides insight into the dependences between variables in the whole group of TIA patients, it is difficult to identify sub-groups where the relationships between variables are significantly different – which would suggest that this group may need to be managed differently from other patients.

Next we considered on which variables we could split and compared the AIC-motivated criterion to the likelihood-ratio criterion. There was a high degree of agreement between the two criteria, see Fig. 5. All the possible splits where there was an improvement in the AIC score were highly significant on the likelihood-ratio test ($p < 0.001$) and vice versa. The top five possible splits were *atherosclerosis, myocardial infarction, cerebral infarction, heart failure,* and *orthostatic hypertension.* The first, atherosclerosis, is somewhat of an outlier and this is almost never diagnosed directly. Instead, this may indicate patients which have

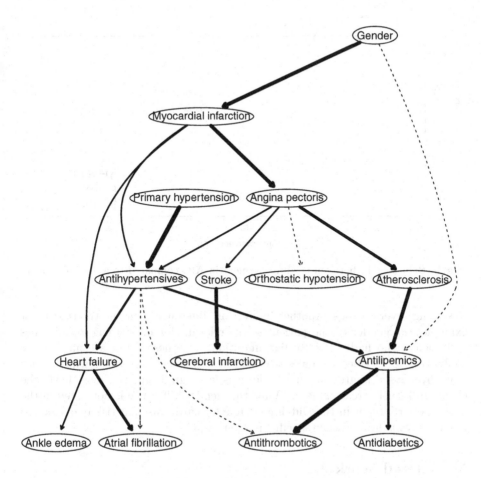

Fig. 4. Bayesian network structure learnt from patient data consisting of TIA patients

several cardiovascular diseases. The others are clearly patient-groups who were at higher risk than other patients.

To illustrate the results of this analysis, we take the most significant one, which was myocardial infarction. The data were split to find differences in network structure that allow explaining differences in the course of the disease, as shown in Figs. 6 and 7. These differences are related to both the patient characteristics and the way that patients are treated. For example, in the group of myocardial infarction, there is no clear (other) association with heart failure, because heart failure is very common in this group and the remaining patients are at high risk for this in any case. In the other group, heart failure is related to antilipemics (patients treated for high cholesterol) and antihypertensives (patients treated for high blood pressure). Clearly, in this patient group it makes sense to reduce the

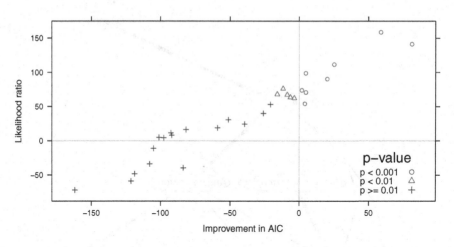

Fig. 5. Relationship between the improvement in AIC compared to a likelihood ratio

risk using several drugs. Another interesting difference is in the treatment: for example, the gender of the patient seems relevant for prescribing antilipemics to patients who had a myocardial infarction, i.e., these drugs are much more likely to be prescribed to males who had heart attacks. For those who did not have myocardial infarction, the gender was less significant, i.e., most likely the cholesterol level is reason alone. While this gender difference is not noted in the guideline for TIA or in the Dutch guideline for cardiovascular risk management (2006), statins have gender-specific differences [32].

5   Related Work

As already mentioned, the representation that was discussed here can be seen as a multinet [30]. These multinets were proposed to represent contextual independence, whereas we learn these networks to discover different subpopulations. As a consequence, by recursively applying the learning approach, we obtain a much richer representation than multinets alone. However, it is beyond of this paper to learn a complete automaton, as we focused on the identification of states.

A more related approach to learn Bayesian networks in context of subgroup discovery is by Duivesteijn et al. [33]. The idea of this paper is to compare structural differences between subgroups. This ideas is different from our paper, which aims to actually use subgroup discovery to uncover potentially different care paths. As a consequence, we proposed statistical criteria based on the AIC and the likelihood-ratio test. Furthermore, we aim to extend this approach to learn automata of Bayesian networks, rather than do subgroup discovery alone.

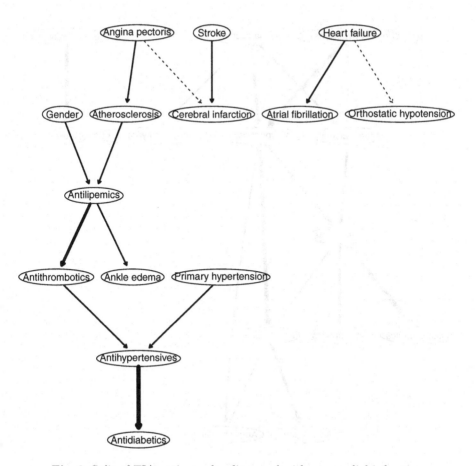

Fig. 6. Split of TIA patients also diagnosed with myocardial infarction

Furthermore, there have been some proposals to induce guidelines from data. For example, one could look upon learning guidelines as learning a decision tree [34], and possibly integrate these models with additional medical background knowledge [35]. Another approach uses process mining techniques [36–38], where the idea is to extract process models from event logs [36, 37]. The main difference is that in process mining there is no abstraction of the events into (probabilistic) states. We think this is an important step, especially for learning clinical models, as it is important for clinicians have understandable models that describe a certain healthcare process. Since there are both probabilistic aspects in guidelines as well as the patients that are being treated by a guideline, a probabilistic model of the process seems more appropriate. Nonetheless, some of the ideas from the process mining field could be combined with abstraction into states, as presented in this paper.

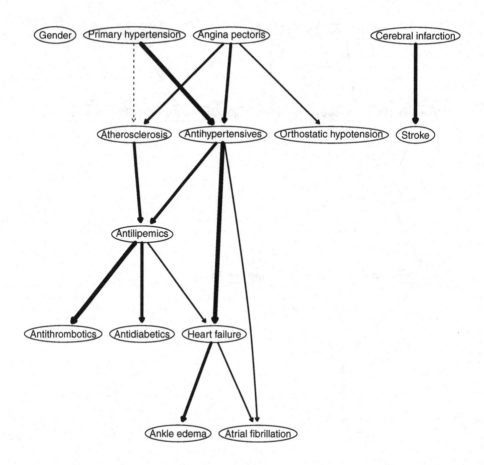

Fig. 7. Split of TIA patients who have not been diagnosed with myocardial infarction

6   Conclusions

In this paper, we introduced a new method for discovery of structure in epidemiological datasets. We view this as the essential step to learn automata that describe care processes. In this paper, we introduced the necessary learning methods and applied these ideas to a dataset consisting of patients diagnosed with a TIA. We argued that the technique identifies subpopulations that can be seen as groups that are different from the others.

The evaluation we presented in this paper is still fairly static: we included all TIA patients, regardless of temporal relationships between events. In future work, we will include time, so that complete automata can be learned from the data. We believe that this can be used to learn representations of the *actual* care, which can then be compared more formally to the care recommended by guidelines.

References

1. ten Teije, A., Marcos, M., Balser, M., van Croonenborgd, J., Duellic, C., van Harmelena, F., Lucas, P., Miksch, S., Reif, W., Rosenbrand, K., Seyfang, A.: Improving medical protocols by formal methods. Artificial Intelligence in Medicine 63(3), 193–209 (2006)
2. Hommersom, A., Groot, P., Lucas, P., Balser, M., Schmitt, J.: Verification of medical guidelines using background knowledge in task networks. IEEE Transactions on Knowledge and Data Engineering 19(6), 832–846 (2007)
3. Bottrighi, A., Giordano, L., Molino, G., Montani, S., Terenziani, P., Torchio, M.: Adopting model checking techniques for clinical guidelines verification. Artificial Intelligence in Medicine 48(1), 1–19 (2010)
4. Quaglini, S.: Compliance with clinical practice guidelines. In: Teije, A.T., Miksch, S., Lucas, P. (eds.) Computer-Based Medical Guidelines and Protocols: A Primer and Current Trends. Studies in Health Technology and Informatics, vol. 139, pp. 160–179. IOS Press (2008)
5. Field, M., Lohr, K. (eds.): Clinical Practice Guidelines: Directions for a New Program. National Academy Press, Institute of Medicine, Washington, D.C (1990)
6. ten Teije, A., Miksch, S., Lucas, P. (eds.): Computer-based Clinical Guidelines and Protocols: a Primer and Current Trends. IOS Press, Amsterdam (2008)
7. Fox, J., Das, S.: Safe and Sound: Artificial Intelligence in Hazardous Applications. AAAI Press (2000)
8. Peleg, M., Boxwala, A., Ogunyemi, O., Zeng, P., Tu, S., Lacson, R., Begnstam, E., Ash, N.: GLIF3: The evolution of a guideline representation format. In: Proc. AMIA Annual Symposium, pp. 645–649 (2000)
9. Fox, J., Johns, N., Rahmanzadeh, A., Thomson, R.: PRO*forma*: a general technology for clinical decision support systems. Computer Methods and Programs in Biomedicine 54, 59–67 (1997)
10. Shahar, Y., Miksch, S., Johnson, P.: The Asgaard project: A task-specific framework for the application and critiquing of time-orientied clinical guidelines. Artificial Intelligence in Medicine 14, 29–51 (1998)
11. Tu, S., Musen, M.: From guideline modeling to guideline execution: Defining guideline based decision-support services. In: Proceedings of American Medical Informatics Association Symposium, Los Angeles, CA, pp. 863–867 (1999)
12. Hommersom, A., Groot, P., Lucas, P., Balser, M., Schmitt, J.: Verification of medical guidelines using background knowledge in task networks. IEEE Transactions on Knowledge and Data Engineering 19(6), 832–846 (2007)
13. Pearl, J.: Probabilistic Reasoning in Intelligent Systems: Networks of Plausible Inference. Morgan Kaufmann, San Francisco (1988)
14. Andreassen, S.: Planning of therapy and tests in causal probabilistic networks. Artificial Intelligence in Medicine 4(3), 227–241 (1992)
15. Lucas, P., van der Gaag, L., Abu-Hanna, A.: Bayesian networks in biomedicine and health-care. Artificial Intelligence in Medicine 30, 201–214 (2004)
16. Dagum, P., Galper, A., Horvitz, E.: Dynamic network models for forecasting. In: Proceedings of UAI 1992, pp. 41–48 (1992)
17. Neapolitan, R.: Learning Bayesian Networks. Pearson (2004)
18. Robinson, R.: Counting unlabeled acyclic graphs. In: LNM, vol. 622, pp. 220–227. Springer, NY (1977)

19. Gillespie, S.B., Perlman, M.D.: Enumerating Markov Equivalence Classes of Acyclic Digraph Models. In: UAI 2001 (2001)
20. Ghahramani, Z.: Learning dynamic bayesian networks. In: Giles, C.L., Gori, M. (eds.) IIASS-EMFCSC-School 1997. LNCS (LNAI), vol. 1387, pp. 168–197. Springer, Heidelberg (1998)
21. Cook, J.E., Wolf, A.L.: Discovering models of software processes from event-based data. ACM Trans. Softw. Eng. Methodol. 7, 215–249 (1998)
22. Lee, D., Yannakakis, M.: Principles and methods of testing finite state machines - a survey. Proceedings of the IEEE 84, 1090–1123 (1996)
23. Bertolino, A., Inverardi, P., Pelliccione, P., Tivoli, M.: Automatic synthesis of behavior protocols for composable web-services. In: Proceedings of the Joint Meeting of the European Software Engineering Conference and the ACM SIGSOFT Symposium on the Foundations of Software Engineering, pp. 141–150. ACM (2009)
24. Aarts, F., Schmaltz, J., Vaandrager, F.: Inference and abstraction of the biometric passport. In: Margaria, T., Steffen, B. (eds.) ISoLA 2010, Part I. LNCS, vol. 6415, pp. 673–686. Springer, Heidelberg (2010)
25. Walkinshaw, N., Bogdanov, K., Holcombe, M., Salahuddin, S.: Reverse engineering state machines by interactive grammar inference. In: Proceedings of the 14th Working Conference on Reverse Engineering, pp. 209–218. IEEE (2007)
26. de la Higuera, C.: Grammatical Inference: Learning Automata and Grammars. Cambridge University Press, New York (2010)
27. Sudkamp, T.A.: Languages and Machines: an introduction to the theory of computer science, 3rd edn. Addison-Wesley (2006)
28. Dupont, P., Denis, F., Esposito, Y.: Links between probabilistic automata and hidden Markov models: probability distributions, learning models and induction algorithms. Pattern Recognition 38, 1349–1371 (2005)
29. Boutilier, C., Dearden, R., Goldszmidt, M.: Exploiting structure in policy construction. In: IJCAI. AAAI (1995)
30. Geiger, D., Heckerman, D.: Knowledge representation and inference in similarity networks and Bayesian multinets. Artificial Intelligence 82, 45–74 (1996)
31. Visscher, S., Lucas, P.J.F., Flesch, I., Schurink, K.: Using temporal context-specific independence information in the exploratory analysis of disease processes. In: Bellazzi, R., Abu-Hanna, A., Hunter, J. (eds.) AIME 2007. LNCS (LNAI), vol. 4594, pp. 87–96. Springer, Heidelberg (2007)
32. Gutierrez, J., Ramirez, G., Rundek, T., Sacco, R.L.: Statin therapy in the prevention of recurrent cardiovascular events: a sex-based meta-analysis. Arch. Intern. Med. 172(12), 909–919 (2012)
33. Duivesteijn, W., Knobbe, A., Feelders, A., van Leeuwen, M.: Subgroup discovery meets bayesian networks – an exceptional model mining approach. In: Proceedings of the 2010 IEEE International Conference on Data Mining, ICDM 2010, pp. 158–167. IEEE Computer Society, Washington, DC (2010)
34. Bohada, J.A., Riaño, D., López-Vallverdú, J.A.: Automatic generation of clinical algorithms within the state-decision-action model. Expert Systems with Applications 39(12), 10709–10721 (2012)
35. López-Vallverdú, J.A., Riaño, D., Bohada, J.A.: Improving medical decision trees by combining relevant health-care criteria. Expert Systems with Applications 39(14), 11782–11791 (2012)

36. Van der Aalst, W., Weijters, T., Maruster, L.: Workflow mining: Discovering process models from event logs. IEEE Transactions on Knowledge and Data Engineering 16(9), 1128–1142 (2004)
37. Mans, R.S., van der Aalst, W.M.P., Vanwersch, R.J.B., Moleman, A.J.: Process mining in healthcare data challenges when answering frequently posed questions. In: Lenz, R., Miksch, S., Peleg, M., Reichert, M., Riaño, D., ten Teije, A. (eds.) ProHealth 2012 and KR4HC 2012. LNCS, vol. 7738, pp. 140–153. Springer, Heidelberg (2013)
38. Kaymak, U., Mans, R., van de Steeg, T., Dierks, M.: On process mining in health care. In: SMC, pp. 1859–1864 (2012)

Implementation of a System for Intelligent Summarization of Longitudinal Clinical Records

Ayelet Goldstein and Yuval Shahar

Ben Gurion University of the Negev, Beer-Sheva, Israel
{gayelet,yshahar}@bgu.ac.il

Abstract. Physicians are required to interpret, abstract and present in free-text large amounts of clinical data in their daily tasks. This is especially true for chronic-disease domains, but also in other clinical domains. In our previous work, we have suggested a general framework for performing this task, given a time-oriented clinical database, and appropriate formal abstraction and summarization knowledge. We have recently developed a prototype system, CliniText, which demonstrates our ideas. Our prototype combines knowledge-based temporal data abstraction, textual summarization, abduction, and natural-language generation techniques, to generate an intelligent textual summary of longitudinal clinical data. We demonstrate both our methodology, and the feasibility of providing a free-text summary of longitudinal electronic patient records, by generating a discharge summary of a patient from the MIMIC database, who had undergone a Coronary Artery Bypass Graft operation.

1 Introduction

Many clinical tasks require dealing with an enormous amount of time-oriented patient data. Physicians, who have to make diagnostic or therapeutic decisions regarding these patients, may be inundated by the volume of data if their ability to reason does not scale up to the amount of data.

We provide a verbal (free-text) summary of electronic patient records that include time-stamped data that have accumulated during an extended time period, such as during hospitalization, or over years of medical care. Such summaries might help care providers in their daily tasks, and support several decision-making processes.

In our previous work [1], we had proposed an architecture that supports a process of transforming longitudinal data into an intelligent, concise, text-based summary. In the current study, we have implemented the proposed architecture as a prototype System – the **CliniText** system. In this paper, we describe the inner workings of the CliniText system, using a detailed example of how each module contributes to the process of automatically transforming time-based data from a typical case in the MIMICII public database, into a discharge summary.

The input to the CliniText system includes longitudinal data and a domain-specific knowledge. The output of the system is a condensed textual summary of the patient's data. In our current prototype, the output textual summary is in the form of a

D. Riaño et al. (Eds.): KR4HC 2013/ProHealth 2013, LNAI 8268, pp. 68–82, 2013.

discharge summary, since we aim to generate text that resembles the corresponding human discharge summary of the same data, as found in the database.

2   Background

Visualization is an effective approach to facilitate analysis and presentation of high volume data, specifically when dealing with huge amounts of data [2]. However, recent findings showed that graphical representation is not always more effective than other methods, and, in the medical domain, clinical decision-making was not necessarily improved by the use of a graphical display. Another study [3] showed that when dealing with large volumes of complex clinical data, a textual presentation is even advantageous over a graphical one, for the purpose of certain clinical tasks.

Temporal abstraction (TA) is the task of producing context-sensitive and qualitative interval-based representations (interpretations). The output of the TA task can be defined as a set of time intervals, each interval representing a certain state holding over a period of time, with its respective context-sensitive concept value [4]. In the medical domain, in which data abstraction is crucial, decision making can be greatly benefited by information (trends, irregularities) derived directly from the data [5].

The *Natural Language Generation* (NLG) task deals with the generation of natural language from a machine-language form input [6]. Although the NLG task has been implemented in different domains [7], in most of the implemented systems the data are relatively well-defined, not requiring advanced data analysis techniques. Furthermore, in the case of the summary of small data sets, only brief summaries are produced, which significantly reduces the complexity of many NLG tasks. In the medical domain, existing NLG systems are far from optimal [7]. A more recent NLG system, BT-45[8], which focuses on decision support, also performs temporal data abstraction; however, the abstraction process is relatively simple, and does not consider different contexts when determining the importance of an event. In addition, it considers only short and pre-defined periods of data. Dealing with different periods of time, especially longer periods, as is common in chronic-disease patients, requires additional temporal-information handling techniques.

The main contributions of our system, are that the input data are allowed to be (1) heterogeneous, which makes the NLG task significantly more complex, (2) of high density, which means that the summaries will not be brief and (3) longitudinal over unlimited time periods. Unlike the approach we took, most existing approaches are not based on the use of complex knowledge specific to the application domain, and thus cannot automatically create any meaningful domain-specific interpretations. Furthermore, these systems cannot decide what data or interpretations are potentially redundant by using a robust domain-specific knowledge base (KB) and formal interpretation theory. Similarly, they cannot determine which facts are crucial to report in different contexts. Moreover, existing systems do not have the capability for interactive exploration of the resulting text summaries at various domain-specific, semantically meaningful and levels of abstraction, a capability for which our system provides the infrastructure.

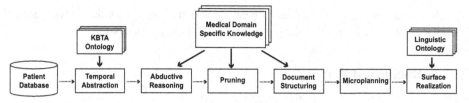

Fig. 1. The architecture of the Clinitext System. Knowledge is used by the temporal abstraction module to abstract the data. Additional knowledge is used in further modules to perform abduction, pruning and document structuring of the data. In the microplanning and surface realization modules we use standard medical dictionaries, such as UMLS to realize the text. Dashed horizontal arrows = control/data flow; Bold vertical arrows = knowledge flow.

3   Methods

Our input data arrives from a time-oriented clinical database. The required medical knowledge is specified through a graphical knowledge specification tool called Gesher [9]. We define both declarative (e.g. What Is mild-anemia in a pregnant women) and procedural (e.g. How to manage the patient, by administering two drugs in parallel) knowledge, necessary in the abstraction process. As we show, the knowledge is also exploited in other modules of the system.

We implemented the CliniText system using a framework composed of several modules, each performing a specific task. The architecture of the system, composed of six main modules, is displayed in Figure 1.

The flow of the data between the components defines the workflow of the process: Longitudinal raw data coming from the time-oriented database is abstracted by the *Temporal Abstraction* module, adding abstract data to the original raw data. Additional data are inferred from it through abduction in the *Abductive Reasoning* module. Raw, abstract and abducted data, are then pruned in the *Pruning* module, responsible to select the important and domain-relevant data, leaving only the information that will take part in the final text. The *Document Structuring* module structure these data, determining the order they should appear in the final text. The *Microplanning* component groups and prepares the structured data to the format expected by the *Surface Realization* module, which finally realizes the data into the final text.

Below we describe each component and its contribution to the process.

3.1   Temporal Abstraction (TA)

The TA step is responsible for the performance of the abstraction of time-oriented data. In the implementation of this module, we used a variation of the IDAN temporal-abstraction mediator [10], which implements Shahar's Knowledge-Based temporal-Abstraction (KBTA) Method [4]. The input to the TA module is time-stamped raw concepts (e.g., red-blood-cell "RBC-BLOOD" values). In Table 1 we list an example of input raw data and the output data, derived abstractions of the raw concepts. Note: The number of input concepts can be different from that of derived abstractions.

Table 1. A: An example of the input to the temporal-abstraction module. B: an example of the temporal-abstraction output. The first column lists the concepts; the second column specifies the number of *instances* in the database (e.g. 7 raw measurements of White Blood Cells Counts (WBC) denoted in the database as the raw concept "WBC-BLOOD"). Note: two or more instances of a raw concept can be transformed into one abstract concept interval, through the KBTA method's temporal interpolation (as is the case for the hematocrit state abstraction). Furthermore, one abstraction might be a function of two or more raw data-type instances.

A – Examples of the input of the TA process step		B – Examples of the output of the TA process step	
Raw concept	**instances**	**Abstraction concept**	**instances**
WBC-BLOOD	7	WBC State	7
RBC-BLOOD	7	RBC State	7
Hematocrit	9	Hematocrit State	8
Heart Rate	112	Heart Rate State	86

The abstraction of the data is performed using the KB defined in Gesher. Figure 2 shows an example of the partial declarative knowledge definition for the derivation of the abstract concept "WBC State" from the raw concept "WBC-BLOOD".

3.2   Abductive Reasoning

The abductive reasoning step is essential, since not all important concepts, such as events or actions performed, can always be found in the input data. However, in some cases, these events can be inferred by abduction from the existing data, with a high probability, albeit not necessarily with complete certainty, using *abduction knowldge*. For example, knowing that a Swan-Ganz catheter (SG) is used to measure the pulmonary artery systolic/diastolic pressure (PAP) concept, even though the event of inserting a SG (SG-in) does not appear in the database we can hypothesize that the event SG-in occurred through an instance of the PAP concept in the database.

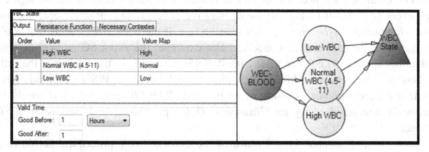

Fig. 2. The Gesher tool declarative-knowledge derivation of the abstract concept "WBC-State" from the Raw concept "WBC-BLOOD". On the right, the abstraction definition of the raw concept into the "WBC State" abstract concept: The raw-concept is initially mapped into value-abstractions which abstract the different values of the WBC-BLOOD (e.g. "Low WBC" = WBC-BLOOD < 4.5). These value-abstractions are then mapped into the different values of the State abstraction, as shown on the left. (e.g. "Low WBC" is mapped to the value "Low").

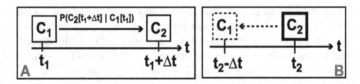

Fig. 3. A: An example of abduction knowledge: concept C_1 is followed with probability $P(C_2[t_0+\Delta t_i] \mid C_i[t_0])$ by concept C_2 within a period of up to Δt. B: The abduction process: From concept C_2 with a timestamp of t_2 we abduct concept C_1 with a timestamp between t_2 and $t_2-\Delta t$.

We can say that knowing that concept C_1 enables the existence of concept C_2, within a certain time Δt, allows through the existence of C_2 in the database, with a timestamp of t_2, the abduction of C_1 with a timestamp between $t_2-\Delta t$ and t_2, as shown in Figure 3.

Formally, we compute ahead of time $\forall i\ P(C_i[t_2 - \Delta t_i] \mid C_2[t_2])$: The probability of each concept C_i, given the concept C_2, t_2 (timestamp of C_2), P_0^i (a-priori probability of each related concept C_i), $P(C_2[t_0+\Delta t_i] \mid C_i[t_0])$ (relation probability of C_2, given C_i) and Δt_i (the interval of time during which C_i can be interpreted. For simplification, we consider only a uniform distribution of probabilities.). The computation applies the standard Bayes theorem, as used in Bayesian diagnostic problem solving [11].

From a knowledge representation point of view, the abduction knowledge typically links the declarative knowledge to the procedural knowledge, although other combinations are possible. (An example of linkage between two instances of procedural knowledge could be the event "syringe-insertion" allowing the abduction of the event "skin-sterilization" 5-10 seconds before). The relationship between the concepts can be either causal (A causes B) or associative (A occurs together with B). Note that in general, the temporal relation between the two concepts might include other temporal relations, such as "overlaps". At this point, we are focusing only on the "before" temporal relation.

To perform abduction, we need to explicitly represent abduction knowledge in the KB. For example, we need to specify beforehand in the procedural knowledge for each event (e.g. SG-in) what are the declarative concepts (e.g. PAP) it enables, and what's the probability/strength of this relation (e.g. if there are other events that could also generate this declarative concept). For example, the event SG-in, with a prior probability quite low, enables PAP with P=0.95; However, in the ICU, it is the only method used to measure PAP. Thus, within the ICU context, P(SG | PAP)=1. Note that in a different context, outside of an ICU, the PAP S/D concept value would be commonly measured using an Ultrasound (U/S) procedure, and not using a SG catheter.

In our case, we enable the inference of the existence of a procedural action (e.g. SG-in) by the existence of a declarative concept (e.g. PAP). Since we deal with a medical domain, we abduct only concepts that have a probability near to certainty.

Fortunately, we usually work in domains in which, although the probability of the existence of the database item that is *accessible* (*explicit*) given the one that is *hidden* (*implicit*) is not necessarily 100% (for example, the SG catheter does not necessarily lead to measurement of PAP S/D with certainty-that depends on the success of the procedure), the number of potential implicit concepts that can be inferred from those that explicitly exist in the database, Ci ($i = 1..N$), is such that N = 1 (e.g., there is only one potential enabler to the measurement of PAP S/D, as rare as that enabler might be); or there might be a huge difference in the prior probabilities, so we can still infer with certainty, or at least very high confidence, the abducted event.

If that is not the case, and there is any significant doubt, and we suspect that even a very likely implicit event or concept inferred from the explicit data is potentially hazardous to infer, we prefer to not include the inferred event in the text, recognizing the huge cost of adding a false item, compared to the omission of an inferred event.

We denote events abducted from declarative concepts as *implicit interventions*.

In table 2, we show an example of interventions inferred through abduction.

Table 2. Declarative concepts used to generate "implicit interventions". Each implicit intervention can have one or more values (e.g. Arterial Line can be "inserted" or "removed"), according to the values of the raw concept it was deducted from.

Declarative (raw) concept(s)	Abducted events (Implicit interventions)	# instances
[PAP S/D]	Swan Ganz catheter (PROC)	1
[CVP], [Arterial BP]	Arterial Line (PROC)	3
[Airway Size], [ETT Mark/Location]	Artificially breathing (PROC)	1

3.3   Pruning

After enriching our original data with abstractions and abducted interventions, we need to select which information is important and will appear in the final summary and which is unnecessary and should be removed to avoid overloading the user.

We prune the data by using general heuristics and several "independent" parameters (E.g., text length, detail level, profiles, etc). We use *pruning-heuristics* which define which data should be pruned and *maintaining heuristics*, defining which data instances should be maintained (and which override the *pruning-heuristics*).

The current *Pruning-heuristic* include: (1) Ignoring expected or "standard" values, within a specific context; during the knowledge acquisition process, we tag certain concept values as "Non-descript" (i.e., not to be mentioned without a special reason). (2) Preferring derived concepts over the concepts from which they are derived; the user can still see the raw concept from which the abstraction is derived by navigation of the text, since we keep links between the abstracted concepts and their deriving concepts. (3) When several interpretations of the same concept exist, within multiple contexts, report only on the interpretation within the most specific context.

Maintaining heuristics include: (4) Data instances that must be described; this is determined according to the domain, although certain events appear in every domain, such as death of the patient. (5) Maintaining extreme raw data values; In this case, even though they have an abstract value, we might want to maintain also the raw data.

In table 3 we show some of the heuristics used to prune the data.

Table 3. Raw and abstracted concepts before and after the pruning step, with the respective heuristic that was used in pruning: (H1) ignoring expected or "standard" values; (H2) Giving preference for derived concepts over the concepts from which they are derived; (H3) Within multiple contexts, report the interpretation with the most specific value. (H4) Data always described; (H5) Maintaining extreme raw data values

Raw concepts				Abstracted concepts			
Concept	Before	After	Heuristic	Concept	Before	After	Heuristic
Date of Birth	1	1	H4	WBC State	7	0	H1
Gender	1	1	H4	RBC State	7	2	H1
WBC-BLOOD	7	0	H2	HematocritState	8	8	none
Hematocrit	9	0	H2	Ectopy status	8	2	H1
PAP S/D	40	0	H2	ArterialBP State	8	4	H1

3.4 Document Structuring (DS)

After considering which data will appear in the final text, we define how these data will be presented. In the DS module it is decided how much information will be expressed in each phrase, in which order the facts will appear, how they will be organized into paragraphs, etc. The structure of the final text varies according to the output format expected as well as to the domain.

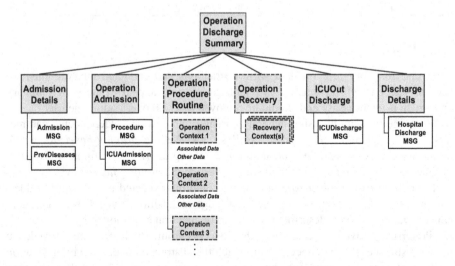

Fig. 4. The DS structures the final text into a tree. The tree defines how the data will be presented – the order, the paragraphs division and also the relation between events. (Gray rectangles are *Document-Block* objects, white rectangles are *Document-Message* objects. *Document-Blocks* can contain one or more *Document-Messages* or *Document-Blocks*.) Dashed-lined blocks represent flexible segments whose structure is defined by the data. Non-dashed blocks represent rigid segments of the text, whose structure was pre-defined.

We use two approaches for the DS: a top-bottom approach, which defines the main structure of the final text (e.g. division of paragraphs), and a bottom-up approach, which groups and combines events until all the events are linked together, by using appropriate discourse relations. The top-bottom approach works well when the structure of the text is very predictable and can be defined beforehand, but is less suitable for structures that vary and cannot be expected in advance. On the other hand, the bottom-up approach is less effective for the creation of paragraphs, and can take a lot of time which is needed to perform extensive searches and optimizations.

The output of this module resembles a tree. We prepare ahead of time, for each domain, a "stub" of the tree which includes the main textual segments in that domain, in a top-bottom approach. We build up from the pruned data a set of intermediate nodes which we try to link to the most appropriate node in the pre-prepared stub, in a bottom-up fashion. We call the leaves of the tree *Document-Messages* and the inner-nodes of the tree *Document-Blocks*. The tree has some parts that are more structured, part of the "stub" pre-defined, and others that are more flexible, with their structure affected and defined by the patient's data. In Figure 4 we show the tree used to create a Discharge Summary text. It defines for example, that each immediate child of the root ("Operation discharge Summary") becomes a new paragraph in the final text.

Document-blocks can be rigid or flexible. For example the Document-blocks: "Admission Details", "Operation Admission", "ICUOutDischarge" and "Discharge Details" have a rigid structure, which was mostly defined before hand, while the blocks "Operation Procedure Routine" and "Operation Recovery" are more flexible and their context will be determined and modeled based on the patient's actual instances of data associated with them. Document-Messages can be generic, as in the case of Drug-Message, Intervention-Message or Data-Message; or specific such as: Admission-Message, PrevDiseases-Message and ICUAdmission-Message.

Structured-blocks will be populated with the specific Document-Messages associated with it. For example, the structured section "Admission Details" will be populated with Document-Messages: Admission-Message and PrevDiseases-Message. Each specific Document-Message has specific data associated with it. Less-structured blocks may contain further Document-Blocks as well as generic Document-Messages. The creation of further Document-Blocks is affected by contexts that the data may generate. For example, the less-structured Document-block OperationRoutine will have further Document-Block children generated by the contexts associated with a specific operation event. Note that in general, the TA process applied by the KBTA method in the first step already generates, in addition to the temporal abstractions, all of the domain-specific contexts.

We denote block-context a document-block that was generated by a context. Each block-context has a start-time and end-time defining when the context starts/ends. This is defined by the start/end time of the event that generated the context and the definitions of the context duration. Figure 5 shows an example of block-contexts created by the CABG-operation event within the context of a CABG operation.

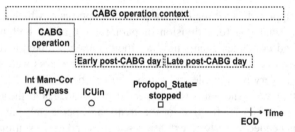

Fig. 5. Raw concepts are denoted by a circle while abstractions are denoted by a square. Contexts are denoted by dashed rectangles and events are denoted by a lined rectangle. The raw concept "Int Mam-Cor Art Bypass", in the context of a CABG operation, creates the event *"CABG Operation"*. The event generates two contexts: *"Early-postCABG day"* and *"Late-postCABG day"*. The start time of the *Early post-CABG day* context is defined by *"ICU In"* and by *"Propofol drug State"*. The *"Late post-CABG day"* context has its StartTime equal to the EndTime of context *"Early post CABG day"* and its EndTime set to the *"CABG operation"* event end of day (EOD).

Data or events that occurred during the context interval are associated with the respective block-context and will become Document-Messages associated with that block.

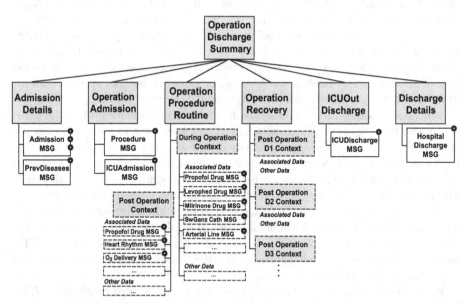

Fig. 6. A DS tree populated by patient's data. Structured blocks (e.g. AdmissionDetails) have specific messages associated to it (e.g. AdmissionMSG). Each Message block hold the patient data (circles). Less-structured blocks (e.g. OperationProcedureRoutine may have further blocks associated to it, according to the contexts generated by the data (e.g. the *"Early-postCABG day"* and *"Late-postCABG day"* context blocks, generated by the CABG operation event). Each context block has *associated* messages containing data related to the respective context interval, followed by *other* date that occurred during the interval.

Each context may have associated data/events, that we expect to occur within this context – based on what was specified in the Guideline (procedural knowledge). Within one block-context we will first add the expected associated data/events, followed by all other data that occurred within that context interval. For example, within the context "Early-postCABG day" we expect to have the events: "insertion of Swan-Ganz", and "start of artificial-breathing" between others. If the expected events indeed occurred we add respective messages to the "Early-postCABG day" block- context; then we add all additional data that took place during the interval.

The structure of the tree establishes the structure of an operation discharge summary for any given patient that has gone through an operation. To produce a Discharge Summary specific for a given patient, we need to populate the tree with the patient's data. An example of a populated tree can be seen in Figure 6. After populating the tree, by traversing the tree in a Depth First Search, we generate the order of the events in the final text.

3.5 Microplanning

In the Microplanning step, we (1) define the words and syntax structures that are used by the final text generator, (2) perform aggregation of the data and (3) generate referring expressions.

In the aggregation process, we define how much information will be expressed in each sentence. Although aggregation was also performed in previous steps, (e.g. in the TA step, which generates abstractions from the raw data) the aggregation here is done at a sentence level. In the aggregation process the semantic order has preference over the chronological order kept until now. Taking into consideration semantic considerations, we group together messages according to their type (drug, intervention or data message types).

In the case of drug messages, we group together different (drugs) with the same value. E.g. instead of: "drug X was started, drug Y was started and drug Z was stopped" we will have: "drug X and Y were started and drug Z was stopped". Note that messages are grouped only if they occur within the same context, although not necessarily during the same time. In the case of interventions and data messages, in addition to grouping different concepts with the same value, we also group same (interventions or data) concepts appearing more than once with the same or variant values. E.g. generating instead of: "Blood transfusion was given, blood transfusion was given" the sentence: "Blood transfusion were given twice [or n times]"; or instead of: "Atrial wires were inserted, ... atrial wires were removed" the sentence: "Atrial wires were inserted then removed".

Referring expression generation is the process of using pronouns to refer to entities. It creates a more natural and human style of the text. While the use of referring expressions can help avoiding repetition, the danger of its wrong usage is not knowing exactly which entity we are referring to. In medical texts, ambiguous meanings can have catastrophic consequences, therefore, we opted for a very conservative and minimalist use of referring expression usage. An example of its use can be seen in the following phrase, (note also the aggregation), in which the second appearance of "the patient's" in a single phrase is substituted by the pronoun his: "The patient's hematocrit, arterial bp and spo2 were Low and **his** temperature was afebrile."

The exact format of the microplanning output depends on the expected format of the step following it: surface realization.

3.6   Surface Realization

Surface Realization is the module responsible for generating the final text. Consequently, this step is language dependent, and observes the grammar rules of the language chosen. We opted to implement the Surface realization module using the existing Java module "SimpleNLG" [12]. Since our previous steps were implemented in C#, using the SimpleNLG module required us to transform our C# objects into Java objets. (Serialize the C# object and unserialize it into a Java object). This was implemented by using Google's protocol buffer whose advantages compared to other serialization methods are described elsewhere [13].

The realization of the text is done per section. Sections were defined within the tree structure, during the DS step. When the tree is flattened, the sections are kept and the flattened list of messages is divided into these sections. Each section is realized separately and in the same order it appears in the flattened list. One section might have sub-sections (generated by contexts). For example, the OperationRoutine section has two contexts: "Early-postCABG day" and "Late-postCABG day". Each context (or sub-section) is also realized separately.

Each section has a relationType (defined in the DS step) defining how messages within the section are related. For example the "sequence" relation defines that they should be realized one after the other, while the "causal" relation defines a cause-effect relationship between the messages.

Rigid (flexible) document-blocks, become rigid-structured (flexible-structured) sections, in the microplanning phase. The realization of structured sections is usually quite straight-forward while the realization of flexible-structured sections first go through aggregation and referring expression before being realized into their final text.

Table 4 compares our generated text summary with the original human-generated discharge summary found in the database. Part of the original summary could not be reproduced, since there was no data in the database that would support it. Presumably, such parts were written using some external data source, or perhaps textual progress notes.

Table 4. Comparison between the human and CliniText generated texts. Striked-trough text between brackets [] indicate text-parts that cannot be generated, i.e., without supporting data. Bold text in the right (left) column indicate data that do not appear in the other column, although they could.

The human discharge summary	The CliniText discharge summary
(1) HOSPITAL COURSE: On ***3285-5-17****, the patient was brought to the Operating Room for a redo coronary artery bypass grafting [~~times two and aortic valve replacement.~~] (2) The patient [~~tolerated the procedure well and~~] was transported intubated to the PACU **in stable condition** on a Levophed drip, Milrinone drip, and a Propofol drip. The patient had atrial wires and a chest tube. (3) On postoperative day #1, the patient was continued on his Levophed drip and Milrinone drip over night. The patient was extubated over night and was on a nasal cannula of 4 Lungs: **oxygen saturation 95% on room air**. The patient's **vital signs were otherwise stable**. (4) The patient had a postoperative hematocrit of 26.8; otherwise laboratory values were all within normal limits. [~~The patient was encouraged to be out of bed.~~] Drips were weaned. [~~The patient was started on his Plavix.~~] (5) On postoperative day #2, the patient was off all drips, [~~was started on Aspirin 325 per day and Captopril 6.25 t.i.d.~~] (6) The patient was afebrile in sinus rhythm. The patient had an **oxygen saturation of 96%** on 2 L nasal cannula. The patient had minimal output from the chest tubes. The patient's white count was 9.7, hematocrit 25.4, otherwise other labs were all within normal limits. [~~patient's chest tubes were removed, and~~ **the patient was transferred to the floor**. ~~On postoperative day #2, the patient was also seen by Physical Therapy.~~] (7) On postoperative day #3, the patient was still in the Intensive Care Unit. [~~The patient was kept in the Intensive Care Unit due to bed availability.~~] (8) The patient was **afebrile with a T-max of 99.7??**. The patient developed atrial fibrillation over night; however, the patient was rate controlled. The patient had an **oxygen saturation of 96%** on 2 L nasal cannula. (9) The patient's hematocrit on postoperative day #3 was 23.9. Other lab values were all within normal limits. [~~The patient was started on Lopressor 12.5, Heparin drip at 600.~~] The patient's wires were removed. (10) The patient self-converted to normal sinus rhythm with **occasional premature atrial contractions**. The patient remained in normal sinus rhythm.[~~and his Heparin drip was held. The patient was continued on Lopressor and Captopril, and tolerating it well.~~] (11) On postoperative day #4, the patient's hematocrit was 22.3. The patient was transfused 2 U packed red blood cells. [~~The patient's Lopressor was increased. The patient was continued on Captopril.~~] The patient was transferred to the floor .	(1) "On the 15/05/2005 Mr.97, a married, 82 years old patient, was admitted to the hospital. The patient's previous history includes peripheral_vascular disease(s). (2) On the 17/05/2005 the patient went through a "CABG" operation and was admitted to the ICU. (3) In the first hours following the CABG procedure, propofol, levophed and milrinone were started. **Swan-ganz catheter, arterial line, chest tube, atrial wires and vent wires were started**, artificially breathing was started, **heart rhythm was Paced**. The patient's hematocrit, **arterial bp and spo2 were Low**, temperature was Afebrile and his urine source was through an external catheter. (4) Later on, propofol was stopped. O2 delivery device was Nasal Cannula, heart rhythm was Normal sinus **and blood transfusion was given**. The patient's O2 Flow State **was 3 then 4** ; hematocrit **and urine output** were Low. (5) On post-oper day #1, the patient's **Arterial BP State remained Low** and Hematocrit remained Low ; **o2 flow was 2**. Levophed and milrinone were stopped. (6) On post-oper day #2, the **patient's BP State remained Hypotension** ; hematocrit was Low, ectopy status was Abnormal, heart rhythm was Atrial Fibrillation and his **arterial bp was High**. Arterial Line (PROC) was removed then inserted;. (7) On post-oper day #3, **the patient's BP State remained Hypotension** ; o2 delivery device was Nasal Cannula, o2 flow was 2, hematocrit was Low, heart rhythm was Normal sinus, **rbc was Very low**, ectopy status was Abnormal, o2 delivery device was None, **nbp_diast was 62 and his nbp_sys was 130**. Atrial wires (PROC) was removed then inserted ; vent wires was inserted. (8) On post-oper day #4, the patient's O2 Delivery Device remained None and **BP State remained Hypotension** ; hematocrit was Low, rbc was Very low and **his urine source was Independent**. Blood Transfusion (PROC) was given twice ; vent wires was removed. (9) The patient was discharged from ICU on 21/05/2005. (10) The patient was discharged from hospital on 23/05/2005."

3.7   Preliminary Evaluation

As a source for the longitudinal clinical data used in the examples, we used data from the Multiparameter Intelligent Monitoring in Intensive Care II database (MIMICII) [14]. There are two types of data in the MIMICII database: clinical data (numeric and textual) and bedside monitor waveforms. Waveforms in the Mimic DB are in fact rapidly sampled (125Hz) digitized signals recorded by the bedside monitors, such a electrocardiograms (ECG) and arterial blood pressure (ABP). Thus, to summarize MIMIC-II "waveforms", we would use the numeric representation of the signals underlying the "waveforms", in which each sample data instance would be represented by a raw data concept; and we could then abstract these data using relevant knowledge, precisely in the same way that we are already applying the temporal-abstraction process to all of the patient's other clinical data. In our current example, we used only clinical data, and mainly numeric data. Textual data was used only to compare our generated text to the original discharge summary. We focused on data of patients in the cardiac domain, more specifically on patients that went through a CABG procedure.

Our current evaluation, an example of which was shown in Table 2, is purely technical, judging the feasibility of the overall process, comparing the generated text to the MIMIC texts, without involving yet any users.

Judging by examples we have gone through such as shown in Table 2, the whole process is quite feasible and shows definite promise; but we have learned from our current preliminary experiments that much additional domain knowledge needs to be added.

Our initial analysis suggests that the amount of effort required to specify the necessary knowledge for a medical domain depends on the information expected to be included in the final summary, and on the amount of input concepts. In addition, each domain will also require a modification of the templates used to realize the text in the rigid blocks.

4   Discussion and Conclusions

It can be noted that in the CliniText summary text there are data items that do not appear in the original text. If some of these data are redundant (something to be defined by a clinical expert), we could prune them by defining additional heuristics in the pruning step, for example.

Another interesting point to be observed is that in the original text the levels of abstraction *varies* as compared to the levels of abstraction that appear in the CliniText summary, in which we always strive to have a uniformly high level of abstraction (e.g. "hematocrit=22.3" vs. "hematocrit state=low"). Allowing the user to *navigate* into the raw concepts that the abstraction was abstracted from can provide them with lower levels of abstraction when required. We are currently adding this capability.

We must take into account that the original text, because it was produced by humans, may sometimes contain wrong information. In our example (see Table 2), we can see that it's stated in paragraph #6 that the patient was discharged from the ICU, and in paragraph #7 the mistake is corrected by saying that the patient was actually kept in the ICU due to bed availability. Such mistakes can't occur in the CliniText summary, if the data are correct. On the other hand, when there are bad data, we can't avoid generating a wrong text. An additional layer of data-validity-check (for example specifying that a dead patient can't have a heart rate) could be added to the process to clean the data before the text starts to be generated. The definition of this layer requires the support of a clinical expert, and additional knowledge.

One of the advantages of having a discharge summary text being produced automatically is that the output format is structured and doesn't depend on subjective factors (e.g. how tired is the physician writing it, or how many discharge summaries she already wrote). Furthermore, the information to be included or omitted has been defined by objective consistent criteria, resulting in an objective data-and-knowledge-based summary.

We were limited during the prototype implementation by the clinical knowledge available and also regarding the data we had access to. Having access to clinical data involves legal and privacy concerns; Furthermore, finding a database which includes data and text summaries that can be related to each other isn't always easy.

The main purpose of building the described prototype was to demonstrate the feasibility of creating a system that can generate a complex knowledge-based textual summary of arbitrarily long time-oriented clinical data. We showed that it is possible to produce a readable text, and include the main events and data, according to what was defined in our KB.

In the future, we might try different implementations, for example, using a grammar instead of a tree representation in the Document Structuring step, or other modules of Surface Realization. We intend to evaluate the CliniText system regarding the aspects of *quality* of the generated text, *usability* and *functionality* for relevant predefined tasks. The evaluation process will involve a technical evaluation as well as involve user opinions.

Acknowledgements. Part of this work was supported the EU 7th Framework MobiGuide project, grant No. 287811.

References

1. Goldstein, A., Shahar, Y.: A Framework for Automated Knowledge-Based Textual Summarization of Longitudinal Medical Records. In: KR4HC Workshop, Tallinn, Estonia (2012)
2. Combi, C., Shahar, Y., Keravnou-Papailiou, E.: Temporal Information Systems in Medicine. Springer, New York (2010)
3. Portet, F., Reiter, E., Hunter, J., Sripada, S.: Automatic generation of textual summaries from neonatal intensive care data. AI in Med., 227–236 (2007)
4. Shahar, Y.: A framework for knowledge-based temporal abstraction. AI 90, 79–133 (1997)
5. Lavrač, N., Kononenko, I., Keravnou, E., Kukar, M., Zupan, B.: Intelligent data analysis for medical diagnosis: using machine learning and temporal abstraction. AI Communications 11, 191–218 (1999)

6. McDonald, D.D., Bolc, L.: Natural Language Generation Systems. Springer, New York (1988)
7. Huske-Kraus, D.: Text generation in clinical medicine-a review. Meth. Info. Med. 42, 51–60 (2003)
8. Portet, F., et al.: Automatic generation of textual summaries from neonatal intensive care data. Artificial Intelligence (2009), doi:10.1016/j.artint.2008.12.002
9. Hatsek, A., Shahar, Y., Taieb-Maimon, M., Shalom, E., Klimov, D., Lunenfeld, E.: A scalable architecture for incremental specification and maintenance of procedural decision-support knowledge. Open. Med. Info., 255–277 (2010)
10. Boaz, D., Shahar, Y.: Idan: A distributed temporal-abstraction mediator for medical databases. AI in Medicine, 21–30 (2003)
11. Owens, D., Sox, H.: Biomedical Decision Making: Probabilistic Clinical Reasoning. In: Biomedical Informatics (Shortliffe and Cimino), ch. 3, pp. 80–129 (2006)
12. https://code.google.com/p/simplenlg/
13. https://code.google.com/p/protobuf/
14. The Laboratory for Computational Physiology, http://www.physionet.org

Knowledge-Based Patient Data Generation

Zhisheng Huang, Frank van Harmelen, Annette ten Teije, and Kathrin Dentler

Department of Computer Science,
VU University Amsterdam, The Netherlands
{huang,Frank.van.Harmelen,annette,k.dentler}@cs.vu.nl

Abstract. The development and investigation of medical applications require patient data from various Electronic Health Records (EHR) or Clinical Records (CR). However, in practice, patient data is and should be protected and monitored to avoid unauthorized access or publicity, because of many reasons including privacy, security, ethics, and confidentiality. Thus, many researchers and developers encounter the problem to access required patient data for their research or make patient data available for example to demonstrate the reproducibility of their results. In this paper, we propose a knowledge-based approach of synthesizing large scale patient data. Our main goal is to make the generated patient data as realistic as possible, by using domain knowledge to control the data generation process. Such domain knowledge can be collected from biomedical publications such as PubMed, from medical textbooks, or web resources (e.g. Wikipedia and medical websites). Collected knowledge is formalized in the Patient Data Definition Language (PDDL) for the patient data generation. We have implemented the proposed approach in our Advanced Patient Data Generator (APDG). We have used APDG to generate large scale data for breast cancer patients in the experiments of SemanticCT, a semantically-enabled system for clinical trials. The results show that the generated patient data are useful for various tests in the system.

1 Introduction

Research and development of medical applications require the use of electronic patient data. This patient data can be obtained either from Electronic Health Records (EHR), which are systematic collections of electronic health information about individual patients or populations, or from Clinical Records (CR), which are collections of personal medical information recorded by clinicians[2]. However, in practice, patient data is protected and monitored to avoid unauthorized access or publicity, because of many reasons, such as privacy, security, ethics, confidentiality, etc. These circumstances make the use of patient data for research hard, and block the publicity of relevant patient data used in the research for public evaluation.

Therefore, an important research question is *"whether it is possible to develop a tool which can be used to create virtual and most importantly realistic patient data?"* The advantage of generated patient data is obvious, as it would not lead to any privacy problems.

We consider the following use cases of the generated patient data:

D. Riaño et al. (Eds.): KR4HC 2013/ProHealth 2013, LNAI 8268, pp. 83–96, 2013.

- **Availability.** The generated patient data can be used by developers to test and evaluate prototypes, without waiting for the approval from the authority or even the patients themselves. Developers mainly care about the format and the quality of the data. By defining the required format, data can easily be generated based on realistic distributions. Such required patient data would always be available for system developers for tests. Public datasets might also prove to be useful for comparison and benchmark of medical applications.
- **Publicity.** The generated patient data can be published and made available for public in any circumstance. Researchers can use those data for explanation of experiments and evaluation of their research. Those generated patient data are sufficient for the experiments in the developments of medical knowledge/information systems.
- **Complementary.** The quality of real patient data is not perfect. Some data values may be missing, erroneous, noisy, or inconsistent. The quality of generated patient data might depend on the preferences of the user. The generator could produce high-quality data for researchers and developers who prefer high quality of data as well as more realistic data.
- **Rarity.** We can use the patient data generator to create some patient data of rare diseases, because their original data is too rare to be obtained. The patient data generator can generate the required patient data, based on existing medical findings, and make those rare data available for demonstration of a prototyping system.
- **Typicality.** For the evaluation and benchmarking of an e-Health system or tool, sometimes we require that the benchmarks or tested data are not biased towards any data feature. Namely, the benchmarks should be typical enough to cover wide range of realistic data. The patient data generator can be used to create those typical data.

It is quite clear that the use cases above are useful for system developers and researchers. Thus, the next research question is: *"How can such a tool for patient data generation be built, with the generated data as realistic as possible?"* This is exactly the question we answer in this paper. The main idea is to use all the domain knowledge we can collect to control the patient data generation. Such domain knowledge can be collected from biomedical publications such as PubMed, domain knowledge from medical textbooks, and web resources such as Wikipedia and medical webpages.

In this paper, we propose a knowledge-based approach of synthesizing large scale patient data. Collected knowledge is formalized in the Patient Data Definition Language (PDDL) and used for the patient data generation. We have implemented the proposed approach in Advanced Patient Data Generator (APDG)[1], and used APDG to create patient data, which includes large data sets for breast cancer patients for the experiments in the SemanticCT system, a semantically-enabled knowledge system for clinical trials[7,6]. Those experiments include patient recruitment service (i.e., identifying eligible patients for a trial), trial finding service (i.e., finding suitable trials for a patient), and protocol feasibility service

---

[1] http://wasp.cs.vu.nl/apdg

(i.e., design eligibility criteria for a trial). The results show that the generated patient data is useful for various tests in the system.

This paper is organized as follows: Section 2 presents a framework of knowledge-based patient data generation. Section 3 proposes the patient data definition language (PDDL). Section 4 discusses the implementation of APDG. Section 5 reports several experiments of APDG. After a discussion of related work in Section 6, the last section includes conclusions and future work.

2   Framework

2.1   Patient Data

We are going to design a system which can generate patient data, based on the formalized domain knowledge. In particular we will focus on the generation of EHR data. Naturally, the first question here is what kinds of standardization for the data would be used for our system. There have been several initiatives to standardize a generic EHR architecture of patient data. Well-known EHR architectures are the archetype-based ones[1], like openEHR[2]. Those archetype-based EHR architectures introduce the two-level approach, reference model level and archetype level, for the specification of the structure and semantics of patient data. Archetypes are reusable and domain-specific definitions of clinical concepts in the structured and constrained combinations of entities of the reference model, which represents the generic and stable properties of patient data. From the perspective of computer science, we call those entities of the reference model *slots*.

In APDG, we introduce a similar architecture of patient data, like those archetype-based EHR ones. We consider the architecture of patient data as a set of data which consists of the following three levels: Session-Archetype-Slot. Namely, sessions are considered to be a collection of archetypes which have been instantiated with slots from a reference model.

2.2   Knowledge for Patient Data Generation

As we have discussed above, we will collect relevant domain knowledge for patient data generation. This domain knowledge can be collected from the following resources.

– **Biomedical publications.** Biomedical publications such as PubMed and medical books provide rich information about diseases and patients. For example, we can find the description of distant metastases for breast cancer patients from a publication in PubMed[3]:

> *We found distant metastases at the time of primary diagnosis in 19 patients (3.9%). Bone metastases were found in 2.7%, liver metastases in 1.0%, and pulmonary metastases in 0.4%. However,*

---

[2] http://www.openehr.org/
[3] http://www.ncbi.nlm.nih.gov/pubmed/14605816

in breast tumors smaller than 1 cm, no metastatic lesions were found, whereas 18.2% of the patients with pT4 tumors had metastases. In 2.4% of screening imaging studies, metastases were ruled out by additional imaging.

The knowledge above can be used to define the distant metastases of breast cancer patients and their metastases sites.

– **Web resources.** Web resources such as Wikipedia and medical websites usually provide information about the distribution and its dependence on other variables (such as gender, age, etc.) for diseases. For example, we can find the following information about the distribution of breast cancer stage from the web page[4]

Data on around 17,800 women diagnosed with breast cancer in the East of England in 2006-2009 shows that, of the 92% of cancers for which a stage was recorded, 41% were Stage I, 45% stage II, 9% stage III and 5% stage IV.

This knowledge can be used to generate patient data with the stage information.

Because the information provided by various resources above may be differing, we can design a preference ordering to evaluate those data resources, so that some information would be preferred to other ones in case of inconsistencies between resources. For the temporal aspect, we would prefer the data which occurs latest to data which occurs earlier. For the trust aspect, we would prefer data which appears in scientific publications (e.g., those in PubMed or Medical textbook) to data that appears in websites.

On the other hand, the collected data may not cover exactly what we are expecting to get. However, it would not lead to a serious problem if we consider approximate patient data acceptable. For example, although the distributions above are stated for specific area (East of England) and specific period (2006-2009), we can use this knowledge to provide an approximate estimation for the distribution if we cannot find any information which states that the data is too specific for that area in that period and they are significantly different from other areas or other periods.

We formalize the collected domain knowledge in a formalism which is called *Patient Data Definition Language (PDDL)* for the procedural control of patient data generation. Namely we will embed formalized domain knowledge into the Session-Archetype-Slot structure of patient data for the control. Given a disease, embedded control knowledge is expected to be added by clinical professionals or knowledge engineers, who have trustful knowledge about the disease and know how to formalize the knowledge exactly. However, we would not expect those domain experts to have an intensive training to learn how to formalize comprehensive knowledge in Artificial Intelligence to use APDG. Thus, We design the PDDL to make it based on an XML-based text document, which would make the formulation easy for clinical professionals or knowledge engineers. Furthermore,

---

[4] http://www.cancerresearchuk.org/cancer-info/cancerstats/
types/breast/incidence/uk-breast-cancer-incidence-statistics#stage

we have also implemented a user-friendly GUI for users, so that they need no any intensive knowledge about XML to use the APDG tool[11].

We generate patient data for breast cancer with APDG by modeling the medical knowledge into PDDL by ourselves. The mapping from the knowledge from several sources into the PDDL model needs to be validated with an expert. The contribution of this paper is the possibility of generating patient data on a knowledge intensive way that exploits the available medical knowledge, and can be used in studying several medical tasks like patient recruitment for clinical trials.

3   Patient Data Definition Language (PDDL)

3.1   General Components

The Patient Data Definition Language (PDDL) is designed to be an XML-based language to define the general format of the patient data and its relevant domain knowledge to control the procedure of patient data generation. Thus, PDDL is concerned with the following information.

- **Patient Data Format.** It defines the structure of patient data by stating which Session-Archetype-Slot structure will be used for the generated patient data.
- **Domains and Ranges.** It defines what kinds of domains and ranges of patient data are allowed for the generated patient data.
- **Distribution.** It provides value distribution statements for each slot.
- **Dependence.** It defines value dependence among variables in the patient data.

In the next subsections we discuss those types of information in more detail.

3.2   Patient Data Format

We use the general structure, i.e., 'Session-Archetype-Slot' for patient data generation. That structure is stated with the following XML format:

```
<Session value="DemographicData">
  <Archetype concept = "Patient">
    <Slot value="LastName" type="string"/>
    <Slot value="FirstName" type="string"/>
    <Slot value="Gender" type="string"/>
    <Slot value="BirthYear" type="year"/>
  </Archetype>
</Session>
```

Each entity (i.e. session, archetype, or slot) has a value property to define the entity name. An archetype is allowed to contain other (non-recursive) archetypes or slots. Slots are termination tabs which are used to state the possible values of the slots.

3.3   Domain Ranges

Data ranges in PDDL are defined by using the DataRange tab and the data type specification, like those in the following format which defines the enumeration values:

```
<Slot value="Gender">
  <DataRange>
  <enumeration value="female"/>
  <enumeration value="male"/>
  </DataRange>
  </Slot>
```

or in the following format which defines the range of the allowed values for the slot by using the maxInclusive and minInclusive tabs.

```
<Slot value="BirthYear">
  <DataRange>
    <maxInclusive datatype="http://www.w3.org/2001/XMLSchema#date"
    >2006</maxInclusive>
    <minInclusive datatype="http://www.w3.org/2001/XMLSchema#date"
    >1900</minInclusive>
  </DataRange>
  </Slot>
```

3.4   Distribution

A data distribution is defined inside the DataRange with the special tab 'distribution'. A distribution value is designed to take a real number between 0 and 100, like this:

```
<Slot value="Gender">
  <DataRange>
    <enumeration value="female"/>
    <enumeration value="male"/>
    <Distributions type="enumeration">
      <Distribution item="female" pfrom="0" pto="100"/>
      <Distribution item="male" pfrom="0" pto="0"/>
    </Distributions>
  </DataRange>
  </Slot>
```

Each distribution tab defines its data type of the slot, followed by a list of the distribution which states the value (i.e., item for the enumeration type) and its distribution range by the pair *pfrom* and *pto*. The example above states that the 100 percent (i.e., from 0 to 100) of patients are female, zero percent of patients (i.e. from 0 to 0) are male. For the non-enumeration data range, we use the properties (*from* and *to*) to define the value range, like this[5]:

```
<Slot value="BirthYear">
  <DataRange>
    <Distributions type="year" variable="$birthyear">
      <Distribution from="1998" to="2006" pfrom="0" pto="0"/>
      <Distribution from="1983" to="1997" pfrom="0" pto="0"/>
      <Distribution from="1973" to="1982" pfrom="0" pto="4.36"/>
      ....
      <Distribution from="1900" to="1932" pfrom="84.35" pto="100"/>
    </Distributions>
  </DataRange>
  </Slot>
```

[5] The value of the slot BirthYear will be reused in other slots. Thus, we introduce a variable for it.

If a distribution statement already contains the information of the datatype for the slot (by stating the type), its reference model tabs (like enumeration, maxInclusive, minInclusive, etc.) can be ignored.

A distribution can be stated by its distribution type (e.g., uniform random, normal distribution, etc.) on an enumeration set, like those in the following example:

```
<Slot value="DiagnosisMonth" type="month">
  <DataRange>
    <Distributions type="enumeration">
     <Distribution disttype="uniformrandom"
         set="1,2,3,4,5,6,7,8,9,10,11,12"/>
    </Distributions>
  </DataRange>
</Slot>
```

or by stating a data range (with a type) over the distribution, for instance the data range (minimax) over integers from 1927 to 2000 with the uniform random distribution[6].

```
<Slot value="BirthYear">
 <DataRange>
  <Distributions type="year" variable="$birthyear">
   <Distribution disttype="uniform" datatype="minmax(int)"
               data="1927,2000"/>
  </Distributions></DataRange>
</Slot>
```

which states the data range (minmax) over integers from 1927 to 2000 with the uniform random distribution.

3.5   Dependence

The condition statements are used to state the conditions which depend on some variables which have been defined in the previous distributions slots, like this:

```
<Slot value="MenopausalStatus">
 <DataRange>
  <Distributions type="enumeration" variable="$menopausalstatus">
    <Distribution item="premenopausal" pfrom="0" pto="100"
        condition="$birthyear &gt;1970"/>
    <Distribution item="perimenopausal" pfrom="0" pto="80"
        condition="$birthyear =&lt;1970 AND $birthyear &gt;=1950"/>
     <Distribution item="postmenopausal" pfrom="80" pto="100"
        condition="$birthyear =&lt; 1970 AND $birthyear &gt;= 1950"/>
     <Distribution item="postmenopausal" pfrom="0" pto="100"
        condition="$birthyear &lt; 1950"/>
    </Distributions></DataRange>
 </Slot>
```

The statements above state that the menopausal status is defined in terms of the condition of the variable '$birthyear'. The Boolean operator 'AND' is introduced to specify the composite expressions with the comparison operators, such as '<'(less than), '>'(greater than), '> =' (greater than or equal), etc.

---

[6] For the normal distribution, it needs the two additional parameters, the mean μ and the standard deviation σ, i.e., $normal(\mu, \sigma)$. If those two parameters are omitted, it means that they take the default values, i.e., $\mu = (min + max)/2, \sigma = 0.5$.

However, we may need some variables which do not necessarily correspond with any slot. Thus, we design a pure variable slot which are used to generate some internal information without binding its values to any slot. Those dummy slots are defined by using the tab variable, like this:

```
<Variable value="housenumber">
 <Distributions type="string" variable="$housenumber">
  <Distribution disttype="uniform"
    datatype="minmax(int)" data="1,1000"/>
 </Distributions>
</Variable>
```

Evalution slots are used to define the slots those values are calculated by some built-in predicates in expressions. For example, we use the predicate "concat" to denote the concatenate of strings, like this:

```
<EvaluationSlot value="phonenumber" type="string"
source="concat($nationalcode,-,$areacode,-,$localnumber)"/>
```

We use the predicate "eval" to denote the evaluation of arithmetic expressions, like this:

```
<EvaluationSlot value="lymphocytepc" type="float"
source="eval(100*$lymphocyte/$leukocyte)"/>
```

which means that the percentage of lymphocytes is calculated by the lymphocyt count and the leukocyte count.

3.6   Semantic Interoperability

We use the tab 'ConceptMapping' to map the PDDL entities into their corresponding concepts in the ontologies[9]. For example, the following statement states that the slot 'gender' has the concept in the ontology SNOMED with a concept id '263495000'.

```
<Slot value="Gender">
  <ConceptMapping ontology="snomed" conceptid="263495000"/>
  <DataRange>
  <enumeration value="female"/>
  <enumeration value="male"/>
  </Distributions></DataRange></Slot>
```

In this section we showed how the knowledge is formalized in the Patient Data Definition Language (PDDL) for the patient data generation. In the next section we report on the proposed approach in our Advanced Patient Data Generator (APDG).

4   Implementation

APDG is designed to support different kinds of formats for the generated patient data to make them easy to be accommodated into various EHR systems. Since we have defined the Patient Data Definition Language (PDDL) in XML, it would be convenient to use XSLT to transform XML-based patient data into the required data formats. The architecture of APDG is shown in Figure 1.

In order to control the generation of patient data, users can input some generation parameters into the system. Those generation parameters include

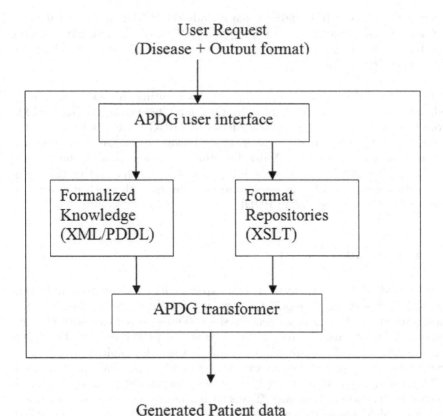

Fig. 1. The architecture of APGD

- Number of patients. Namely, how many patients will be covered by the generated data. Usually we create a single file for each patient. With the support of the extended APDG system (i.e., the APDG system supports for the extension of the patient data based on the existing data), a single patient may have multiple data files which cover different sessions.
- Identification number of Patient (Patient ID). We want to design unique patient IDs for generated patient data, so that generated patient data can be loaded into any data store (typically, triple stores) without having to worry about ID conflict with other data. The Patient IDs consist of the following parts: the creator ID, which is used to identify the creator of the patient data, the session ID, which is used to identify different patient data sets which are generated by same creators, the disease ID, an additional ID which is designed to identify certain kinds of patients, and a patient number, which is used to identify a single patient which is created in the same session. The initial patient number (like 1000000) is used to create those patient numbers accordingly.
- Patient data format. The patient data format is used to specify what kinds of patient data format will be generated. We have provided the support for

several formats of RDF data, which include the NTriple data format (with the extension names 'nt' or 'ntriples) and RDF/XML data format (with the extension name 'xml')[7]. Each data format corresponds to an XSLT file for the data generation.

Those generation parameters are set by editing a text file named 'apdg.properties', or inputting into the GUI interface of the APDG tool[11], before launching the APDG system. After the APDG system is launched, the system will load the formalized patient generation knowledge (i.e., those are formalized in PDDL) and the XSLT file which corresponds with the selected data format. The APDG transformer is a java system which calls the XSLT converter with the support of some Java libraries to interpret the patient generation knowledge which are encoded in PDDL.

5 Experiments

We have used APDG to perform several experiments on the patient data generation. In this section, we report the case of data generation for female breast cancer patients. In this case, we generated 10,000 female patients with the first diagnosis of breast cancers, and use those generated patient data for the experiments in SemanticCT, a semantically enabled system for clinical trials[7,6].

SemanticCT[8] [7] provides semantic integration of various data in clinical trials. The system is semantically enabled for decision support in various scenarios in medical applications. SemanticCT has been semantically integrated with various data, which include trial documents with semantically annotated eligibility criteria and large amount of patient data with structured EHR and clinical medical records. Well-known medical terminologies and ontologies, such as SNOMED, LOINC, etc., have been used for the semantic interoperability.

SemanticCT is built on the top of LarKC (Large Knowledge Collider), a platform for scalable semantic data processing[9][5,10]. With the built-in reasoning support for large-scale RDF/OWL data of LarKC, SemanticCT is able to provide various reasoning and data processing services for clinical trials, which include faster identification of eligible patients for recruitment service and efficient identification of eligible trials for patients.

The 10,000 generated breast cancer patients have been used in the tests of SemanticCT for automatic patient recruitment and trial finding. The generated patient data covers the main properties of clinical trials for female patients with the first diagnosis of breast cancer. Those main properties include:

- Gender. Since we want to create female patient data, we set the gender to 'female' with 100 percent in the PDDL and map the concept to SNOMED CT as follows:

---

[7] We thank José Alberto Maldonado for creating the support of RDF/XML format.
[8] http://wasp.cs.vu.nl/sct
[9] http://www.larkc.eu

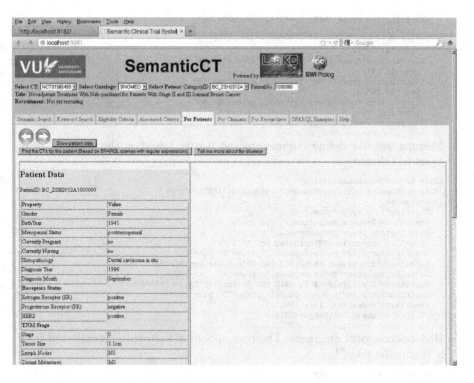

Fig. 2. The Patient Data in SemanticCT

```
<Slot value="Gender">
 <ConceptMapping ontology="snomed" conceptid="263495000"/>
 <DataRange>
  <enumeration value="female"/>
  <enumeration value="male"/>
  <Distributions type="enumeration">
   <Distribution item="female" pfrom="0" pto="100"/>
   <Distribution item="male" pfrom="0" pto="0"/>
  </Distributions></DataRange></Slot>
```

– Age. The age is an important variable which will be used to define the
  menopausal status and distribution of other properties. We collect the age
  distribution of female breast cancer from a cancer research website [10] and
  define this knowledge in PDDL as follows:

```
<Slot value="BirthYear">
 <ConceptMapping ontology="snomed" conceptid="397669002"/>
 <DataRange>
  <maxInclusive datatype="http://www.w3.org/2001/XMLSchema#date">
    1982</maxInclusive>
  <minInclusive datatype="http://www.w3.org/2001/XMLSchema#date">
    1900</minInclusive>
  <Distributions type="year" variable="$birthyear">
    <Distribution from="1973" to="1982" pfrom="0" pto="4.36"/>
```

---

[10] http://info.cancerresearchuk.org/cancerstats/types/
breast/incidence/uk-breast-cancer-incidence-statistics

```
<Distribution from="1963" to="1972" pfrom="4.36"
    pto="19.32"/>
<Distribution from="1953" to="1962" pfrom="19.32"
    pto="41.29"/>
<Distribution from="1943" to="1952" pfrom="41.29"
    pto="67.12"/>
<Distribution from="1933" to="1942" pfrom="67.12"
    pto="84.35"/>
<Distribution from="1900" to="1932" pfrom="84.35"
    pto="100"/>
</Distributions></DataRange></Slot>
```

– Menopausal. We define the menopausal status, based on the age (i.e., birth year) as follows:

```
<Slot value="MenopausalStatus">
<ConceptMapping ontology="snomed" conceptid="161712005"/>
<DataRange>
  <Distributions type="enumeration"
    variable="$menopausalstatus">
  <Distribution item="premenopausal" pfrom="0"
    pto="100" condition="$birthyear &gt;1970"/>
  <Distribution item="perimenopausal" pfrom="0" pto="80"
    condition="$birthyear =&lt;1970 AND $birthyear &gt;=1950"/>
  <Distribution item="postmenopausal" pfrom="80" pto="100"
    condition="$birthyear =&lt; 1970 AND $birthyear &gt;= 1950"/>
  <Distribution item="postmenopausal" pfrom="0" pto="100"
    condition="$birthyear &lt; 1950"/>
  </Distributions></DataRange></Slot>
```

– Histopathological diagnosis. The corresponding knowledge is collected from a Wikipedia page[11].

```
<Slot value="Histopathology">
  <DataRange>
    <enumeration value="Invasive ductal carcinoma">
    <ConceptMapping ontology="snomed" conceptid="408643008"/>
    </enumeration>
    <enumeration value="Ductal carcinoma in situ">
    <ConceptMapping ontology="snomed" conceptid="399935008"/>
    </enumeration>
    <enumeration value="Invasive lobular carcinoma">
    <ConceptMapping ontology="snomed" conceptid="444057000"/>
    </enumeration>
    <Distributions type="enumeration" variable="$diagnosis">
      <Distribution item="Invasive ductal carcinoma"
        pfrom="0" pto="55"/>
      <Distribution item="Ductal carcinoma in situ"
        pfrom="55" pto="68"/>
      <Distribution item="Invasive lobular carcinoma"
        pfrom="68" pto="73"/>
      <Distribution item="Lobular carcinoma in situ"
        pfrom="73" pto="100"/>
    </Distributions></DataRange></Slot>
```

Figure 2 shows a screen shot of the patient data in SemanticCT. For the experiment of patient recruitment service. We have picked up 10 clinical trials randomly and formalized their eligibility criteria by using the rule-based formalization [6]. We have tested the system for automatically identifying eligible patients for those selected trials. For the experiment of trial finding service, we use SPARQL queries with regular expressions over eligibility criteria to find the trials which are suitable for the patients. The results show that the generated patient data are useful for various tests in the system[7,6].

---

[11] http://en.wikipedia.org/wiki/Breast_cancer_classification

6   Discussion and Conclusion

6.1   Related Work

Clinical avatars[12] developed by the Laboratory for Personalized Medicine are virtual representations of people for the purpose of conducting personalized medicine simulations. Similar with APDG, Clinical Avatars are configured so that their statistical distribution matches the requirements of a particular population. The Conditional Probability Table which describes the distribution of the avatar attributes are used to configure Clinical Avatars.

In [4], an approach of synthetic patient data is developed. It consists of an OWL schema that describes the data needed to calculate the exemplary indicators (TBox, i.e. terminological background knowledge), and the patient data (ABox, i.e. knowledge about individuals). It can generate both the OWL schema and the patient data in OWL 2 with the OWL API. [4] uses unique random distribution only for the generation of patient data.

[8,3] propose a data-driven approach for creating synthetic electronic medical records. The approach consists of the three major steps: 1) synthetic patient identity and basic information generation; 2) identification of care patterns that the synthetic patients would receive based on the information present in real EMR data for similar health problems; 3) adaptation of these care patterns to the synthetic patient population. A distance measure is used to identify the closest patient care descriptor to the desired inject.

APDG supports for comprehensive configuration of domain-knowledge and description of statistical distribution and variable dependence. Thus, it provide a more powerful tool to generate various patient data which meets different requirements. Furthermore, in APDG, the Patient Data Definition Language PDDL is designed based on the XML format. Thus, it is much more convenient and flexible to convert the PDDL data into ones with other kinds of data formats.

6.2   Concluding Remarks

We have proposed a knowledge-based approach of synthesizing large scale patient data. This synthesis is to use various domain knowledge we can collect to control the patient data generation. Those domain knowledge can be collected from biomedical publications or web resources. The collected knowledge are formalized in an XML-based language PDDL to describe required patient data and their distributions.

There are many interesting issues for future work of APDG. The existing APDG supports for the generation of the RDF data formats (RDF/NTriple and RDF/XML) only. We are going to create more XSLT files to make APDG to cover wider range of data formats. We are going to extend the PDDL so that it can cover wider range of data distribution declaration and more powerful expressions for variable dependence description.

---

[12] http://clinicalavatars.org/

Acknowledgments. This work is partially supported by the European Commission under the 7th framework programme EURECA Project (FP7-ICT-2011-7, Grant 288048). We thank José Alberto Maldonado of the Universidad Politecnica de Valencia Spain, who contributes to the XSLT file for the generation of RDF/XML in APDG. Thanks to Minghui Zhang and the team in Wuhan University of Science and Technology China, who contribute to the design and the implementation of the visual interface tools for APDG.

References

1. Beale, T.: Archetypes: Constraint-based domain models for future-proof information systems. In: OOPSLA 2002 Workshop on Behavioural Semantics (2002)
2. Bucur, A., ten Teije, A., van Harmelen, F., Tagni, G., Kondylakis, H., van Leeuwen, J., Schepper, K.D., Huang, Z.: Formalization of eligibility conditions of CT and a patient recruitment method, D6.1. Technical report, EURECA Project (2012)
3. Buczak, A., Babin, S., Moniz, L.: Data-driven approach for creating synthetic electronic medical records. BMC Medical Informatics and Decision Making 10(59) (2010)
4. Dentler, K., ten Teije, A., Cornet, R., de Keizer, N.: Towards the automated calculation of clinical quality indicators. In: Riaño, D., ten Teije, A., Miksch, S. (eds.) KR4HC 2011. LNCS, vol. 6924, pp. 51–64. Springer, Heidelberg (2012)
5. Fensel, D., van Harmelen, F., Andersson, B., Brennan, P., Cunningham, H., Della Valle, E., Fischer, F., Huang, Z., Kiryakov, A., Lee, T., School, L., Tresp, V., Wesner, S., Witbrock, M., Zhong, N.: Towards LarKC: a platform for web-scale reasoning. In: Proceedings of the IEEE International Conference on Semantic Computing (ICSC 2008). IEEE Computer Society Press, CA (2008)
6. Huang, Z., ten Teije, A., van Harmelen, F.: Rule-based formalization of eligibility criteria for clinical trials. In: Peek, N., Marín Morales, R., Peleg, M. (eds.) AIME 2013. LNCS, vol. 7885, pp. 38–47. Springer, Heidelberg (2013)
7. Huang, Z., ten Teije, A., van Harmelen, F.: SemanticCT: A semantically enabled clinical trial system. In: Lenz, R., Mikszh, S., Peleg, M., Reichert, M., ten Teije, D.R.A. (eds.) Process Support and Knowledge Representation in Health Care. LNCS (LNAI), Springer (2013)
8. Moniz, L., Buczak, A.L., Hung, L., Babin, S., Dorko, M., Lombardo, J.: Construction and validation of synthetic electronic medical records. Journal of Public Health 1(1), 1–36 (2009)
9. Spackman, K.: Managing clinical terminology hierarchies using algorithmic calculation of subsumption: Experience with snomed-rt. Journal of the American Medical Informatics Association (2000)
10. Witbrock, M., Fortuna, B., Bradesko, L., Kerrigan, M., Bishop, B., van Harmelen, F., ten Teije, A., Oren, E., Momtchev, V., Tenschert, A., Cheptsov, A., Roller, S., Gallizo, G.: D5.3.1 - requirements analysis and report on lessons learned during prototyping. Larkc project deliverable (June 2009)
11. Zhang, M., Huang, Z., Gu, J.: Visual interface tools for advanced patient data generator. In: Chinese Digital Medicine (to appear, 2013)

An Ontology-Driven Personalization Framework for Designing Theory-Driven Self-management Interventions

Syed Sibte Raza Abidi[1] and Samina Abidi[1,2]

[1] NICHE Research Lab, Faculty of Computer Science, Dalhousie University, Canada
[2] Medical Informatics, Faculty of Medicine, Dalhousie University, Canada
sraza@cs.dal.ca, samina.abidi@Dal.ca

Abstract. We present a patient-centered self-management framework that aims to assist individuals to achieve self-efficacy in terms of self-management of their chronic condition. We have incorporated an evidence-driven behavior model—i.e. the Social Cognition Theory (SCT)—to personalize the self-management educational content based on the individual's health and psychosocial profile. We have taken a knowledge management approach to the development of the self-management framework where we have modeled the SCT, educational content and strategies, assessment tools and the personalization logic using an OWL-DL based ontology. The execution of the knowledge encapsulated within the SCT ontology allows for the dynamic generation of a patient's profile and the selection of the relevant self-management strategies, educational and motivational messages. We applied our self-management framework to develop a self-management program for cardiac conditions.

1 Introduction

Chronic diseases place a significant burden both on the patient and the healthcare system. Effective management of chronic diseases involve a longitudinal care program in which the patient is expected to be (a) an informed decision maker; and (b) an active partner engaging in disease management activities. Patient engagement in their care process, vis-à-vis self-management programs is an important element of the patient's longitudinal care program, where the patient is encouraged and expected to achieve self-efficacy in the self-management of the disease through a regime of educational and behavioral modification strategies. To ensure the effectiveness and efficacy of self-management programs, it is important that the proposed self-management interventions are (a) personalized to the unique needs and constraints of the patient; (b) based on sound theoretical health models so that the design of the intervention and the patient's responses to the intervention can be objectively determined; (c) based on validated health and behavior assessment tools to determine the patient's physical and behavioral dispositions; and (d) be interactive and readily accessible to the patient through a ubiquitous medium, such as smart phones or the web.

We argue that health education and disease-specific self-management programs for chronic disease management should not just focus on changing the patient's

D. Riaño et al. (Eds.): KR4HC 2013/ProHealth 2013, LNAI 8268, pp. 97–112, 2013.

awareness of the disease, rather they need to focus on improving the ability of the patient to make the right decisions and choices to achieve effective disease self-management. To this end, theory driven, evidence based behavioral models have been successfully integrated within patient self-management programs to influence the patient's behavior in adhering to their self-management programs. Some examples include: (i) diabetes management interventions [1-3], (ii) increasing low motivation to make a lifestyle change using stages of change [4,5], (iii) supporting effective behavior modification when motivation is present using theory of planned behavior [6, 7], social cognitive theory [8,9] and motivational interviewing [10], and (iv) addressing emotional and relational barriers to change [11,12].

Computerized patient education and self-management programs have been used to influence behavior change and to help individuals to make informed choices about therapeutic options, risk assessments and lifestyle modification, etc. More so, personalized patient education programs are noted to be more effective because individualized patient-specific educational interventions are more likely to be read, remembered and experienced as relevant and in turn personalized recommendations have a larger impact in motivating individuals to modify and adopt healthy behaviors [13, 14].

The effectiveness of a self-management program is contingent on the patient's ability and motivation to adhere to it—if a patient is not motivated or is incapable of following the self-management program then the expected health targets are likely to be underachieved or even the health of the patient may be compromised. Therefore, our approach to personalized self-management is to not just prescribe a disease-specific self-management program, but also to assist patients achieve the right level of knowledge, self-efficacy and self-regulation so that they are able to adhere to their self-management program and in turn achieve the targeted health benefits. This demands working with patients to understand their compliance challenges and to help them achieve positive behavior modification so that they become both motivated and capable to adhere to their self-management program. To incorporate behavior modification in self-management program planning we use the Social Cognition Theory (SCT) [21], where we focus on the patient's self-efficacy expectations and their perceived capabilities to learn or perform self-care actions [21]. Self-efficacy attainment has been shown to influence a patient's motivation, accomplishments, self-regulation and efforts to perform self-care actions [21-25]. To help patient achieve self-efficacy in the self-management of their disease, we propose to develop computerized interventions to: (i) help patients to self-identify their behavior modification challenges through self-observation and barrier identification exercises; and (ii) help patients to set personal goals and actions plans to achieve behavioral self-efficacy and self-regulation in overcoming their behavioral challenges through a series a personalized behavioral interventions. To this end, we propose to computerize the knowledge pertaining to theory-driven evidence-based behavior change models guided by SCT to design personalized behavior-driven and competence-driven self-management program that also include self-efficacy attainment strategies to help patients achieve positive behavior changes to improve compliance to their self-management program.

We believe that health knowledge management approaches can be used to model and integrate disease-specific clinical guidelines, evidence-driven behavior models and self-management strategies, where an interplay between these knowledge elements will help to develop personalized evidence-driven self-management programs for chronic disease patients. The key advantage of a knowledge model is the ability to interrelate concepts about the disease, clinical guidelines recommendations on self-management, behavior change models, validated self-management strategies and patient health, behavior and QoL assessment tools. This integrated, yet generic, knowledge model can be instantiated with disease-specific knowledge to design disease-specific self-management programs that can be further fine-tuned based on the patient's current health and behavior profile to generate personalized, persuasive and persistent self-management programs. The self-management programs will address behavioral issues pertaining to self-efficacy and compliance as well, and can be administered in a private learning environment where by educational and motivational reinforcements are delivered to patients to help them self-manage their condition. For developing the proposed knowledge model we use ontologies to represent the underlying concepts, their relationships, constraints and rules [26].

In this paper, we present our *Personalized Self-management Intervention Design (PSID)* framework to design personalized self-management educational and motivational interventions to empower, educate and engage patients in the self-management of their chronic conditions. The general objective of PSIDF is to provide a knowledge management environment to (a) model a high-level self-management program personalization strategy that takes into account both the health maintenance and behavioral compliance aspects of self-management programs; (b) computerize existing health and behavior assessment tools, evidence-based behavior models and self-management and self-efficacy attainment interventions; and (c) design condition- and patient-specific self-management programs based on the personalization strategy and the modeled knowledge. We have taken a semantic web approach to develop PSIDF, where we have developed a *Self-Management Program Personalization* (SPP) ontology that serves as the unified and scalable knowledge model to semantically represent and interrelate: (i) SCT-driven behavior models used to influence behavior change, (ii) a generic self-management program personalization strategy, (iii) health and behavior assessment tools, and (iv) self-efficacy related educational and motivational content. The knowledge encapsulated within the SPP ontology is re-used and re-configured by a reasoning based personalization engine—based on a patient's profile, the personalization strategy and self-efficacy goals—to generate a personalized self-management program that comprises self-efficacy attainment strategies to help patient's self-manage their condition and also to overcome any challenges they face in complying to their self-management program. In this paper, we discuss our self-management program personalization strategy and its manifestation in terms of the SPP ontology.

2   Social Cognition Theory: Background and Rationale

The Social Cognitive Theory (SCT) [16] provides a theoretical framework for developing interventions to modify a variety of health behaviors. According to SCT, motivational enhancements can ultimately lead to behavior modification [16]. From the SCT point of view, an educational intervention that is designed to provide information, behavioral strategies and incentives to motivate individuals to meet health-specific goals have two purposes: (i) to help the individual modify their behaviors, and (ii) to enhance the individual's perceived self-efficacy and outcome expectations. This is an interesting health educational dimension as SCT aims to instill self-efficacy and self-regulation in individuals in order to ensure permanent behavior change. In this regard, SCT postulates that a behavior is affected by (i) expectation of self-efficacy, i.e. the belief that a patient can successfully execute a necessary behavior and (ii) outcome expectation, i.e. belief that the behavior will produce desired outcome [16]. These expectations and cognitive competencies are developed and modified by social and environmental influences such as: social environments, encouragement and persuasions from credible people, observing other people's behaviors, and making judgments whether it has resulted in desired outcomes [17]. We note that the application of SCT has demonstrated positive effects on health behaviors in many chronic disease settings such as: Diabetes [18] and heart disease [19]. SCT has also been successfully applied to cessation of many negative behaviors such as smoking [18], and sedentary life style [20], and to acquire positive behaviors [21].

Our aim is to develop self-management programs that establish relationships between the interventions provided and the behavioral outcomes achieved. We believe that health education and self-management programs for chronic disease management should not just focus on changing the patient's awareness of the disease, rather they should focus on enhancing the ability of the patient to make the right choices to achieve effective disease management. In our framework, by modeling and computerizing SCT we aim to generate personalized self-efficacy attainment strategies addressing motivation to change, motivational enhancement strategies, behavior modification (goal-setting, behavior shaping, stimulus control and reinforcement management), emotion management and stress management issues [26, 27].

3   Strategy for Designing Personalized Self-management Programs

We have developed a personalized self-management program design strategy that incorporates SCT as the theoretical foundation to personalize educational content and behavior change strategies based on psychosocial determinants of self-efficacy, self-regulation, skill mastery and outcome-expectation [16]. In line with the principles of SCT, we engage the patient to: (a) self-identify their perceived barriers to achieving the self-management targets; and (b) self-select specific behavior modification strategies to help them overcome the perceived barriers that are inhibiting their attainment of self-efficacy to self-manage their condition.

The intent of our personalized self-management program design approach is to develop a fine-grained profile of a patient, where the profile comprises both health and psychosocial elements, and then use the profile to select relevant educational and motivational messages that aim to educate, empower and engage patients to develop skills, knowledge and self-confidence so that patients are able to self-manage their chronic condition, lifestyle and behavior. Personalization of the self-management program is achieved by the presentation of personalized behavior modification and self-efficacy related motivational messages that are in line with (i) the patient's self-selected behavior modification goals, and (ii) the patient's profile. Our personalized self-management program design approach is as follows:

1. *Develop the patient's health profile* using a range of validated health assessment tools to determine his/her health status. The health profile characterizes the patient's health along a set of disease-specific parameters that are to be used to personalize the health and behavior change interventions. For instance, to develop a health profile for cardiac patients we determine their level of stress, lifestyle, blood pressure, etc.

2. *Develop a behavioral profile* using evidence-driven behavior models, such as health belief model, social cognition theory, motivational interviewing, etc. The behavioral profile highlights the behavioral and psychosocial dispositions of a patient towards disease self-management. The behavioral profile is then to be used to tailor the self-management programs so that it complies with the interests, needs and challenges of the individual. For the management of cardiovascular risks, we have employed the social cognition theory to develop the behavioral profile using the following SCT markers:

   a. *Self-Efficacy* (SE) refers to a person's belief in his/her own ability to succeed in a specific situation [16].

   b. *Self-Regulation* enables a patient to control his/her response or behavior when encountered with externally inflicted incitements [16]. According to SCT both self-efficacy and outcome expectations in part, influence behavior through self-regulation [28].

   c. *Social Support* (SS) includes support and encouragement one can expect from care providers to help maintain a healthy life.

   d. *Outcome Expectation* (OE) is a belief about the likelihood of the behavior leading to specific outcome [16]. OE beliefs are self-evaluative and are dependent on a patient's self-efficacy beliefs.

   e. *Socioeconomic Status* (SES) depends on a combination of number of variables including income, education, wealth and employment.

3. *Develop the patient's personalization profile* by integrating the health and behavior profiles. SCT markers, such as socioeconomic status, perceptions of self-regulation, social support, etc., are used to further enrich the patient's personalization profile.

4. *Identify barriers* that the patient perceives to be the reasons for the non-compliance behavior which is then negatively impacting the self-management of the disease, for instance identifying the barriers to drug compliance, regular exercise, healthy lifestyle etc. Our strategy involves engagement with the patient to help him/her to self-identify their behavior modification barriers through self-observation and barrier identification exercises.

5. *Identify self-efficacy goals* that the individual will like to achieve to counter the noted barriers, for instance 'I want to comply with my drug plan'. We ask patients to set personal self-efficacy goals and to select specific actions plans (the action plans are shortlisted based on their profile and pre-identified barriers) that they will like to follow to achieve behavioral self-efficacy and self-regulation as a means to overcome their barriers that are hindering their self-management of their condition.

• *Design and deliver personalized self-management strategies* that are based on the individual's personalization profile (step 3), barriers to overcome (step 4) and goals to be attained (step 5). The personalized self-management programs, constituting self-efficacy attainment strategies, are designed to help the patient modify his/her behavior, and as outcome achieve positive self-efficacy and self-regulation in self-managing the disease and in turn to achieve positive health outcomes.

6. *Pursue the self-management improvement strategy* for a specified period (say 2 – 4 weeks). During this intervention period personalized educational and motivational messages reinforcing the prescribed self-management program's activities are proactively delivered to the individual to achieve self-efficacy to overcome the barriers.

7. *Monitor the individual*'s compliance to the stipulated self-management plan and the messages being delivered during the intervention period.

8. *Reassess the individual's self-efficacy* to successfully self-manage his/her disease based on validated assessment tools. Depending on the assessment results, the individual can select a new barrier or continue to reinforce the current one.

4   Ontology Based Modeling of SCT Based Personalization Approach for Self-management

Note that as per our strategy to personalize self-management programs at the first level a patient is categorized based on his/her health status and at the second level he/she is categorized based on very specific SCT markers. In this way, the educational and motivational interventions, associated with the selected self-efficacy strategy, that are deemed relevant at the first level are further personalized at the second level.

We take a semantic web approach in designing the personalization approach whereby we have developed an OWL-DL based personalization ontology to (a) model the theoretical framework of SCT in terms of SCT concepts; (b) model health assessment tools; (c) instantiate the self-management strategies and related educational messages; and (d) model the personalization rules that integrate the health and SCT models with the educational messages. The SPP ontology serves as a generic theory-driven health knowledge model that can be specialized by adding problem/disease-specific content to design problem/disease-specific self-management plans. For illustration purposes, we have modeled knowledge pertaining to the self-management of cardiac risk factors, and in particular are focusing on the helping individuals achieve self-efficacy towards healthy eating.

Figure 1 shows a high-level class hierarchy of the SPP ontology, whereas Figure 2 shows the conceptual relationships between the classes to realize the individual's profile—individual is the focal point (i.e. main class) and the associated classes are designed to model the health and behavioral profiles, the interventional strategies as per SCT and the intervention strategies.

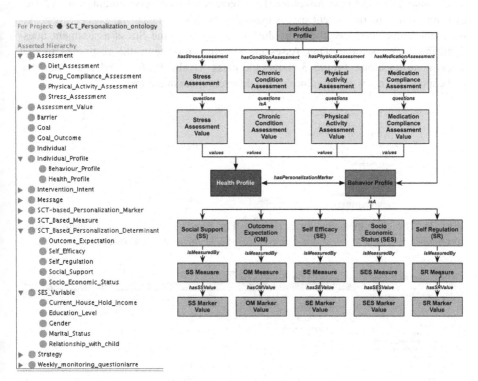

Fig. 1. High level concept hierarchy for the SPP ontology

Fig. 2. High level SCT-based self-management program personalization module highlighting just the behavior profile aspect of the SPP ontology

4.1   Ontological Modeling of the Health Profile

In this section we describe the modeling of the elements leading to the determination of a patient's health profile (shown in Fig 1) within the SPP ontology. Note that the health profile is derived from validated health assessment questionnaires—each questionnaire may focus at a specific health aspect, such as stress, physical activity, diet, medication compliance, etc. The health profile can be a systematic and informed synthesis of these independent assessments to realize a holistic health profile. The modeling challenge is capturing the questions within the assessments and the individual's response to the questions in a semantic framework such that the questions and their responses are semantically related and conformant to prior value ranges. We show below our ontological approach to represent the assessments in the personalization ontology, illustrating the highest-level classes, properties and instantiations.

'Individual' represents the person for whom the self-management plan is being designed. At the next level we have a series of assessment classes, such as 'Stress Assessment', 'Physical Activity Assessment', that represent the respective assessment questionnaire. At the next lower level we have a series of assessment value classes that are related to the parent assessment classes. For instance the class 'Stress Assessment Value' captures the individual's responses to the Stress assessment questionnaire. Likewise, the 'Diet Assessment Value' represents the responses to diet assessment questions. Figure 3 shows the class 'Health Profile' and properties that will capture the assessment values of the different assessment tests.

Fig. 3a. The class hierarchy for a patient profile

Fig. 3b. The properties of a health profile –i.e. health assessment values

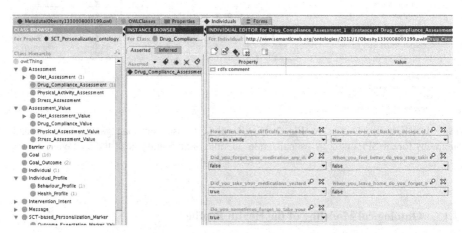

Fig. 4. Ontology section about drug compliance assessment class, showing the properties that are derived from the assessment tool and are instantiated with responses by the individual

The values of each element of the health profile are determined by assessment tests modeled by the class 'Assessment' and their corresponding values by the class 'Assessment_Value'. We implemented all the assessment questionnaires as an object, and the questions within them as their properties. The questions with responses having a range of allowable values were modeled as datatype properties, whereas questions that require representable knowledge content as a response (e.g. What is the highest level of education you have achieved?) were represented as object type properties. We found this approach towards representation of questionnaires to be effective and reliable, since we were able to use property restrictions, such as cardinality restrictions, range (both for object type and data type) and allowed values to ensure on-line data integrity. Moreover, in our modeling approach, each instance of an individual is related to an instance of each of the assessment questionnaires, thereby seamlessly providing well-identified data for developing the individual's profile. Figure 4 shows the drug compliance assessment, and Figure 5 shows the data type properties for capturing the individual's responses to the questions.

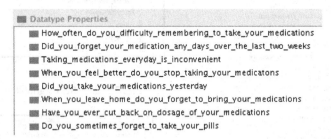

Fig. 5. Ontology section about drug compliance assessment class, showing the assessment questions (as data type properties) that are derived from an assessment tool

In summary, the health profile is developed as per the responses of the individual to the various health assessment tools. The health profile is related to the behavior profile as jointly they represent the patient's personalization profile. It may be noted that the SPP ontology is quite scalable and reusable. The health assessment questions are individuals and can be re-used for different assessment tools, and new health assessment tools and even specific questions can be included to the SPP ontology.

4.2   Ontological Modeling of Behavior Profile

The design of the behavior profile is guided by SCT whereby the profile's elements are derived through a series of SCT based assessments. The modeling of the behavior profile is as follows—we first identified the SCT determinants that are to be used to define a patient, then we modeled a set of SCT based assessments to establish the elements of the profile and finally we modeled the responses of the assessment questions—it is the responses of the SCT based assessment questions for each SCT element that is represented in the behavior profile (see Fig. 9). The class hierarchy for representing the behavior profile is shown in Fig. 6 that illustrates the three main classes related with each other through a series of object properties.

'SCT Based Personalization Determinant' represents the five SCT based determinants—'Self Efficacy', 'Social Regulation', 'Social Status', 'Outcome Expectation', 'Socioeconomic Status'—that are used to develop the SCT-driven behavior profile. The socioeconomic determinant is modeled as the separate class 'SES Variable' with five sub-classes each focusing on a specific socio-economic element (see Fig. 7) and each sub-class having its own set of instances, for instance 'Current Household Income' has salary ranges as instances (shown in Fig. 8).

'SCT Based Measure' represents the individual questionnaires used to assess each of the five SCT determinants. The SCT questionnaires for the five SCT determinants are modeled in a similar manner as the health assessment questionnaires.

'SCT Based Personalization Marker' represents the individual's responses to the questions posed by the SCT based measures.

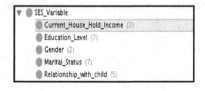

Fig. 7. Class 'SES Variable'

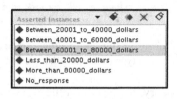

Fig. 6. SCT Classes used to develop the behavior profile

Fig. 8. Instances of the Subclass 'Current Household Income'

Fig. 9a. Class hierarchy of Individual profile

Fig. 9b. The elements of the behavior profile. Some of the properties have their range 'SCT Based Measure'

4.3   Ontological Modeling of Self-efficacy Strategies Based on SCT

The SPP ontology models health and behavioral aspects to design personalized self-efficacy strategies to overcome the barriers faced by patients in adhering to their self-management programs. Based on a patient's personalization profile, our approach is to identify a self-efficacy goal, find out what are the barriers to the attainment of this

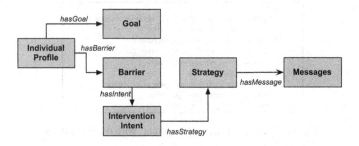

Fig. 10. SCT based strategy for designing personalized self-management programs

goal and then pursue the achievement of this goal through a selective strategy. This triangulation of concepts is modeled in the SPP ontology as shown in Figure 10.

'Goal' represents a self-management goal that the patient plans to achieve through the self-efficacy development interventions. Typical goals are compliance to drugs, healthy eating, active lifestyle, reduction of weight, stress, etc.

'Barrier' represents the perceived barriers (as noted in the literature) to the list of goals. Typical barriers that hinder the attainment of healthy goals are lack of knowledge, low motivation, busy lifestyle, financial considerations, social challenges, etc. Figure 11 shows the barriers for healthy diet and drug compliance instantiated as instances of the class 'Barrier'.

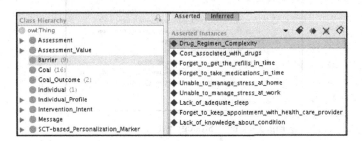

Fig. 11. The class 'Barrier' with some instances of the noted 'Barrier'

'Intervention Intent' represents specific focus areas that are based on barriers and contain all the strategies related to a specific focus. The literature suggests a range of strategy foci for a barrier. The modeling challenge here is the semantic annotation of the strategy foci and their links with actual strategy content, personalization profile and the messages. The 'Intervention Intent' was classified into 9 sub-classes (shown in Figure 12) based on the noted barriers to drug compliance (as shown in Figure 11). For example a subclass for 'Intervention Intent' is 'Improve skills to deal with drug regimen complexity' that is based on the barrier '*drug regimen complexity*'.

Each 'Intervention Intent' sub-class is instantiated with a list of specific intervention intents that are to be selected by the individual and pursued through a strategy.

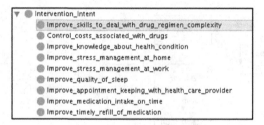

Fig. 12. The class 'Intervention Intent' with its sub-classes

'Strategy' represents a concerted plan to overcome a barrier—a strategy comprises a set of actions with accompanying educational and motivational messages and targets to be achieved during a specific timeframe. The strategies are hierarchically classified into 9 sub-classes (see Figure 13) along the same lines as the sub-class 'Intervention Intent'; in this way each high-level strategy is associated with a specific intent, which in turn is linked to a specific barrier. It is these inter-class relationships that control the tailoring of the strategy messages as per the patient's profile.

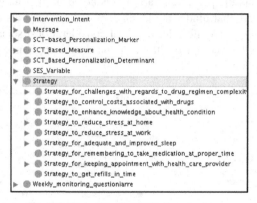

Fig. 13. Class 'Strategy with its sub-classes

Each 'Strategy sub-class' is further classified down the hierarchy so that all the related strategies are grouped together as a sub-class. For example, 'Strategy' sub-class: 'Strategy For Lack Of Availability', has 7 sub-classes, each one of those represent a set of strategies that can be offered to a patient to deal with the particular issue related to lack of availability. Each strategy comprises a set of messages, in the form of short and at times long paragraphs. As a result the datatype property 'has detail' is assigned to class 'Strategy', the range of which is string and the value of each 'has detail' property is a specific strategy text.

Each strategy message is associated with a set of constraints—if the constraints are satisfied the message is deemed relevant to a patient. The range of the hasConstraint property for each message is the health and behavior profile. We use a reasoning engine that determines whether a message is suitable for a patient by comparing the individual profile with the message constraint. Details of the message selection process are to be provided in a separate publication.

4.4   SPP Ontology Evaluation

The evaluation of the SPP ontology was carried out in terms of evaluating the consistency and quality-oriented ontology descriptions, where we evaluated the functional dimension of the SPP ontology [29]. We assume that the conceptualization of domain, as captured by the SPP ontology, corresponds to a large extent to the expertise of the domain experts (who are evaluating the ontology) in making use of the ontology to design a personalized self-management strategy.

In order to establish the quality of the ontology we engaged six domain experts (medical and behavioral scientists) who were asked to review (a) the concept classification and class hierarchy; (b) the relationships between the concepts, especially the domain and range of the relationships; and (c) the instances of the concepts which are the elements of the strategies and their associated messages. The domain experts were first provided an overview of the original content—i.e. the behavior change model documentation, assessment tools and validated self-efficacy strategies, and were explained the intent and purpose of the SPP ontology. Next, the domain experts were asked to evaluate the correctness of the SPP ontology in terms of the representation of the domain content. The experts validated the correctness of the SPP ontology in terms of its concept classification and the instantiation of the domain content. To evaluate the working of the SPP ontology to generate patient specific self-management programs and self-efficacy attainment strategies we asked the domain experts to develop a diverse range of test cases, where each test case comprised health and behavior attributes, barriers that need to be overcome, and potential strategies to be pursued. The patient attributes were instantiated in the SPP ontology to develop the test patient's personalization profile. Domain experts were again engaged to review and work with an instantiated patient profile by selecting various patient-specific barriers and the corresponding behavior change strategies. In response to the selection of the barriers and behavior change strategy, the PSID framework generates a sequence of educational and motivational messages. At this point, the domain experts reviewed the presence and relevance of the educational and motivational messages as per the test patient's profile. The domain experts used a Likert scale to measure the completeness, relevance and clarity of the messages with respect to the selected barrier and strategy and the patient's profile. Overall, the evaluation of the SPP ontology was positive and the domain experts validated the relevance, correctness (in terms of the medical context and behavior strategy) and completeness (in terms of the coverage of the topic) the messages with respect to the barriers and strategies. The evaluation by domain experts established the successful instantiation of the behavior model, questionnaires, barriers and the strategies using the SPP ontology. We concluded that the SSP ontology with its class definitions, generalization and specialization of the classes, and the relations with their domain and range has adequate representational capacity to capture the domain concepts and the personalization strategy to serve as the knowledge model for the development of personalized self-management programs.

To evaluate the consistency of the SPP ontology we used the Pellet reasoner to run subsumption tests to establish the concept satisfiability and consistency. Our results indicated that the ontology is consistent and satisfiable. Since the reasoner did not discover any redundancies in the model, this establishes the conciseness of the ontology [30].

5   Concluding Remarks

To ensure the efficacy of computerized and personalized health educational interventions, it is prudent to also account for behavioral, personal and environmental factors that influence's a patients health decisions. In this regard, we investigated the incorporation of theory-driven evidence-based behavior change models—i.e. SCT—to guide the design and delivery of personalized patient education and self-management plans. The modeling of SCT as an ontology ensures the semantic relatedness and logical consistency of the SCT constructs used to develop a patient's profile and the corresponding selection of self-efficacy development strategies and messages. A key contribution of this research is the semantic web based modeling and execution of theory-driven psychosocial models to personalize self-management content. Our *personalized self-management framework* features (a) a novel self-management oriented individual profiling mechanism that takes into account both the health and psychosocial characteristics of a patient to generate his/her holistic profile; and (b) a semantic web based knowledge model that captures the theoretical foundations of SCT, the personalization strategy and the self-management content in terms of a SPP ontology. We have demonstrated the novel integration of health models, educational content and behavior change strategies using an ontological framework to realize a personalization approach that is guided by validated assessment tools and it selects messages based on theory-driven health models.

We posit that individually tailored, self-administered interventions delivered through a ubiquitous and interactive communication medium can serve as a viable alternative to the traditional face-to-face education around self-management. We argue that the SSP ontology allows for consistent knowledge scalability to support the inclusion of new strategies and messages for the development of new self-management educational programs.

Acknowledgement. The project was supported by grants from Greenshield Canada and CIHR (catalyst grant).

References

1. Fisher, E.B., Fitzgibbon, M.L., Glasgow, R.E., et al.: Behavior matters. American Journal of Preventive Medicine 40(5), e15–e30 (2011)
2. Glasgow, R.E., Fisher, E.B., Anderson, B.J., et al.: Behavioral science in diabetes. Contributions and opportunities. Diabetes Care 22(5), 832–843 (1999)
3. Packer, T.L., Boldy, D., Ghahari, S., Melling, L., Parsons, R., Osborne, R.H.: Self-management programs conducted within a practice setting: Who participates, who benefits and what can be learned? Patient Educ. Couns. 87(1), 93–100 (2012)

4. Jones, H., Edwards, L., Vallis, T.M.: Changes in diabetes self-care behaviors make a difference to glycemic control: the Diabetes Stages of Change (DiSC) study. Diabetes Care 26, 732–737 (2003)
5. Vallis, M., Ruggiero, L., Greene, G., et al.: Stages of change for healthy eating in diabetes: relation to demographic, eating-related, health care utilization, and psychosocial factors. Diabetes Care 26(5), 1468–1474 (2003)
6. Wing, R.R., Goldstein, M.G., Acton, K.J., et al.: Behavioral science research in diabetes: lifestyle changes related to obesity, eating behavior, and physical activity. Diabetes Care 24(1), 117–123 (2001)
7. Nguyen, M.N., Potvin, L., Otis, J.: Regular exercise in 30- to 60-year-old men: combining the stages-of-change model and the theory of planned behavior to identify determinants for targeting heart health interventions. J. Community Health 22(4), 233–246 (1997)
8. King, D.K., Glasgow, R.E., Toobert, D.J., et al.: Self-efficacy, problem solving, and social-environmental support are associated with diabetes self-management behaviors. Diabetes Care 33(4), 751–753 (2010)
9. Mishali, M., Omer, H., Heymann, A.D.: The importance of measuring self-efficacy in patients with diabetes. Fam Pract. 28(1), 82–87 (2011)
10. Miller, W.R., Rose, G.S.: Toward a theory of motivational interviewing. Am. Psychol. 64(6), 527–537 (2009)
11. Soo, H., Lam, S.: Stress management training in diabetes mellitus. J. Health Psychol. 14(7), 933–943 (2009)
12. Fisher, E.B., Thorpe, C.T., Devellis, B.M., Devellis, R.F.: Healthy coping, negative emotions, and diabetes management: a systematic review and appraisal. Diabetes Educ. 33(6), 1080–1103 (2007); discussion 1104-1086
13. Brug, J., Campbell, M., van Assema, P.: The application and impact of computer-generated personalized nutrition education: A review of the literature. Patient Education and Counseling 36, 145–156 (1999)
14. Davis, S., Abidi, S.S.R., Stewart, S.: A compositional personalization approach for designing personalized patient educational interventions for cardiovascular risk management. In: 13th World Cong. on Medical Informatics (2010)
15. Elder, J.P., Ayala, G.X., Harris, S.: Theories and intervention approaches to health behavior change in primary care. American Journal of Preventive Medicine 17(4), 275–284 (1999)
16. Bandura, A.: Health promotion and social cognitive means. Health Edu. Behave. 31(2), 143–164 (2004)
17. Clark, N.M., Dodge, J.A.: Exploring self-efficacy as a predictor of disease management. Health Education and Behavior 26, 72–89 (1999)
18. Aljasem, L., Peyrot, M., Wissow, L., Rubin, R.: The impact of barriers and self-efficacy on self-care behaviors in type 2 diabetes. Diabetes Educator 27, 393–404 (2001)
19. Oka, R.K., DeMarco, T., Haskell, W.L.: Effect of treadmill testing and exercise training on self-efficacy in patients with heart failure. European Journal of Cardiovascular Nursing 4, 215–219 (2005)
20. King, T.K., Marcus, B.H., Pinto, B.M., Emmons, K.M., Abrams, D.B.: Cognitive-behavioral mediators of changing multiple behaviors: smoking and a sedentary lifestyle. Preventive Medicine 25, 684–691 (1996)
21. Haider, T., Sharma, M., Bernard, A.: Using social cognitive theory to predict exercise behavior among South Asian college students. J. Community Med. Health Educ. 2, 155 (2012)

22. Bandura, A.: Social foundations of thought and action; A social cognitive theory. Prentice Hall, Englewood Cliffa (1986)
23. McGowan, P.: The effect of Diabetes patient education and self-management education in Type 2 diabetes. Canadian Journal of Diabetes 35(1), 46–53 (2012)
24. Lorig, K.R., Holman, H.R.: Self-management education: History, definition, outcomes and mechanism. Ann. Behav. Med. 26(1), 1–7
25. Lorig, K.R., Sobel, D.S., Ritter, P.L., Laurent, D., Hobbs, M.: Effect to Self-Management program on patient with chronic disease. Effective Clinical Practice 4(6), 256–261 (2001)
26. Norris, S.L., Lau, J., Smith, S.J., Schmid, C.H., Engelgau, M.M.: Self-management education for adults with type 2 diabetes: a meta-analysis of the effect of glycemic control. Diabetes Care 25, 1159–1171 (2002)
27. Funnell, M.M., Anderson, R.M.: Empowerment and self-management of diabetes. Clin. Diabetes. 22, 123–126 (2004)
28. Anderson, E.S., Winett, R.A., Wojcik, J.R.: Social regulation, self-efficacy, outcome expectation and social support: Social Cognitive Theory and nutritional behavior. Ann. Behav. Med. 34(3), 304–312 (2007)
29. Gangemi, A., Catenacci, C., Ciaramita, M., Lehmann, J.: Modelling ontology evaluation and validation. In: Sure, Y., Domingue, J. (eds.) ESWC 2006. LNCS, vol. 4011, pp. 140–154. Springer, Heidelberg (2006)
30. Gómez-Pérez, A.: Ontology Evaluation. In: Handbook on Ontologies. International Handbooks on Information Systems, pp. 251–273 (2004)

Dynamic Homecare Service Provisioning: A Field Test and Its Results

Alireza Zarghami, Mohammad Zarifi, Marten van Sinderen, and Roel Wieringa

Department of Electrical Engineering, Mathematics and Computer Science,
University of Twente, Enschede, The Netherlands
{a.zarghami,m.zarifi,m.j.vansinderen,r.j.wieringa}@utwente.nl

Abstract. Providing IT-based care support for elderly at home is proposed as a highly promising appraoch to address the aging population problem. With the emergence of homecare application service providers, a homecare system can be seen as a linked set of services. Configuring and composing existing homecare application services to create new homecare composite applications can reduce the application development cost. The idea even looks more promising if the service provisioning is dynamic, i.e., if applications can update their behaviors with respect to the contextual changes without or with minimum manpower. Dynamic service provisioning can play an important role to accept homecare systems in practical settings. This motivated us to develop a Dynamic Homecare Service Provisioning (DHSP) platform to address the homecare context changes in an effective and efficient manner. As a proof of concept, we have developed a software prototype of our platform. The prototype was subsequently used in a real-world field test at a care institution in the Netherlands to validate the approach. This paper describes the design of the field test and reflects on the outcome of the validation experiments.

1 Introduction

The population of many Western-European countries have an increasing percentage of elderly people and, consequently, the healthcare-related cost for these countries is growing [4,10]. Providing automated care support for elderly people in their own home is proposed as a highly promising solution to alleviate the problem of the growing healthcare related cost for elderly [7]. A homecare system is "*a potentially linked set of services ... that provide or support the provision of care in the home*" [12]. With the emergence of homecare application service providers, which provide IT-based healthcare services (e.g., blood pressure measurement service) for elderly people at home, a homecare system can be seen as a linked set of IT-based services, i.e., application services.

The time and cost of homecare application development and provisioning play an important role to have widely-accepted practical homecare systems. With the emergence of the Service-Oriented Architecture (SOA) paradigm, composing applications by reusing existing application services has become technically and economically feasible. The used application services can be provided by different healthcare-related organizations, and programmers can use them to build

D. Riaño et al. (Eds.): KR4HC 2013/ProHealth 2013, LNAI 8268, pp. 113–127, 2013.

a composite homecare application without knowing their internal implementation mechanisms. The idea even looks more encouraging if service provisioning can be dynamic, if these composite applications can update their behaviors with respect to the contextual changes without or with minimum manpower.

People needing homecare applications, such as patients or some elderly people, are generally called care-receivers. They can use their systems in their own ways. Thus many (un)foreseen changes may occur during the provisioning of a homecare application. Care-receivers are subject to different types of contextual changes such as changes in their vital-signs (e.g., blood pressure value), location (e.g., inside or outside home) and their capabilities (e.g., sight, hearing). These changes motivate the use of dynamic service provisioning in the homecare domain.

Dynamic homecare service provisioning is not easy to realize because (1) it must be cheaper (both human and system resources) than the current solution (otherwise the homecare domain stakeholders are not interested), (2) each user must be independently and adequately supported (otherwise the end-users (e.g., care-receivers) are not interested), (3) safety of the care-receivers may not be at risk (otherwise the government and the general public will be opposed). For instance, if the application must send an alert to a care-giver such as nurse, failure in sending that alert could be life-threatening in some specific circumstances.

Our top-level goal is to design a Dynamic Homecare Service Provisioning (DHSP) platform to address the homecare contextual changes in an effective and efficient manner. Although several promising prototypes have been done in academia [11,13,1,5], yet there are many challenges and hurdles to overcome before having a realistic homecare solution [12,9]. Based on our study, we observed that existing solutions have not addressed dynamic provisioning and its requirements as much as other challenges such as distributed and heterogeneous application service providers [23]. Specially, with respect to homecare requirements such as compliance with medical protocols, safety-criticalness and limited human resources (lack of care-givers), a homecare-specific dynamic service provisioning (we call it DHSP) platform is required [22].

We propose a DHSP platform which has been prototyped and tested with real care-givers, care-receivers and homecare application service providers. The contribution of this paper is threefold: a) we describe the design and execution of a field test, b) we present the collected and analyzed data from the field test, and c) we report on interesting results obtained from the field test and considered useful to improve similar systems. The field test is designed in two experiments and the goal of doing them is to study the usability of the platform in terms of effectiveness, efficiency and the end-user's satisfaction.

The rest of the paper is structured as follows. In Section 2, we introduce our DHSP and discuss related concepts. In Section 3, we describe an evaluation strategy for evaluating our approach. Section 4 presents the setup of the field test and the role of involved organizations (including service providers and the care center). Section 5 presents the results of the first experiment, and how the system evolved based on the changes requested by the care-givers. In Section 6 we discuss the results of the second experiment, how the system improved, and the lessons learned from the field test. In Section 7 we conclude the paper with an outlook on our future research.

2   Dynamic Homecare Service Provisioning Platform

We define a DHSP platform as an *adaptive, tailorable* and *evolvable* application service provisioning platform. In dynamic service provisioning, a composite application can be reconfigured. This can happen automatically on-the-fly (called *adaptive* service composition), by end-users such as nurses (which we call *tailorable* service composition) or by a programmer (which we call *evolvable* service composition).

Several dynamic service provisioning approaches have been proposed to facilitate the adaptation of composite applications with respect to contextual changes [14,16]. These changes can be *foreseen* or *unforeseen*. Automated reconfiguration of services must be foreseen at design time, and the composite application must be able to monitor relevant changes and adapt to them at runtime based on predefined application logic (adaptivity). Tailored reconfiguration is different: It is the end-user who recognizes the condition for change, but the possible responses to this change have been predefined and can be configured by the end-user (tailorability). In contrast, unforeseen changes are not known at design time and no possible responses have been planned at design time. Thus, at a later phase in the lifecycle, a programmer of a composite application must modify the application logic to deal with unforeseen changes (evolvability) [3]. The aim of our research is to provide the infrastructure for all three forms of dynamicity in a composite service-oriented application in the homecare domain [20].

Fig. 1 shows how an application is defined and executed on the DHSP platform. To decouple the concerns, we assume that there is a separate tailoring platform that takes care of creation and tailoring of service plans to be executed by the provisioning platform. A homecare system as we propose consists of a tailoring platform, a provisioning platform and several application services. A *service plan* consists of one or more *service building blocks* (SBBs) and describes the configuration and orchestration of instances of these service building blocks with respect to run-time circumstances. The service plan specifies the behavior of a composite application at runtime by specifying which application service will be selected for a SBB and how the selected service will be configured and orchestrated [21] . Each service plan can have several predefined orchestrations (of SBBs) of which one is selected at runtime based on decision making rules. A SBB defines a set of functionalities at the abstract level that can be implemented by alternative application services. The SBBs have several configurations that determine which application service should be selected. For instance, a SBB of medicine dispensing can be implemented by different medicine dispenser devices which might be provided by different vendors.

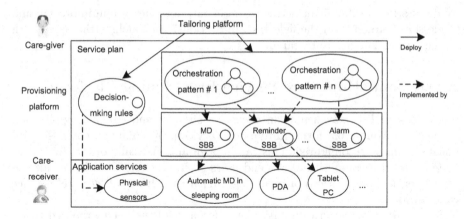

Fig. 1. How a service plan is defined and executed on our DHSP platform

To improve the evolvability, we separate these decision making rules from the orchestrations as a decision service [20]. The decision service can be called by the orchestration patterns. The decision service employs physical sensors through their corresponding application services. Based on the data coming from the physical sensors, the output of decision service determines which orchestration and configurations must be selected.

3   Validation Criteria

We want to improve homecare systems by facilitating dynamic service provisioning. The improvement criteria can be classified as: (a) To adapt a homecare application successfully within a certain time expected by an end-user, (b) To deploy a (re)tailored homecare application successfully within a certain time expected by a care-giver, and (c)To deploy an evolved homecare application successfully within a certain time expected by a programmer.

To investigate the needed time, we need to measure the efficiency of the platform and the efficiency correlates with the level of achieved effectiveness [8]. In the literature, usability is defined as the software quality attribute which comprises the efficiency, effectiveness and satisfaction aspects [8]. Therefore, We have performed a field test to evaluate the usability of the DHSP platform. Usability is a multidimensional characteristic which must be measured in the context of users performing a task with a system in a specific environment [2]. Most usability evaluation methods gather both subjective and objective quantitative data. Subjective data are measures of participants' opinions or attitudes concerning their perception of usability. Objective data are measures of participants performance, such as deployment completion time and successful rate [15].

To evaluate the usability of our DHSP platform, we follow the ISO 9241-11 definition of usability, which is "*Extent to which a product can be used by specified users to achieve specified goals with effectiveness, efficiency and satisfaction*

in a specified context of use" [8]. The standard provides guidelines to measure
the effectiveness and efficiency, which results in objective data (through system
transaction logs), and to measure satisfaction, which delivers subjective data
(through end-users' interviews). Being able to combine objective and subjective
measurements, would be useful to know which level of effectiveness and efficiency
is acceptable in the homecare domain. Moreover, we identified explanations of
our observations that allowed us to understand which parts of our approach need
further improvement.

3.1 Effectiveness

The ISO standard defines effectiveness as *"accuracy and completeness with which
users achieve specified goals"*. In our case, we define it as the number of system
tasks such as sending an alert (adaptivity goals), deploying a service plan (tailorability goals) or modifying the application logic (evolvability goals), which
have been completed within a specific time without systems errors. Since homecare systems are real-time reactive systems [17], task completion is measured
time-dependently. For instance, sending a late alert or sending a reminder when
it is not needed, is considered an error, although the system task is completed.
Moreover, we exclude the care-givers' mistakes. For instance, if a care-giver
makes a mistake in tailoring an application but the deployment process goes
well, we consider it as a completed and successful task. The effectiveness can be
scored on a scale of 0 to 100%. In our field test, to measure the effectiveness,
we will measure successful system task completion rate, i.e, the number of the
system tasks that have been completed within a specific time as a percentage of
the total number of system tasks.

$$successful - system - task - completion - rate = \\ = \frac{completed-system-tasks*100}{total-number-of-system-tasks}$$

3.2 Efficiency

The ISO standard defines efficiency as *"the level of effectiveness achieved to the
expenditure of resources"*. In our case, we define it as the completion time of the
system tasks. To evaluate the completion time, we should compare it with other
homecare systems. Since in our case there are no other systems to compare, we
evaluate the completion times with the care-givers' expectations to see if the
completion times are acceptable or not.

3.3 Satisfaction

The ISO standard defines satisfaction as *"the extent to which users are free from
discomfort, and their attitudes towards the use of the product"*. In our case, we
define it as the perceived effectiveness and perceived efficiency of the system
from the end-users' point of view. The satisfaction has some other aspects which

are more related to interaction with the end-users [6], however, our platform interacts indirectly with the end-users through the application services or the tailoring platform. Thus, to evaluate the satisfaction of the DHSP platform, we only consider the perceived effectiveness and efficiency. Moreover, we are interested to see how satisfaction can be affected by using different application services.

In order to measure satisfaction, we used questionnaires. Since we limit the satisfaction to the perceived effectiveness and efficiency, the existing usability questionnaires, that takes some other aspects into account [6], do not suit our requirements. Therefore, we have designed a questionnaire to ask specific questions about the perceived effectiveness and efficiency for each type of system task. Our questionnaire contains 8 open-end attitudinal questions to uncover end-users' beliefs and thoughts on the effectiveness and efficiency of each type of system task.

These questions are task-specific and designed to measure effectiveness and efficiency of each system task. For instance, (1) does the system remind the care-receivers on time to measure their vital signs or to take their medications?, (2) After measuring the vital signs, does the system show the measured values on the Tablet PC in a reasonable time?, and (3) Does the system stop sending reminders after the care-receiver has measured his/her vital signs? Each question has two answer parts: (1) *answer (yes/no)* and (2) *Comment on the question*. Due to the limited space, we can not explain all the questions in this paper.

4   Setup of the Experiments

The field test has been done in two experiments of two months each, with one month in between to improve existing applications and to add new applications. The field test is an action case study [19], in which we aim to improve the current situation of providing care by using a DHSP platform. We follow the guidelines described by Wieringa in [18] to perform the experiments systematically.

Each series of the experiments was conducted in a near real-world setting in a care institute in the Netherlands and each series lasted for two months. The experiments are close to a real-world setting, because some real-world aspects are present, such as real care-receivers, real institution, real nurses and realistic scenarios, but other aspects are absent, such as only a single homecare institution, a few users and candies instead of real medicines. In this section, first, we explain the scenarios to be used in the experiments, then we describe which actors participate in the experiment and the role of each one (e.g., which service provider provides which application service) and finally, we explain the measurement tools and how we collect data.

4.1   Homecare Applications

In our field test, we have three types of homecare applications: 1) vital-sign monitoring (VsM), 2) medication monitoring (MdM) and 3) social activity monitoring (SaM). For VsM, we consider three types of vital-signs: blood pressure (BP), oxygen saturation (OX) and weight (WT). For MdM, we have two types of monitoring: using an automatic dispenser and using a manual dispenser.

Due to specific requirements of the care-receivers who participated in the field test, we have used combinations of these applications. We involved the care-givers while defining these combinations to make them as realistic as possible.

4.2 Actors

Our field test has been done at Orbis[1], a care-institution in the Netherlands. This institution owns residential blocks where elderly can live and receive care services that are provided by professional care-givers. The aim of this institution is to provide round-the-clock services to their care-receivers and at the same time to enable them to live an independent life as much and as long as possible. The institute provides 8 care-receivers and 3 care-givers as end-users our field test.

There are 3rd-party application services which are used by our homecare applications: calendar, reminder, vital-sign measurement, medicine dispenser and reporting service. The calendar, reminder and vital-sign reporting services are provided by the Biomedical Signals and Systems (BSS) group of the University of Twente[2]. These services are running on Tablet PCs available to the care-givers and care-receivers. The tailoring platform is provided by the Information System (IS) group of the University of Twente[3]. It is running as an application on Tablet PCs available to the care-givers. If the application logic needs to be updated manually to address unforeseen changes, a programmer of IS modifies the application logic and accordingly updates the service plan.

The vital-sign measurement services are provided by the MobiHealth[4] company. Care-receivers use a vital-sign measurement device, which is connected to a server in MobiHealth. The MobiHealth server forwards vital-sign measurement values (e.g., blood pressure), which it receives from the measurement devices, to the DHSP platform. We also have an alert service as an internal application of the provisioning platform. The alert service sends an alert to a care-giver's PDA when there is a hazard situation.

The automatic medicine dispenser is provided by the Innospense[5] company. Care-receivers use the automatic medicine dispenser, which is connected to a server in Innospense. The Innospense server forwards the medicine intake information (e.g., time stamps) to the DHSP platform. For the manual medicine dispenser, we use a simple box in combination with the reminder and alert services.

---

[1] http://www.orbisconcern.nl/

[2] http://www.utwente.nl/ewi/bss/

[3] http://www.utwente.nl/ewi/is/

[4] http://www.mobihealth.com/

[5] http://www.innospense.com

4.3   Measurement Instruments

To collect data, we logged all the interactions among the DHSP platform and application services. The system logs have the timestamp and the data of the interactions. They are stored in a SQL database. At the end of each experiment, we analyze them off-line. To evaluate the evolvability, during the first experiment, we maintain a list of changes, which are requested by the care-givers. These changes have been applied after the first experiment. In the second experiment, we investigate how effective the applied changes are. Furthermore, after each series of the experiments, we have interviewed the care-givers and care-receivers who participated in the experiments using questionnaires. The first interview was about the perceived effectiveness and efficiency and the requested changes by the care-givers to improve the system for the second experiment. The second interview was about the perceived effectiveness and efficiency of the system in the second experiment and also some general aspects such as pros and cons of using the proposed system.

5   Results of the First Experiment

The applications used in the first experiment are: VsM (BP, WT, OX), MdM using a manual medicine dispenser and SaM. We explain the result of the first experiment according to the three types of dynamicity: *adaptivity, tailorability* and *evolvability*, both objectively and subjectively.

5.1   Adaptivity

We group the system tasks into four categories: sending reminders, sending alerts, vital-signs measurements and medications dispensing. For reminder and alert, the functionality consists of sending the reminder/alert messages and receiving the acknowledge from the application service. For vital-sign and medication, the functionality consists of receiving the vital-sign/medication intake data, sending the data to the reporting service and sending back the acknowledge to the vital-sign measurement/medicine dispenser service. Table 1 shows how effective and efficient the application functionalities are adapted in the first experiment according to the system logs. For instance, during the first experiment (which lasted 2 months), with 8 care-receivers using the DHSP platform, the reminder task was in total 339 times executed, and 46 out of the 339 times the execution was not successful; and the duration of a single execution of this task was between 3419 ms and 10974 ms with an average of 6426 ms and standard deviation of 664.

For effectivity, the unsuccessful numbers of activities are calculated based on receiving exception errors or based on feedbacks from the care-givers. There are four reasons for the unsuccessful tasks: 1) operating system update: the DHSP platform was running on a Windows 2008 server. The operating system updates itself every day at 3 AM by default. 2) application update: during the experiment,

Table 1. Effectivity and efficiency of adapting the functionalities of the applications

	Effectiveness			Efficiency (millisecond)			
	#Total	#Unsuccessful	#Success rate	#Min	#Max	#Average	#Sdv
Reminder	339	46	%86.4	3419	10974	6426	664
Alert	171	16	%90.6	180	1379	356	176
Vital-sign	247	21	%91.4	6255	6712	6392	97
Medication	55	12	%78.1	165	11888	922	2217

one of the service providers updates its application services without informing the platform providers. 3) behavioral change of the care-receiver: after introducing the system, some care-receivers measure their vital-signs much earlier than expected, for instance at 5 AM instead of 8 AM, which is the scheduled time. Then if a care-receiver's vital-sign values are too high/low, the application must send the alert immediately after 5 AM. But in the first experiment, the application starts only half an hour before the scheduled time to check the measured values. Thus some alert messages were not sent on time. 4) duplicated vital-sign measurement values: due to the Bluetooth network used by MobiHealth, sometimes a vital-sign value was sent twice to the platform and the platform forwards the value to the reporting service two times accordingly.

For efficiency, the system measures the time from sending (or receiving) data until receiving (or sending) an acknowledge. For instance, the time of vital-sign task is calculated from receiving a vital-sign value until sending back an acknowledge to the vital-sign measurement service.

Based on the results from our first interview, we conclude that care-givers are not satisfied with the effectiveness of the system. Specially missing alerts are considered unacceptable in life-threatening situations. Besides, when care-receivers cannot use the system for several times, they are not interested in technical reasons and they may loose their trust and interest in using the system. However, the efficiency was considered acceptable. The care-givers mention that the alerts must be delivered *immediately* after the vital-signs measurements in case the values are higher/lower than a predefined threshold. We tried to quantify that and we found out that less than one minute would be considered as *immediately* by the care-givers. Looking at the Table 1, we can see that the efficiency of successful tasks are acceptable for the care-givers.

5.2   Tailorability

In the first experiment, care-givers can tailor/create three types of service plans: VsM, MdM (manual) and SaM. The tailorability task consists of receiving a new service plan by the DHSP platform, deploying the service plan to application services and sending back the acknowledge to the tailoring platform. This is done on the fly without interrupting running applications. Table 2 shows how effective and efficient is the tailorability of the applications. For instance, during the first experiment, VsM application was tailored in total 134 times, and 12 out of the 134 times the tailorability task was not successful; and the duration of a single execution of this tailorability task was between 296 ms and 85068 ms with an average of 5252 ms and standard deviation of 13202 ms. Some tailorability tasks were unsuccessful due to duplicated primary key error. This error happened because the tailoring platform enables care-givers to delete an existing service plan by deleting its events from the calendar service and adding a new service plan and its corresponding events. The calendar service used the Ids (i.e., identifier) of deleted events for the new events, while the tailoring platform used these Ids as primary key and does not delete them permanently to keep the activity logs of tailoring tasks. Therefore, for some tailorability tasks, the process was interrupted by the duplicated primary key error.

Table 2. Effectivity and efficiency of tailorability tasks

	effectiveness			Efficiency (millisecond)			
	#Total	#Unsuccessful	#Success rate	#Min	#Max	#Average	#Sdv
VsM	134	12	%91	296	85068	5252	13202
MdD	30	5	%83.3	316	27337	3069	6458
SaM	270	15	%94.4	16425	97654	26780	19876

For efficiency, we measure the time from receiving a service plan until sending back the acknowledge to the tailoring platform. Based on the results from our first interview, we conclude that care-givers are satisfied with both effectiveness and efficiency of the tailorability. The number of unsuccessful tailorability tasks was tolerable by care-givers since there was no effect on the running applications.

5.3   Evolvability

During the first experiment and also our first interview, we collected the changes which are requested by care-givers (i.e.,unforeseen changes). Some of the changes are related to end-user interfaces of application services for instance, showing less text in the calendar service. Some other changes should be addressed on the DHSP platform and thus we investigate how the platform supports the evolvability of the applications. These changes are listed as follows: 1) If care-receivers measure their vital-signs earlier than the scheduled time and the measured values are not in the normal range, the alert must be sent immediately. 2) The vital-sign values should be sent with the alert messages to help care-givers to be prepared in advance. 3) For weight measurement, first we sent an alert when the weight of a care-receiver was either higher or lower than the last measured weight more than a threshold. Later on, care-givers want to receive this alert if the weight of a care-receiver is either higher or lower than a threshold. 4) The nurses can add more than one event per day to the calendar service for each application.

The programmer modifies the application logic manually to evolve the applications based on the unforeseen changes. To address the unforeseen change 1, we add an alert activity at another orchestration pattern that receives vital-sign values from the MobiHealth. The alert activity calls the decision service of VsM application to see whether it is necessary to send alert or not. Since, we have reused the VsM decision service in another orchestration with the same service interface, the modification is accomplished quickly by dragging and dropping an alert activity to the orchestration. To address the unforeseen changes 2, 3 and 4, the modification is required only in the decision service without changing the orchestrations.

We improved evolvability of the applications because of using the decision service. However, using the decision service increased time and data communication to run the applications. In the first experiment, the decision service has been called 256 times. It takes 278 milliseconds by average (min=149,max=1700, Std=176 milliseconds) to call the decision service. This period of time is much less than the time durations of the system tasks (see Table 1) and is not noticeable by care-receivers and care-givers. The data model of messages between the orchestration and the decision service consists of 19 variables (8 String, 7 Integer and 4 Boolean variables). In our field test, the size of data which is exchanged between an instance of orchestration and the decision service is always less than 5 kilobytes for each interaction. Therefore, we have seen that using of the decision service improves evolvability while its cost in terms of time and data communication is rather trivial.

6   Results of the Second Experiment

Two months after the first experiment, the improved version of the system based on the requested changes was validated in the second experiment. The applications used in the second experiment are: VsM (BP, WT), MD (using manual and automatic dispenser) and SaM. In the second experiment, we empowered the system with an extra power supply, disabled automatic operating system update and asked all the service providers not to modify their application services during the experiment. We first evaluate the adaptivity and tailorability of the system to see if the system is improved. After execution of the second experiment, we interviewed the care-givers to measure their perceived *effectiveness and efficiency*. Moreover, we asked the care-givers to give us their opinions about the whole system through open-end (descriptive) questions. Even though the focus of this work is the DHSP platform and its implemented prototype, some of the results reported in this section are in general about the whole system.

6.1   Adaptivity

Based on the result, the effectiveness was improved since we had only four unsuccessful vital-sign tasks. The reason was that the reporting service took longer than the first experiment. Therefore, the DHSP platform sent an acknowledge to the vital-sign measurement service with a delay and it caused an error on care-receivers' PDAs. Although the vital-sign values are received and shown correctly, we consider them as unsuccessful task since showing this error on the PDA was inconvenient for care-receivers. The achieved efficiency of the second experiment is almost the same as the one in the first experiment. Based on our second interview, the care-givers are satisfied with both effectiveness and efficiency of the system tasks' adaptivity.

6.2 Tailorability

We have achieved 100% effectiveness regarding VsM and MdM tailorability. However, we had several failure for SaM tailorability because care-givers create more than 5000 social events per each service plan deployment. Thus, the deployment took more than 3 minutes and they stopped using the application since they thought it was broken. Based on our second interview, care-givers are satisfied with the effectiveness and efficiency of the VsM and MdM tailorability, but not with the SaM tailorability.

6.3 General Feedback

We experienced that not all the care-givers could distinguish the different parts of the system. Therefore, our second interview contains 20 task-independent questions to ask care-givers' opinions regarding the whole system as an integrated application. These are the lessons learned:

- Care-givers believe that the proposed homecare system can work in practice particularly after the second experiment. Note that the system is not used occasionally, but in daily use with more than 400,000 transactions among the services. However, the end-user interfaces for care-receivers must be improved (e.g., showing less text and bigger icons).
- The system would be more useful for private apartments outside of the care-center because it can save lots of traveling time for care-givers. Inside the care-center, it is sometimes faster to reach the care-receiver instead of using the system.
- In close future, care-receivers with less health problems will be advised by the government to stay at home in order to reduce healthcare costs and thus, the system would be even more promising.
- The system reduces physical contact that can decrease care quality. In this case, a voice/video communication can be helpful.
- Although adding vital-signs values to alert messages was useful, it is not sufficient to decide what they should do before visiting care-receivers. So, a video communication can help care-givers to judge.
- It is highly desirable that care-receivers measure their vital-signs without waiting for a care-giver particularly when they want to leave their apartments. However, care-receivers would be obliged to get back home, if they were outside their apartments at the scheduled time. Therefore, it is useful if they can carry the measurement devices with themselves.
- The field test can be improved if it takes longer than 4 months with better target group of care-receivers (e.g., 70-80 years old).

– An automatic dispenser is more successful than the manual one because first, it has an embedded reminder beep and pressing a button on the dispenser device is easier than pressing a message box on Tablet PC, and second, it cuts the bag that contains the medicine.

7   Conclusion

In this work, we discussed a field test of our dynamic homecare service provisioning (DHSP) platform. We investigated whether the following goals can be supported by the platform: (a) To adapt a homecare application successfully within a certain time expected by an end-user, (b) To deploy a (re)tailored homecare application successfully within a certain time expected by a care-giver, and (c) To deploy an evolved homecare application successfully within a certain time expected by a programmer. At least one of the above goals should be achieved in order to justify using the proposed DHSP platform. With respect to the these goals, we investigated the usability, i.e., efficiency, effectiveness and satisfaction (perceived efficiency and effectiveness) of the homecare applications running on the platform.

We believe that dynamic homecare applications provisioning must be efficient for the platform, care-giver, and programmer, i.e., the required time for adapting, (re)tailoring and evolving the applications with respect to the contextual changes must be as less as possible. Our interviews indicated that a desirable property of the DHSP platform is to decrease the work load of the care-givers, thus saving costs for the care centers and care-provider organizations. In addition, saving cost on manpower (needed for manual tasks) should not be annihilated by extra costs for system resources and application programmers. This cost saving for addressing new contextual changes is very important in the homecare domain since its environment is often subject to several types of changes. Our field test shows that the efficiency of adaptivity is acceptable for the care-giver although the response time is higher than that of a stand-alone application due to distributed application services. The efficiency of tailorability is also acceptable for the care-givers except for the SaM application due to the large numbers deployed events in each tailoring task. Separating the decision making rules from the orchestrations improves the evolvability of the applications since almost all the changes have been handled within the decision rules without redeploying the orchestration patterns.

Regarding the effectiveness, the first experiment was not successful due to several system failures. These failures caused several safety and availability risks using our proposed platform. However, it motivated us to develop a risks identification method which we applied after the first experiment to prevent similar risks in the second experiment. As a result, the effectiveness of the homecare applications in the second experiment is acceptable for the care-givers.

The care-givers believe that having a DHSP platform enables them to use alternative application services (e.g., manual or automatic medicine dispenser) for a specific homecare application (e.g., MdM application) without affecting how the care-givers tailor and how the care-receivers use that homecare application.

This would be useful to decrease the required time from both care-givers and care-receivers to learn how to use a new homecare application. Moreover, using the DHSP platform enables the care-giver to create applications with more realistic and useful functionalities. For instance, in our field test, the care-givers created a new application to ask a care-receiver to take a medication if his blood pressure is in a specific range, which can be done by integrating a medicine dispenser and blood pressure measurement devices.

Our conclusion from the field test is that the DHSP platform is usable (by care-givers and care-receivers) at least in our field test. However, the number of homecare applications and end-users involved in our field test is limited. To be able to provide statistical analysis, we plan to provision more homecare applications with more care-givers and care-receivers as our future work. In addition, our field test shows that both care-givers and care-receiver are interested to see more often measured vital-sign values. But it is important (1) how to show this data to the end-users (e.g., using graphical interface or statistical analysis) and (2) to export the data automatically to other healthcare applications (e.g., hospital patient record). As such, using application services with data processing user-interfaces and integrating the vital-sign measurement and medication intake data with other existing healthcare information systems are considered in our future plan.

Acknowledgements. This work is part of the IOP GenCom U-Care project (http://ucare.ewi.utwente.nl) which is sponsored by the Dutch Ministry of Economic Affairs under contract IGC0816.

References

1. Batet, M., Isern, D., Marin, L., Martinez, S., Moreno, A., Sanchez, D., Valls, A., Gibert, K.: Knowledge-driven delivery of home care services. Journal of Intelligent Information Systems, 1–36 (2010)
2. Bevan, N., Kirakowski, J., Maissel, J.: What is Usability? In: Human Aspects in Computing: Design and Use of Interactive Systems with Terminals, pp. 651–655. Elsevier (1991)
3. Breivold, H., Crnkovic, I., Eriksson, P.: Evaluating software evolvability. Software Engineering Research and Practice in Sweden, 96 (2007)
4. European Commission: Ageing well in the information society - an i2010 initiative - action plan on information and communication technologies and ageing. Tech. rep., EU (June 2007)
5. Fraile, J.A., Bajo, J., Abraham, A., Corchado, J.M.: HoCaMA: Home Care Hybrid Multiagent Architecture. In: Pervasive Computing. Computer Communications and Networks, pp. 259–285. Springer, London (2010)
6. Frøkjær, E., Hertzum, M., Hornbæk, K.: Measuring usability: are effectiveness, efficiency, and satisfaction really correlated? In: Proceedings of the SIGCHI Conference on Human Factors in Computing Systems, pp. 345–352. ACM (2000)
7. Gabner, K., Conrad, M.: ICT enabled independent living for elderly, A status-quo analysis on products and the research landscape in the field of Ambient Assisted Living in EU-27. prepared by VDI/VDE Innovation und Technik GmbH (March 2010)

8. ISO: Ergonomic requirements for office work with visual display terminals (VDTs) - Part 11: Guidance on usability. International Standard 9241-11 (1998)
9. Kleinberger, T., Becker, M., Ras, E., Holzinger, A., Müller, P.: Ambient intelligence in assisted living: enable elderly people to handle future interfaces. In: Universal Access in Human-Computer Interaction. Ambient Interaction, pp. 103–112. Springer (2007)
10. Malanowski, N., Ozcivelek, R., Cabrera, M.: Active Ageing and Independent Living Services, The Role of Information and Communication Technology. European Communitiy (2008), http://www.umic.pt/images/stories/publicacoes2/JRC41496.pdf
11. MATCH: Mobilising Advanced Technologies for Care at Home (2005-2012), http://www.match-project.org.uk/main/main.html (last visited: September 2012)
12. McGee-Lennon, M.R.: Requirements engineering for home care technology. In: 26th Annual SIGCHI Conf. on Human Factors in Computing Systems, pp. 1439–1442 (2008)
13. MPOWER: Middleware Platform for eMPOWERing cognitive disabled and elderly (2006-2009), http://www.sintef.no/Projectweb/MPOWER
14. Rao, J., Su, X.: A Survey of Automated Web Service Composition Methods. In: Cardoso, J., Sheth, A.P. (eds.) SWSWPC 2004. LNCS, vol. 3387, pp. 43–54. Springer, Heidelberg (2005)
15. Shackel, B.: The concept of usability. In: Visual Display Terminals: Usability Issues and Health Concerns, pp. 45–87. Prentice-Hall, Englewood Cliffs (1984)
16. Urbieta, A., Barrutieta, G., Parra, J., Uribarren, A.: A survey of dynamic service composition approaches for ambient systems. In: Proceedings of the 2008 Ambi-Sys Workshop on Software Organisation and MonIToring of Ambient Systems, SOMI-TAS 2008, pp. 1:1–1:8. ICST (Institute for Computer Sciences, Social-Informatics and Telecommunications Engineering), Brussels (2008)
17. Wieringa, R.: Design Methods for Reactive Systems: Yourdon, Statemate, and the UML. Morgan Kaufmann (2003)
18. Wieringa, R.: A unified checklist for observational and experimental research in software engineering (version 1) (March 2012), http://doc.utwente.nl/79890/
19. Wieringa, R., Moralı, A.: Technical Action Research as a Validation Method in Information Systems Design Science. In: Peffers, K., Rothenberger, M., Kuechler, B. (eds.) DESRIST 2012. LNCS, vol. 7286, pp. 220–238. Springer, Heidelberg (2012)
20. Zarghami, A., Sapkota, B., Zarifi Eslami, M., van Sinderen, M.: Decision as a Service: Separating Decision-making from Application Process Logic. In: The 16h IEEE Int.l Enterprise Distributed Object Computing Conference (EDOC), pp. 103–112. IEEE (2012)
21. Zarghami, A., Zarifi Eslami, M., Sapkota, B., van Sinderen, M.: Dynamic Homecare Service Provisioning Architecture. In: 9th Int. Conf. on Service-Oriented Computing and Applications (SOCA), pp. 292–299 (2011)
22. Zarghami, A., Zarifi Eslami, M., Sapkota, B., van Sinderen, M.: Service Realization and Compositions Issues in the Homecare Domain. In: 6th International Conference on Software and Data Technologies (ICSOFT), vol. 1, pp. 347–356. SciTePress (July 2011)
23. Zarghami, A., Zarifi Eslami, M., Sapkota, B., van Sinderen, M.: Toward Dynamic Service Provisioning in the Homecare Domain. In: 5th International Conference on Pervasive Computing Technologies for Healthcare (PervasiveHealth), Workshop on Designing and Integrating Independent Living Technology, pp. 292–299. IEEE (May 2011)

iALARM: An Intelligent Alert Language for Activation, Response, and Monitoring of Medical Alerts

Denis Klimov and Yuval Shahar

Medical Informatics Research Center, Department of Information System Engineering,
Ben Gurion University of the Negev, P.O.B. 653, Beer-Sheva, 84105, Israel
{klimov,yshahar}@bgu.ac.il

Abstract. Management of alerts triggered by unexpected or hazardous changes in a patient's state is a key task in continuous monitoring of patients. Using domain knowledge enables us to specify more sophisticated triggering patterns for alerts, based on temporal patterns detected in a stream of patient data, which include both the temporal element and significant domain knowledge, such as "rapidly increasing fever" instead of monitoring of only raw vital signals, such as "temperature higher than 39 C". In the current study, we introduce iALARM, a two-tier computational architecture, accompanied by a language for specification of intelligent alerts, which represents an additional computational [meta] level above the temporal-abstraction level. Alerts in the iALARM language consist of (a) the *target population* part (*Who* is to be monitored?); (b) a *declarative* part (*What* is the triggering pattern?), i.e., a set of time and value constraints, specifying the triggering pattern to be computed by the bottom tier; and (c) a *procedural* part (*How* should we raise the alarm? *How* should we continue the monitoring and follow-up?), i.e., an action or a whole plan to apply when the alert is triggered, and a list of *meta-properties* of the alert and action. One of our underlying principles is to avoid *alert fatigue* as much as possible; for instance, one can specify that a certain alert should be activated only the first time that the triggering pattern is detected, or only if it has not been raised over the past hour. Thus, we introduce a complete *life cycle* for alerts. Finally, we discuss the implied requirements for the knowledge-acquisition tool and for the alert monitoring and procedural application engines to support the iALARM language. We intend to evaluate our architecture in several clinical domains, within a large project for remote patient monitoring.

Keywords: Alert, Monitoring, Knowledge representation, Temporal abstraction, Temporal reasoning, Medical informatics.

1   Introduction

Caring for patients, in particular chronic-disease patients, requires monitoring the patients, recognizing problems, raising alerts as necessary, and managing the patients accordingly – just as is the case in more standard business processes [1]. For example, alerting the clinical team (or the patient!) when the state of a patient changes (often

D. Riaño et al. (Eds.): KR4HC 2013/ProHealth 2013, LNAI 8268, pp. 128–142, 2013.
© Springer International Publishing Switzerland 2013

for the worse) is a key task for successful treatment of the patient, especially in potentially life-threatening situations.

Although multiple types of medical monitoring and alerting systems had been developed, most of them are device-oriented, with a basic functionality for monitoring of vital signals, such as medical monitors [2, 3], or alert devices for emergency situations [4]. Furthermore, due to common false-positive errors when monitoring raw data, the continuous sounding of the alarms of several medical devices used for monitoring often confuses the medical stuff and leads to an erroneous response [5] and to the "*alert fatigue*" phenomenon. Thus, much more control in designing an alert is required, such as determining when it will fire again, or what response to expect.

In addition, recognition of a specific combination of several continuously monitored parameters (i.e., a complex temporal pattern such as the development of pneumonia in a ventilated patient [6], or an infection such as sepsis [7]), cannot be accomplished without a comprehensive analysis of the historical data of the patient [8]. An example is "worsening gas exchange over the past twelve hours."

These observations represent several requirements for monitoring and alerting.

To significantly enhance the monitoring and alerting capabilities, we propose the *intelligent Alert Language for Activation, Response and Monitoring (iALARM)*. The iALARM language is a syntactic representation of the semantics of a monitoring philosophy that refers to a *two-tier computational architecture*: (1) continuous temporal-abstraction computation, and (2) monitoring, acting, and follow up (Figure 1).

Underlying the iALARM language is the assumption that we have access to a domain knowledge base and to the results of an ongoing computation of temporal-patterns from time-stamped [clinical] data. Thus, in the first tier, we extract from the continuous longitudinal raw data meaningful interval-based interpretations, known as *temporal abstractions (TAs)* (or abstract concepts), derived from the raw time-oriented data by using the domain knowledge, including temporal-abstraction patterns, i.e., complex combinations of time and value constraints that hold over medical concepts. In our study, we use the *knowledge-based temporal-abstraction (KBTA)* method [9] and to its implementation via a *temporal-abstraction mediator* [10] that mediates (using a domain temporal-abstraction knowledge base) between the monitoring level and a time-oriented domain database. However, in general, the trigger pattern of an iALARM alert can refer to any temporal pattern that is [pre] computed by any external system.

Thus, the unique features of the iALARM monitoring language, *which exists at the second, top tier,* are independent of the method used for computation of the TAs.

Furthermore, care providers might want to be alerted only when the triggering condition arises for the first time, and perhaps an additional alert if the condition still exists after a certain sufficiently long time period, or if the care provider has not responded appropriately; but not otherwise. Else, alert fatigue is only to be expected.

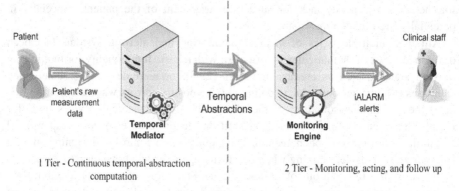

Fig. 1. The iALARM conceptual architecture

The following features distinguish iALARM from other monitoring frameworks:

- iALARM is a *generic* [meta] language for specification of alerts. It could be applied in different medical domains, and even in other time-oriented domains (e.g., finance, information security, etc). Moreover, iALARM alerts are activated according to the changes in either raw concepts or in TAs, computed by an external TA system, e.g., by using an enhanced version of a data-driven TA mediator that we have previously developed [11], but dedicating it to the purpose of continuously monitoring a group of subjects over time;
- iALARM monitoring and associated alert specifications are applied to a *whole population of patients,* defined once and then dynamically updated with respect to its members, according to a set of static (non-temporal), dynamic (temporal), and knowledge-based constraints.
- iALARM tries to reduce alert fatigue while enhancing compliance, by using unique *meta-properties*, such as the *refractory period* and *reminder*s.
- iALARM is acquired by using a knowledge specification tool [12] dedicated to the purpose of acquisition of *declarative* (definitional, such as temporal patterns) and *procedural* (workflow, such as clinical guidelines) domain knowledge.
- To handle all aspects of alarm triggering, activation, response, and inactivation, we introduce a novel view of a complete *life cycle* for alerts. The philosophy represented by this lifecycle underlies the iALARM language and its meta-properties.

2   Background

2.1   Using Temporal Abstractions in Medical Domains

TA is the process of aggregation of a time-stamped series of data into a succinct, symbolic, interval-based representation, suitable for decision making, monitoring, or analysis [13]. Examples include "moderate anemia" (a state abstraction derived from raw Hemoglobin values) and "decreasing liver-functions" (a gradient (change) abstraction, derived from consecutive values of the "liver function" state abstraction, which is derived from values of Bilirubin and several liver enzymes.

The KBTA method [9; 14], which happens to be the default TA methodology in our framework, enables us, using a domain-specific temporal-abstraction knowledge base acquired from a domain expert, to specify context-sensitive temporal patterns. These patterns can be assumed to exist as symbols, and thus can be used in the iALARM language, with appropriate additional *meta-constraints,* as triggering conditions for alerts such as "notify the physician when a patient has *<a period of more than two months of moderate or severe anemia, followed within up to three months by decreasing liver-functions>*". The definitions and properties of medical concepts (terms) such as "moderate anemia" and "decreasing liver-functions" are often sensitive to the context of a particular therapy protocol, the patient's gender and age, etc., and exist in the TA knowledge base.

Over the years, especially within the medical domain, several studies have investigated different techniques for temporal abstraction. For example, combining temporal data abstraction techniques with data mining approaches to update the prior domain knowledge [15], or methods that do not require predefined domain knowledge [16, 17]. A useful survey of temporal abstraction for intelligent clinical data analysis is provided by Stacey and McGregor [13].

In 1993, Mora et al. [8] introduced the concept of *intelligent monitoring* and had shown the importance of using knowledge-based alerts to monitor patients, such as taking into account the treatment history of an arrhythmic patient in a coronary care unit.

2.2   Event-Based Monitoring Systems

The research area of event-based monitoring, or as it is recently referred to, complex-event processing [18], is very closed to the monitoring-alerting approach suggested by iALARM alerts. However, as we described below, the iALARM architecture and [meta] language is different due to a combination of properties, which are usually found separately in different event-based monitoring systems, or not found at all.

The central *"if statement then action"* rule of the production systems is the basic operation of any monitoring systems. Rule engines such as those based on the RETE algorithm [19] are able to detect the combination of various components within the rules and more complex inter-relations between production rules, enabling us to specify more complex scenarios of monitoring-activation-reminder-response sequences. However, the *temporal* aspect, which is very important in a medicine, is very difficult to model in such simple structures of rules.

In *Event-Condition-Action* (ECA) paradigm rules are of the form "*On Event If Condition Do Action*" which means: when Event occurs, if Condition is verified, then execute Action [20]. The ECA rules and general event-driven approaches are used in medicine, e.g., [21, 22, 23 24].

By using the combination of *Event* and *Condition* parts the user is able to specify rules for monitoring of raw data measurements. To support continuous interval-based temporal abstraction, and add to it meta-constraints, as we are suggesting in iALARM system, an enhanced capability for application of different types of time constraints at different levels is required.

Moreover, the Action part in the iALARM language includes the enhanced capabilities for reminders and for delaying of the alerts, as we will see.

2.3   Alert Languages in Medical Domains

The main focus in medical domains is on alerts with respect to medication, as reviewed by [25] and evaluated with the intent of understanding the impact of medical alerts on clinicians' prescribing behavior by McCoy et al. [26] and by Schedlebauer et al. [27]. However, the iALARM alerts are activated according to changes in the *time-oriented* patient's data. Moreover Schedelbauer et al. pointed out that in the literature there are no clear distinctions made between "reminders", "alerts", and "prompts", which might explain why we failed to find a standard for representation of medical monitoring alerts (i.e,, both the triggering pattern, as well as how to proceed when it is triggered). In most medical "alert" systems reviewed by us, only a sub-part of the desiderata we consider relevant to the design of the iALARM schema is discussed. For example, in a study by Lee et al. [28], alerts included properties such severity, type, and trigger event, but only with respect to drugs.

Standards for alerts are common only in the area of networking: CAP, ASF, DMTF, etc. However, these standards do not include the meta-properties we consider as necessary for clinical monitoring.

3   The iALARM Schema

We now introduce the iALARM schema for specification of medical alerts.

Recall that we are defining in fact a *meta-language* (with *meta-properties* regarding the behavior of the monitoring mechanism itself) at the top tier of the iALARM architecture, assuming a continuous temporal-abstraction process at the bottom tier, whose output is accessible for querying by the monitoring mechanism.

We use the following notation: *terms in italics* refer to the property of the concept, square brackets [] denote an optional property, | denotes a disjunction, and < > refers to a complex expression to be specified later. The alert in iALARM language includes three parts as follows:

<Alert> ≡ *(<Population Expression>,*
        <Declarative Expression>, <Procedural Expression>),

Where *<Population Expression>* includes the criteria for selecting episodically the patients who should be monitored, *<Declarative Expression>* consists of the triggering concept to be monitored and a list of time and value constraints, and *<Procedural Expression>* refers to the actions to-apply when an alert is triggered, and how to continue the monitoring process.

In the following section, we describe in detail each of the expressions.

3.1   Specification of the Target Population

To support the specification of the populations of patients of the same type that should be monitored through some particular monitoring alert (e.g., "pregnant women above the age of 35 who have had moderately high blood pressure over the past three weeks") a *Population Expression* is introduced.

<Population Expression> ≡*(patients|<context, [rate]>),* where

- *patients* is an enumerated list of patients' identification data (i.e., patient IDs). The intent here is to specify a monitoring alert relevant to a fixed group of patients, including a single patient.
- *context* is patient's state as characterized by demographic features (e.g., age, gender, location, socioeconomic status), medical conditions, or in general, any concept or pattern from the knowledge base. For example, pregnant women under the age of 35 who are known to be diagnosed as having gestational diabetes; or pregnant women for whom more than two episodes of HIGH diastolic blood pressure have been reported within the current pregnancy. The context is periodically computed at a certain *rate* (e.g., ONCE, in the first time that the monitoring alert is applied to the overall patient population, such as when the patient is enrolled in some study and monitored from that point on, or PER_DAY, etc.), thus significantly reducing the computational burden; otherwise, the context is checked each time a new data item arrives.

The temporal-abstraction mediator is responsible for continuously computing (as new data arrive) the abstract concepts, from which the context is defined. Thus, a list of patients for monitoring can be dynamically or episodically, as needed, modified, according to the accumulating patients' data. For example, the population to be monitored might change every day.

3.2   Specification of the Triggering Pattern

The *Declarative definition* relates to the alert's triggering concept or pattern and the constraints on it, using purely declarative knowledge:

<Declarative definition> ≡*(concept-name,<value constraints>,<time constraints>),* where

- *concept-name* is the unique name of the concept (raw data or abstract concept) or of the (linear or repeating) pattern, as it appear in the knowledge base.
- *<value constraints>* ≡ (*min value, max value*), in which *min value* and *max value* are the constraints on the minimal and maximal values of the selected concept. Since the concepts and their values are selected from the knowledge base, they are always associated with a standardized measured unit.

  For example, "the White blood cell (WBC) count is less than 3000 cells/ml," in the case of a raw concept; or "Hemoglobin-state is abstracted as "moderately-low" or higher, as defined in the context of a pregnant woman", in the case of an abstract concept.

  By using the value constraints the user can directly focus on the specific values of the concept. In the case of a concept that is in fact a complex temporal pattern, the default value constraint, TRUE, is often sufficient, but other values are possible, depending on the values allowed in the domain knowledge base.
- *<time constraints>* ≡(*Now* | *<retrospective constraints>*), where *Now* is a macro that refers to a function returning the *current* time point (i.e., now) to specify real-time monitoring (the default value), *retrospective constraints* refer to the case in which the alert relates to some data in the past (for example chemotherapy during the past year), although the alert is activated during the current time, in which the temporal constraints hold.

The *retrospective constraints* are expressed as follows:

<retrospective constraints> ≡(*earliest-time, latest-time,*
$$minimal\text{-}duration, maximal\text{-}duration), \text{ where}$$

earliest-time and *latest-time* refer to the *envelope* time period [earliest-time, latest-time] of the valid time of the existence of the raw or abstract triggering concept or pattern that was computed by the underlying continuous TA framework, relative to the time returned by the current-time function that NOW uses (thus, the default value of *Now* means actually an envelope of [0,0]); *minimal-duration* and *maximal-duration* refer to the minimal and maximal length of the time period duration in which it was true. (The default is an instantaneous event: *minimal-duration = maximal-duration* = 0).

Note that these constraints are meta-constraints over the time at which the triggering temporal pattern is detected, and are not the constraints over the components of the linear or periodic TA pattern itself; to express these, we use other, more expressive languages, such as CAPSUL [29, 30].

Note that the need for retrospective monitoring is that the valid time of performing the actual observations or measurements on which the triggering pattern is based could be quite different from the transaction time, in which the data are stored in the database. This is especially important in the medical domain, in which, quite often, the measured data are available, by definition, after a certain time lag (for example, the results of a microbiological laboratory culture).

3.3   The Triggered Action or Plan

The *Procedural definition* relates to the actions that need to be notified of the alert when it is activated:

$<$*Procedural definition*$>$ $\equiv$ (*actor*$^+$, $<$*action*|*plan*$>$, *significance*,
$\qquad\qquad\qquad$ $<$*clipping-expression*$>$, $<$*refractory-period*$>$), where

- *actor* indicates at least one person to whom the alert is addressed. In the medical domain, usually at least three types of actors are involved: a patient, a nurse and an attending physician. However, in certain cases the alert could be addressed to the patient herself, or to relatives caring for the patient, or to other clinicians from relevant areas, or even to paramedical professionals such as a physiotherapist.
- *Action* is a particular action to perform when the trigger is activated, one of an enumerated lists of procedures with predefined arguments, such as: $<$send_message, *medium, message content*$>$ which sends a message to the actor via some *medium* such as an SMS, with the specified *content*.
- *Plan* is a pointer to a plan in an external guideline library, such as the DeGeL digital guidelines library [31]. The assumption is that an external guideline-application engine, such as Picard [32] will then apply the whole plan (i.e., guideline) to the patient.
- *significance* relates to the importance, or urgency, of the alert. To indicate the significance, we propose to use an ordered scale from 1 (least important) to 10 (most important). The significance property aims at enabling an ordering of the alerts in a list, for a single patient or a whole group of patients.
- $<$*clipping-expression*$>$ defines the pattern that will deactivate the alert, and includes also a specification of possible *reminders* until deactivation occurs.
- $<$*refractory-period-expression*$>$ refers to the minimal period to pass before the alert can be re-activated, to avoid alarm fatigue, i.e., overloading the user by repeating alerts.

The last two properties are fully described below.

3.3.1   An Intelligent Alert's Lifecycle

An activation of an alert typically aims to focus the attention of the attending care provider(s) to a change in the patient's state, possibly due to some multivariate combination of the patient's monitored concepts. Therefore, the desired response to the alert is often the reaction of the actor, usually the medical personnel, but possibly the patient or their family, acknowledging the alert and hopefully even performing a certain action that can detected and verified. However, in some situations, confirmation of the alert might not be forthcoming; thus one or more reminders might need to be activated, until the desired response arrives, or until the alert is deactivated, such as when the alert is deemed to be no longer relevant.

The lifecycle of alerts underlying the iALARM schema includes three steps: activation by a triggering pattern, a response, and follow-up monitoring via reminders, as shown in Figure 2.

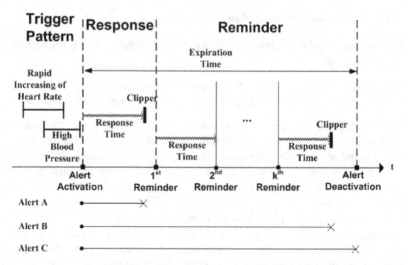

Fig. 2. Three phases in an alert's lifecycle. Alert A is deactivated within the suggested response interval. Alert B is deactivated after k reminders. Alert C is finally deactivated when its deactivation time arrives and it becomes irrelevant.

Below we describe the schema of clipping and reminding properties.

$$<clipping\text{-}expression> \equiv (<actor\ action,\ waiting\text{-}period,\ [mandatory]>^{+},$$
$$<clipper\ pattern,\ waiting\text{-}period,\ [mandatory]>^{+},$$
$$expiration\text{-}time,\ reminders\text{-}cardinality),\ where$$

- *actor action* refers to an action (Default: a confirmation/acknowledgment) by the target actor. The corresponding *waiting-period* denotes the maximal time period allowed to wait for a response by the actor. The corresponding optional *mandatory* flag denotes whether that action is mandatory. The symbol "+" denotes one or more actor actions as response to the alert.
- *clipper pattern* refers to the existence of some pattern in the patient's database, such as evidence for an administration of a recommended medication, or for the results of the performance of a necessary measurement (the default pattern is *Nil*, i.e., no clipper.). The corresponding *waiting-period* denotes the maximal time period allowed for waiting to such a pattern to appear. The corresponding optional *mandatory* flag denotes whether appearance of the pattern is mandatory. The symbol "+" denotes one or more clipper patterns as response to the alert.

Note that at least one clipper, either an *actor action* or a *clipper pattern*, must be specified.

- *expiration-time* refers to the maximal period of time during which the alert is relevant: after that time, the alert is de-activated regardless of the other constraints (the default if not specified is 0, which activates the alert and immediately turns it off). Note that the expiration time determines the maximal lifecycle period for the same alert instance.

- *reminders-cardinality* is the maximal number of reminders that can be sent for the same alert instance. After the suggested time period for each response is over, an [additional] reminder is activated.

By using the *mandatory* option, the user is able to define the required reaction of the actor to an alert. For example, when defining an alert triggered by a measurement, for the third time within one day, of a High Diastolic Blood Pressure, we might want to notify the nurse about a possible worsening in the patient's condition and the need to measure it again, and, in addition, verify that another measurement was indeed performed and some result of measuring a diastolic blood pressure appears within a reasonable time period in the patient's record. We might even want to monitor the Diastolic Blood Pressure until it becomes sufficiently low. In such a case, we might want to specify that only when both the actor action (acknowledgment and measurement) and the clipper pattern (low blood pressure) are satisfied, the alert is deactivated.

3.3.2 The Refractory Period

In continuous monitoring, for example of Blood pressure and heart rate in an intensive care unit, when alerts are triggered by the existence of some temporal pattern, the same alert (e.g., "5 consecutive measurements of heart rate above 180") might be activated each minute (or even each second), as new measurements arrive. To avoid the overloading of the users by consecutive instances of the same alert, we introduce the refractory period.

The refractory period is the minimal time period from the activation of an alert instance, until another instance of an alert of the same class is allowed to be activated (even if the pattern triggering the alert has been detected again, perhaps even continuously).

<refractory-period-expression> ≡ *(refractory period, cardinality, refresh time)*, where

- *refractory period* is the minimal waiting time period for activation of the new instance of the same alert.
- *cardinality* k limits the monitoring engine to sending up to k different instances of the same alert type, within a certain overall *"refresh time"* period p. That is, we can send up to k different instances of alerts of the same type within the period $<0, p>$. the reference time 0 is initialized when the triggering pattern activating the first alert of the k alerts was detected. Note that this is a dynamic global constraint, which ensures that the rate of sending alerts is never more than k/p. The default is $k = 1$, which limits the alerting mechanism to the sending an alert only when the triggering pattern is first detected, whatever the refresh time is, and no more.

4   Implementation of iALARM Alerts

4.1   Specification of the Alerts Using a Knowledge-Acquisition Tool

Figure 3 shows an example of an iALARM alert specification, using the Gesher knowledge-acquisition tool [12], in this case, in the Atrial Fibrillation (AF) (a type of cardiac arrhythmia) domain.   In addition to the support for the specification of procedural knowledge, Gesher enables a user to define a declarative *knowledge map* that specifies complex patterns and their properties. The alert's intent is to notify a patient, who is remotely monitored through bodily sensors and a mobile device (and also notify her physician), when the second episode of Atrial Fibrillation occurs, even in the case of taking a pill after a first episode of Atrial Fibrillation.   In other words, there might be a sequence of AF -> Pill taken -> AF, where the AF pattern is defined by a set of time and value constraints on the Heart Rate measurement.

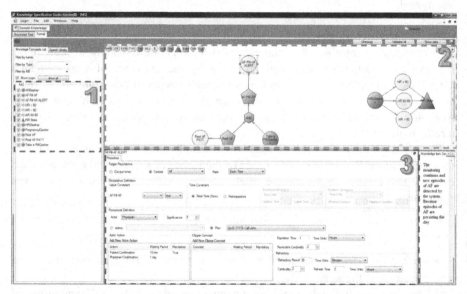

Fig. 3. The Gesher interface for specification of alerts. The list of concepts in the declarative knowledge base is denoted by the label "1". The Gesher knowledge map (denoted by the label "2") shows the concepts and their inter-relations; thus the "AF-Pill-AF" Alert (selected) is derived from the "AF-Pill-AF" pattern. The lower Panel (denoted by the label "3") shows the properties of the alert, as explained in the text.

4.2   Enhancing the Monitoring Engine to Support iALARM Alerts

Figure 4 shows the architecture, which includes the previously explained bottom tier of external components, such as the TA mediator, and the core intelligent monitoring engine. The TA mediator computes the derived TAs as new data arrives, using the domain-specific TA knowledge base [11]. The Monitoring Engine checks the triggered TAs according to a list of subscribed alerts. When the triggered pattern

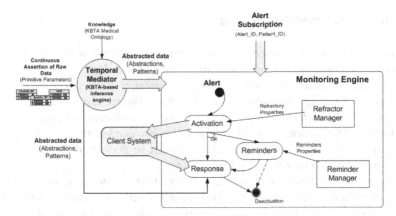

Fig. 4. The current design of the iALARM monitoring engine

matches the computed TA, an alert is activated according to the meta-properties, in particular, the refractory properties. If activation is successful, the Client System is notified about the alert. Based on the user action provided by the Client System or on the clipper pattern computed by the Temporal Mediator, the alert is deactivated; otherwise the reminders are applied according to the reminding properties. If after several reminders there was no appropriate response to the alert, the alert is deactivated in an unexpected (failed) manner, denoted by the dashed arrow.

By separating the knowledge-based TA computation and the [meta] monitoring tasks, we are exploiting the benefits and future enhancements in both methodologies.

The need for the use of sophisticated mechanisms such as shown in Figure 4, for clinical monitoring, to support the continuous triggering of alerts while adhering to the reminders' constraints and the refractory-period definition, can be demonstrated by following example.

In data-intensive domains such as the AF domain, in which vital signs (such as Heart Rate) are measured at least each minute or even each second, and when patients are remotely monitored, we might need to monitor for a pattern such as AF->Take-a-Pill-Recommendation->AF (i.e., an additional episode of AF in spite of our recommendation to the patient to take a pre-prescribed pill after the detection of the first episode). Detection of an additional AF episode might then trigger another alarm and another recommendation to the patient. However, the monitoring engine should trigger the alert according to the relevant reminders (i.e., perhaps we are still waiting for a response to the first reminder) or according to the refractory period constraint (i.e., we might already have reached the maximal number of different instances of the same alert type, within the "refresh time" period). Such considerations are extremely important, to ensure patient compliance as well as reduce risk of over medication.

We have designed the monitoring engine as discussed, and we are currently implementing it.

5   Summary and Discussion

Hudson [33] defined the process of monitoring of patients as the *"Repeated or continuous observations or measurements of the patient, his or her physiological function, and the function of life support equipment, for the purpose of guiding management decisions, including when to make therapeutic interventions, and assessment of those interventions"*. There are two main objectives in that definition: (1) detection of the patient's clinical conditions, whose combination triggers the alert, and (2) application of the clinical actions that must be performed, at the right time, while monitoring also the results of these actions.

In this study, we represented the iALARM two-tiered intelligent monitoring and alerting architecture and the iALARM language's schema, which together fulfill Hudson's objectives. Moreover, to avoid the cognitive overload of alert fatigue, caused by overloading the user, we added special *meta-assertions* to the procedural aspect of the alert's definition, such as the refractory period.

In addition, the user is able to apply the alert to whole population groups, whose members are either pre-specified or are dynamically (periodically) computed and updated according to an appropriate contextual definition, i.e., a combination of the patient's demographic features and of the knowledge-based time-oriented patterns in their historical record.

Based on the underlying architecture, we have introduced a novel view of a complete *life cycle* for alerts. The philosophy represented by this lifecycle underlies the iALARM language and its various meta-properties.

Obviously, we need to evaluate a complete implementation of the iALARM architecture to assess its value. We intend to evaluate the iALARM schema and the monitoring engine developed accordantly to this schema in the gestational diabetes and cardiac arrhythmia domains. The evaluation will be carried out in the context of the MobiGuide project [34] whose aim is to monitor chronic patients using body sensors and the patient's mobile device, and to provide guideline-based decision-support to the patients and to their care providers.

Acknowledgments. This research was supported by the European Commission under the 7th Framework Program, as part of the MobiGuide project (Award FP7-287811).

References

[1] vom Brocke, J., Rosemann, M.: Handbook on Business Process Management-I:Introduction, Methods, and Information Systems. International Handbooks on Information Systems. Springer (2010)

[2] Curtis, D.W., Pino, E.J., Bailey, J.M., Shih, E.I., Waterman, J., Vinterbo, S.A., Stair, T.O., Guttag, J.V., Greenes, R.A., Ohno-Machado, L.: SMART–an integrated wireless system for monitoring unattended patients. J. Am. Med. Inform. Assoc. 15(1), 44–53 (2008)

[3] Chipara, O., Brooks, C., Bhattacharya, S., Lu, C., Chamberlain, R., Roman, G.-C., Bailey, T.C.: Reliable real-time clinical monitoring using sensor network technology. In: Proceedings of AMIA (2009)

[4] 2013 Best Medical Alert Service Comparisons and Reviews, http://medical-alert-systems-review.toptenreviews.com/

[5] Kowalczyk, L.: Patient alarms often unheard, unheeded. The Boston Globe (February 13, 2011), http://www.boston.com/lifestyle/health/articles/2011/02/13/patient_alarms_often_unheard_unheeded/

[6] Centers for Disease Control (CDC) and Prevention. National Healthcare Safety Network. Guidelines and procedures for monitoring VAP (March 2009), http://www.cdc.gov/nhsn/PDFs/pscManual/6pscVAPcurrent.pdf

[7] Rooney, Z., Nadel, S.: Optimizing intensive care management in paediatric sepsis. Curr. Opin. Infect. Dis. 22(3), 264–271 (2009)

[8] Mora, F., Passarielllo, G., Carrault, G., Le Pichon, J.P.: Intelligent patient monitoring and Management Systems: A review. IEEE Eng. Med., Biol. Mag. 12, 23–33 (1993)

[9] Shahar, Y.: A framework for knowledge-based temporal abstraction. Artificial Intelligence 90(1-2), 79–133 (1997)

[10] Boaz, D., Shahar, Y.: A distributed temporal-abstraction mediation architecture for medical databases. Artificial Intelligence in Medicine 34(1), 3–24 (2005)

[11] Spokoiny, A., Shahar, Y.: An active database architecture for knowledge-based incremental abstraction of complex concepts from continuously arriving time-oriented raw data. Journal of Intelligent Information Systems 28(3), 199–231 (2007)

[12] Hatsek, A., Shahar, Y., Taieb-Maimon, M., Shalom, E., Klimov, D., Lunenfeld, E.: A scalable architecture for incremental specification and maintenance of procedural decision-support knowledge. The Open Medical Informatics Journal 4, 255–277 (2010)

[13] Stacey, M., Mcgregor, C.: Temporal abstraction in intelligent clinical data analysis: A survey. Artificial Intelligence in Medicine 39, 1–24 (2007)

[14] Shahar, Y., Musen, M.A.: Knowledge-based temporal abstraction in clinical domains. Artificial Intelligence in Medicine 8(3), 267–298 (1996)

[15] Silvent, A.-S., Dojat, M., Garbay, C.: Multi-level temporal abstraction for medical scenario construction. Int. J. Adapt. Control 19, 377–394 (2005)

[16] Miksch, S., Horn, W., Popow, C., Paky, F.: Utilizing temporal data abstraction for data validation and therapy planning for artificially ventilated newborn infants. Artif. Intell. Med. 8, 543–576 (1996)

[17] Combi, C., Chittaro, L.: Abstraction on clinical data sequences: an object-oriented data model and a query language based on the event calculus. Art. Intell. Med. 17, 271–301 (1999)

[18] Etzion, O.: Temporal Perspectives in Event Processing. Principles and Applications of Distributed Event-Based Systems, pp. 75–89 (2010)

[19] Rete, F.C.: A Fast Algorithm for the Many Pattern/Many Object Pattern Match Problem. Artificial Intelligence 19, 17–37 (1982)

[20] Alferes, J., Banti, F., Brogi, A.: An event-condition-action logic programming language. In: Proc. of the 10th European Conference on Logics in Artificial Intelligence, UK (2006)

[21] Dube, K., Wu, B., Grimson, J.B.: Using ECA Rules in Database Systems to Support Clinical Protocols. In: Hameurlain, A., Cicchetti, R., Traunmüller, R. (eds.) DEXA 2002. LNCS, vol. 2453, pp. 226–235. Springer, Heidelberg (2002)

[22] Greiner, U., Ramsch, J., Heller, B., Löffler, M., Müller, R., Rahm, E.: Adaptive Guideline-based Treatment Workflows with AdaptFlow. In: Kaiser, K., Miksch, S., Tu, S.W. (eds.) Proceedings of the Symposium on Computerized Guidelines and Protocols (CGP 2004), Computer-Based Support for Clinical Guidelines and Protocols, pp. 113–117. IOS Press (2004)

[23] Mansour, E., Wu, B., Dube, K., Li, J.: An Event-Driven Approach to Computerizing Clinical Guidelines Using XML. In: Proceedings of the IEEE Services Computing Workshops, September 18-22, pp. 13–20 (2006)

[24] Mouttham, A., Peyton, L., Eze, B., Saddik, A.: Event-Driven Data Integration for Personal Health Monitoring. Journal of Emerging Technologies in Web Intelligence 1 (2009)

[25] Kuperman, G.J., Bobb, A., Payne, T.H., et al.: Medication-related clinical decision support in computerized provider order entry systems: A review. J. Am. Med. Inform. Assoc. 14(1), 29–40 (2007)

[26] McCoy, A.B., Waitman, L.R., Lewis, J.B., Wright, J.A., Choma, D.P., Miller, R.A., et al.: A framework for evaluating the appropriateness of clinical decision support alerts and responses. JAMIA (2011)

[27] Schedlebauer, A., Prasad, V., Mulvaney, C., Phansalkar, S., Stanton, W., Bates, D.W., Avery, A.J.: What evidence supports the use of computerized alerts and prompts to improve clinicians' prescribing behavior? JAMIA 13, 531–538 (2009)

[28] Lee, E.K., Mejia, A.F., Senior, T., et al.: Improving patient safety through medical alert management: an automated decision tool to reduce alert fatigue. In: AMIA Annu. Symp. Proc., pp. 417–421 (2010)

[29] Chakravarty, S., Shahar, Y.: A constraint-based specification of periodic patterns in time-oriented data. Annals of Mathematics and Artificial Intelligence 30(1-4) (2000)

[30] Chakravarty, S., Shahar, Y.: Specification and detection of periodicity in clinical data. Methods of Information in Medicine 40(5), 296–306 (2001); Reprinted in: Haux, R., and Kulikowski, C. (eds.): Yearbook of Medical Informatics 2003, pp. 296–306. F.K. Schattauer and The International Medical Informatics Association, Stuttgart (2001)

[31] Shahar, Y., Young, O., Shalom, E., Mayaffit, A., Moskovitch, R., Hessing, A., Galperin, M.: A hybrid, multiple-ontology framework for specification and retrieval of clinical guidelines. The Journal of Biomedical Informatics 37(5), 325–344 (2004)

[32] Shalom, E., Fridman, I., Shahar, Y., Hatsek, A., Lunenfeld, E.: Towards a realistic clinical-guidelines application framework: Desiderata, Applications, and lessons learned. In: Lenz, R., Miksch, S., Peleg, M., Reichert, M., Riaño, D., ten Teije, A. (eds.) ProHealth 2012 and KR4HC 2012. LNCS, vol. 7738, pp. 56–70. Springer, Heidelberg (2013)

[33] Hudson, D.: Design of the intensive care unit from a monitoring point of view. Respir Care V 30, 549–559 (1985)

[34] MobiGuide: Guiding patients anytime everywhere, http://www.mobiguide-project.eu/

GLM-CDS: A Standards-Based Verifiable Guideline Model for Decision Support in Clinical Applications

Marco Iannaccone, Massimo Esposito, and Giuseppe De Pietro

National Research Council of Italy - Institute for High Performance
Computing and Networking (ICAR), Naples, Italy
{iannaccone.m,esposito.m,depietro.g}@na.icar.cnr.it

Abstract. In the last years, many parties have been engaged in developing models for encoding clinical practice guidelines in a computer-interpretable form. Despite the attempts involved to specify and adopt a single, common model, to date, there is no de facto standard solution. Moreover, the effort in defining new models has not been coupled by a parallel effort in supporting a seamless integration with the clinical workflow and existing health information systems. In such a direction, this paper proposes a standards-based verifiable guideline model, named GLM-CDS (GuideLine Model for Clinical Decision Support), whose main features can be summarized in the following points: i) its control-flow model is a formal Task-Network Model devised to represent guidelines on multiple levels of abstraction by focusing only on issues pertaining the clinical decision support; ii) its information model is expressly built on the top of the simplified patient information model standardized as HL7 Virtual Medical Record for Clinical Decision Support; iii) its terminological model is essentially constructed on the top of standard medical terminologies; iv) its computer-interpretable encoding is built in terms of both a formal, semantically well-defined and verifiable ontology for describing control-flow and information models, and a logical rule formalism for specifying decision criteria.

Keywords: Clinical Practice Guidelines, Decision Support Systems, Workflow Management, Ontology.

1 Introduction

Clinical Practice Guidelines (hereafter, CPGs) are systematically developed statements aimed at supporting general practitioners in making clinical decisions and managing medical actions about appropriate healthcare for specific clinical circumstances [1]. CPGs typically capture both literature-based and practice-based evidence in a paper-based format. Their adoption is advocated to represent an important step for improving the quality of care for the patients, minimizing the variance in the care, cutting down costs of medical services, and standardizing clinical procedures [1,2].

However, even if, during the last decade, a variety of CPGs has been developed, focusing on different application domains and modality of usage, their actual potential in improving health outcomes is yet to be realized [3]. Indeed, unfortunately, the

D. Riaño et al. (Eds.): KR4HC 2013/ProHealth 2013, LNAI 8268, pp. 143–157, 2013.

dissemination of CPGs as educational paper-based documents is revealed as not effective in improving the general practitioners' behaviour [3]. As a consequence of that, implementing CPGs in computer-based decision support systems (hereafter, DSSs) is crucial for improving adherence over paper-based guidelines and, thus, for facilitating their broad acceptance and application in daily practice [4]. Indeed, these systems could be proficiently used to monitor actions and observations of care providers and, contextually, provide patient-specific advice at the point of care [4,5].

In the last years, many parties have been engaged in developing formalisms based on Task-Network Models (hereafter, TNMs) for marking up or encoding CPGs in the form of computer-interpretable guidelines (hereafter, CIGs) for DSSs. Even if these formalisms have in common a process-flow-like model that decomposes CPGs into a network of tasks that unfold over time, they differ from each other in their approaches to addressing particular modeling challenges [6]. This is an important drawback because there is any de facto standard formalism, so as to prevent the development of tools in the same way [7]. Moreover, the effort in defining new TNMs for encoding CPGs has not been coupled by a parallel effort in defining a systematic approach for embedding medical concepts and data items used in electronic health records (hereafter, EHRs) directly within a CIG and, thus, for enabling a seamless integration with the clinical workflow and existing health information systems in order to facilitate the automatic provision of advice at the time and place where decisions are made [8].

On the one hand, such an integration could favourite the sharing of CIGs built by exploiting generic clinical concepts and patient data items instead of using institution-specific data models and codes. On the other hand, it could save clinicians from entering patient data already existing in EHRs, thus reducing data-entry errors [9]. However, this integration is usually achieved by means of knowledge-data mappings, where high-level concepts are linked to low-level data. For this reason, it is a long and complicated process, where the largest barrier consists in the variety with which similar data are represented in heterogeneous EHRs [9].

Summarizing, in order to face these open problems, this paper proposes a standards-based verifiable guideline model, named GLM-CDS (hereafter, GuideLine Model for Clinical Decision Support), whose main features can be summarized in the following points: i) its control-flow model, devised as a formal TNM able to represent CPGs on multiple levels of abstraction, synthesizes prior work done in the guideline modeling community and integrates the model standardized as Health Level 7 Virtual Medical Record for Clinical Decision Support (hereafter, HL7 vMR)[10], by focusing only on issues pertaining the clinical decision support; ii) its information model is expressly built on the top of the HL7 vMR, i.e. it embeds and, in some cases, extends information model and data types of the HL7 vMR in order to create only one mapping to different EHRs by directly describing data about the patient's clinical history as well as care interventions and recommendations; iii) its terminological model is essentially constructed on the top of standard medical terminologies; iv) its computer-interpretable encoding is built in terms of both a formal, semantically well-defined and verifiable ontology for describing control-flow and information models, and a logical rule formalism for specifying decision criteria.

The rest of the paper is organised as follows. Section 2 outlines an overview of the state-of-the-art solutions existing in literature. In Section 3, the formulation of the proposed model is described. Section 4 depicts an example application of the proposed model to an existing guideline. Finally, Section 5 concludes the work.

2 Related Work

In the last decades, the Health Level 7 Clinical Decision Support and Arden Syntax Work Groups have worked to specify and adopt a single, common CIG language, i.e. the Arden Syntax, but this attempt to date has been unsuccessful [7]. Indeed, the Arden Syntax has been essentially devised to encode machine-executable clinical rules and, thus, it has been considered as not adequate to model temporal and control-flow patterns existing in CPGs due to authoring and maintenance difficulties.

Recent efforts, such as SAGE [11], GLIF [12], Asbru [13], EON [14] and PROforma [15], have sought to address this issue by proposing process-flow-like models for representing CPGs. However, despite the similarities about a common set of control-flow patterns, none of these approaches, designed with a different coverage and particularities, has been to date recognized as a de facto standard formalism by the guideline modeling community. One critical point to be tackled in order to favourite the broad adoption of a guideline model for clinical use is how to conceptualize CIGs, i.e. how to explicitly define concepts and data that are used in a CIG, such as patient demographics, results of laboratory tests, prescriptions of drugs, so that they can be mapped to EHR entries in clinical information systems.

Several solutions have been proposed to face this issue. One of the first approaches has been proposed in [16], consisting in the definition of a shared schema of EHR, referred to as Virtual Medical Record (hereafter, vMR), which is devised to specify a broad set of classes of information to be integrated in a CIG. This solution consists in creating mappings from a vMR to actual EHR systems. Conversely, concepts and data that are used in a CIG are encoded against the vMR, and at execution time, their references in the vMR are resolved to entries in physical EHRs. A drawback of this approach, similarly proposed also in SAGE and EON languages, relies on the usage of a proprietary simplified information model, partially defined and not yet standardized.

In order to face this lack of standardization, the KDOM framework [9] proposes a vMR model based on a simplified version of the HL7 Reference Information Model [17] (hereafter, HL7 RIM) as the basis for developing a standard interface to EHR systems. It allows specifying CIGs using clinical abstractions, which are mapped to different EHRs by means of the proposed vMR model, adopted as common data model. However, the use of HL7 RIM is not properly adequate to this goal since it entails much more complexity than is required or desirable for a CIG language.

Only recently, a project has begun within the HL7 Clinical Decision Support Work Group (hereafter, CDS-WG) to establish a standard for the vMR [10]. This standard, named HL7 vMR, is a simplified patient information model for describing data coming from health information systems and recommendations to be delivered to clinicians [10]. It attempts to build a shared information model for EHR systems and clinical DSSs in order to support a portable mapping of patient data references used in guidelines to EHRs. Some approaches have been described in literature [18,19], which use the HL7 vMR model to map knowledge in CIGs to patient data encoded in EHR systems. The approach proposed in [18] is devised to facilitate both the integration of patient data with a guideline-based clinical DSS and the representation of the DSS outcome. It consists in combining openEHR archetypes and the HL7 vMR standard, supported by a service-oriented framework for data exchange. The solution proposed in [19] is aimed at realizing a service-oriented architecture for integrating a clinical DSS with the HL7 vMR standard, used as common information model.

Summarizing, in guideline modelling community a range of approaches and solutions has been addressed for integrating CIGs with EHRs systems, but, to the best of our knowledge, none of them is concerned with directly embedding the HL7 vMR standard as the basis of a CIG formalism. The guideline model here proposed has been conceived and developed in this direction, as described in the following sections.

3   The GuideLine Model for Clinical Decision Support

GLM-CDS synthesizes prior work done in the guideline modeling community and integrates the Domain Analysis Model, Release 1 of the HL7 vMR standard (hereafter, HL7 vMR-DAM) issued by HL7 CDS-WG, by focusing on issues pertaining the clinical decision support. It consists of a control-flow part, which is based on a formal TNM for representing CPGs on multiple levels of abstraction, in terms of structured tasks, representing clinical actions and decisions, connected with transition dependencies between them from an initial state of the patient. Moreover, its information model in terms of guideline knowledge is coded coherently with the HL7 vMR-DAM.

The GLM-CDS is object-oriented and has been formally defined in form of ontology. An ontology relies on a well-defined semantics grounded in Description Logics, based on the notion of concepts (unary predicates, classes), individuals (instances of concepts), abstract roles (binary predicates between concepts) and concrete roles (binary predicates between concepts and data values). The choice of using an ontology is due to the possibility of defining both the structure and semantics of the whole model, not only in terms of its basic elements and relationships between them, but also by specifying a set of modeling primitives, such as axioms and constraints, for granting well-formed and semantically correct CIGs.

In the following, data types are preliminary introduced, and, next, concepts, roles and formal axioms defined for all the elements constituting the CIG are reported. Finally, the standard terminologies supported are indicated.

3.1   Data Types

Data types used in GLM-CDS resemble the ones defined in the HL7 vMR DAM, which gives a simplified/constrained version of ISO 21090 data types, based on the abstract HL7 version 3 data types specification, release 2 [17]. A synthetic outline of the main data types used is reported in Table 1. For major details, please refer to [10].

Table 1. The main data types used in GLM-CDS

Data type	Definition
INT	Integer numbers
PQ	A dimensioned quantity expressing the result of a measurement
REAL	Fractional numbers
RTO	A quantity constructed as the quotient of a numerator divided by a denominator
TS	A quantity specifying a point in time
IVL_XX	An interval of INT or PQ or REAL or RTO or TS
CD	Reference to a concept defined in an external code system, terminology, or ontology
ST	Text data
ANY	Abstract data type specialized in the other concrete ones
BL	Boolean values

3.2 Guideline, EntryPoint, ExitPoint and Task

Each guideline TNM is described in terms of four main concepts: *Guideline, EntryPoint, ExitPoint,* and *Task* as depicted in the UML class diagram in Figure 1.

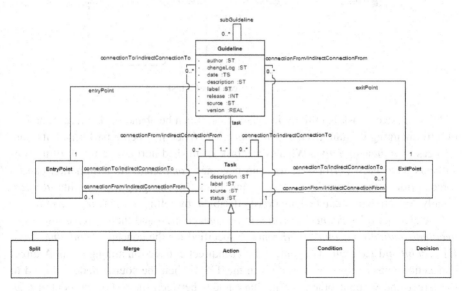

Fig. 1. The concepts *Guideline, EntryPoint, ExitPoint, Task* arranged as UML class diagram

In more detail, each (sub)guideline is represented by the concept *Guideline*, whose individuals are the actual CIGs. This concept is defined in terms of a number of concrete roles for expressing descriptive information, such as textual *label, description* and *source*, and versioning information. It is also connected with the other concepts *EntryPoint, ExitPoint, Guideline* and *Task* by means of the abstract roles *entryPoint, exitPoint, subguideline* and *task,* in order to enable the creation of a collection of tasks or sub-guidelines linked together in a TNM. Each *Guideline* must be characterized by a *label* and made by exactly one *EntryPoint,* one *ExitPoint* and at least one *Task*.

The concepts *EntryPoint* and *ExitPoint* represent start and end points of a TNM representing a guideline. They are mutually exclusive in sense that an individual of *EntryPoint* cannot be simultaneously also an individual of *ExitPoint*.

The concept *Task* is generic and specialized into the following sub-concepts: *Condition, Action, Decision, Split* and *Merge*. It is defined in terms of a number of concrete roles for expressing descriptive information, such as textual *label, description* and *source*, and an abstract role, named *status,* for specifying a number of states a task can assume. For each *Task*, *label* and *status* are mandatory roles. The possible values the role *status* can assume are *new, active, cancelled, aborted, suspended* and *completed*. They resemble codes representing the states of an *Act* as defined in the HL7 v3 RIM. The lifecycle of a task is shown in Figure 2.

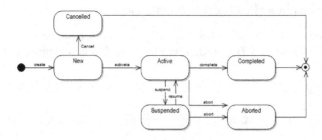

Fig. 2. The lifecycle of a task

In detail, every task is initially in a *new* state. It can be abandoned before its activation by changing its state from *new* to *cancelled*. When it is being performed, its state changes from *new* to *active*. Whenever a task is finished normally after all of its constituents have been performed, its state becomes *completed*. Its termination can be forced prior to the originally intended completion, by changing its state into *aborted*. Finally, an active task can be temporarily disabled, by setting its state as *suspended*.

The abstract roles *connectionTo/indirectConnectionTo* and their inverse roles *connectionFrom/indirectConnectionFrom* are specified for the concepts *Guideline, Task, EntryPoint* and *ExitPoint* to enable a direct/indirect connection among them. A direct connection exists between two nodes in the TNM when the source node is linked to the target one without other intermediary nodes between them. On the contrary, an indirect connection exists between two nodes when the target node is reachable from the source one through a path of links connecting other intermediary nodes.

It is worth noting that each *EntryPoint* and *ExitPoint* are admissible to have a direct connection only to and from a *Task* or *Guideline,* respectively, so avoiding the possibility of creating empty guidelines. The concepts *Guideline, EntryPoint, Exit-Point* and *Task* are building blocks of the final TNM and, for this reason, are defined by means of ontology axioms and restrictions as shown in Table 2.

Table 2. Ontology axioms for the concepts *Guideline, EntryPoint, ExitPoint* and *Task*

Concept	Axioms
EntryPoint	*EntryPoint* ≡ ¬ (*ExitPoint* ⊔ *Task*) ⊓ ¬(∃*connectionTo. ExitPoint*) ⊓≥1*connectionTo.*(*Task* ⊔ *Guideline*) ⊓ ≤1*connectionTo.*(*Task* ⊔ *Guideline*) ⊓ ¬ (∃*connectionFrom.*⊤)
ExitPoint	*ExitPoint* ≡ ¬ (*EntryPoint* ⊔ *Task*) ⊓ ¬ (∃*connectionFrom.EntryPoint*) ⊓ ≥1 *connection-From.*(*Task* ⊔ *Guideline*) ⊓ ≤1 *connectionFrom.*(*Task* ⊔ *Guideline*) ⊓ ¬ (∃*connectionTo.*⊤)
Task	*Task* ≡ ¬ (*EntryPoint* ⊔ *ExitPoint*) ⊓ ≥1 *connectionTo.*⊤ ⊓ ≤1 *connectionTo. ExitPoint* ⊓ ≥1 *connectionFrom.*⊤ ⊓ ≤1 *connectionFrom.EntryPoint* ⊓ ≥1 *status* ⊓ ≤1 *status* ⊓ ≥1 *label* ⊓ ≤1 *label*
Guideline	*Guideline* ⊑ ≥1 *entryPoint* ⊓ ≤1 *entryPoint* ⊓ ≥1 *exitPoint* ⊓ ≤1 *exitPoint* ⊓ ≥1 *task* ⊓ ≥1 *label* ⊓ ≤1 *label*

3.3   Action: Observation, Supply, Encounter, Procedure and SubstanceAdministration

The first sub-concept of *Task* here described is the concept *Action*. It is generic and models a high-level action to be performed, which encapsulates a list of one or more elementary action items expressed in terms of the HL7 vMR-DAM. In other words, each action can generate one or more action items, coded coherently with the HL7 vMR-DAM, which are sent to external health systems for their execution and the retrieval of expected results. The resulting piece of model is shown in Figure 3.

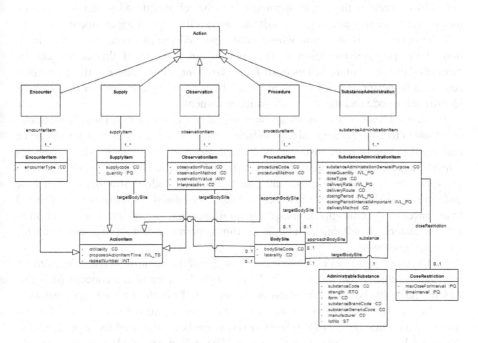

Fig. 3. Concepts and roles for encoding actions

In detail, the concept *Action* is specialized into the concepts *Observation, Supply, Encounter, Procedure* and *SubstanceAdministration,* and inherits abstract and concrete roles defined for its super-concept *Task.* These sub-concepts are associated to ad-hoc action items, modeled with the concepts *ObservationItem, SupplyItem, EncounterItem, ProcedureItem* and *SubstanceAdministrationItem,* which are specialization of the generic concept *ActionItem.* Among the concrete roles defined for *ActionItem,* the role *repeatNumber* is mostly relevant since it allows the iteration of an action item for a specific number of times.

In more detail, *Observation* is an action aimed at determining a measurement, a laboratory test or a user input value. An instance of this action can be associated to one or more instances of *ObservationItem,* which represents the single observation of a specific object and is typified by a set of concrete roles indicating its focus, the approach for its enactment, the observed value and its explanation.

Supply is an action whose aim is to provide some clinical material or equipment to the patient. An instance of this action can be linked to one or more instances of *SupplyItem,* which indicates the single supply to be delivered and is typified by concrete roles to express the code identifying the material to supply and its amount.

Encounter models an action aimed at requesting an appointment between a patient and healthcare participants for providing patient services or assessing his health status. An instance of this action can be linked to one or more instances of *EncounterItem,* which specifies the single appointment to be scheduled and is characterized by the concrete role *encounterType* to indicate the specific type of appointment.

Procedure models an action whose immediate and primary outcome is the alteration of the physical condition of the subject. An instance of this action can be associated to one or more instances of *ProcedureItem,* which indicates the single procedure to be performed and is characterized by a set of concrete roles expressing its identification code and the approach for its enactment

SubstanceAdministration is an action whose aim is to give a material of a particular constitution to a patient for enabling a clinical effect. An instance of this action can be connected to one or more instances of *SubstanceAdministrationItem,* which indicates a single request of a substance administration and is typified by a set of concrete roles to express, for instance, purpose, rate and frequency of administration, type of dose and amount of substance. An instance of *SubstanceAdministrationItem* is also linked to instances of the concepts *AdministrableSubstance* and *DoseRestriction,* which indicate the material to administer and the maximum permissible dose in a specified time interval, respectively.

Furthermore, instances of *ObservationItem, SupplyItem, SubstanceAdministrationItem* and *ProcedureItem* are associated to a single instance of the concept *BodySite,* which models the body site involved in the action to be performed, whereas instances of *SubstanceAdministrationItem* and *ProcedureItem* are also linked to another instance of the same concept *BodySite* to express the body site used for approaching to the target body site involved in the action. The definitions of *Observation, Supply, Encounter, Procedure* and *SubstanceAdministration,* which are further building blocks of the TNM, are formally shown in Table 3.

Table 3. Ontology axioms for the concept *Action* and its sub-concepts

Name	Axioms
Action	*Action* ≡ *Task* ⊓ ¬ (*Decision* ⊔ *Condition* ⊔ *Split* ⊔ *Merge*)
Encounter	*Encounter* ⊑ *Action* ⊓ ≥1 *encounterItem.EncounterItem*
Procedure	*Procedure* ⊑ *Action* ⊓ ≥1 *procedureItem.ProcedureItem*
Supply	*Supply* ⊑ *Action* ⊓ ≥1 *supplyItem.SupplyItem*
Observation	*Observation* ⊑ *Action* ⊓ ≥1 *observationItem. ObservationItem*
Substance Administration	*SubstanceAdministration* ⊑ *Action* ⊓ ≥1 *substanceAdministrationItem. SubstanceAdministrationItem*

3.4   Condition, Split and Merge

The concept *Condition* is defined as an observable state of the patient that persists over time and tends to require intervention or management. Such a definition is coherent with the one given in HL7 RIM for the class *ActCondition*. This concept allows synchronizing the management of a patient with the corresponding guideline or parts of it and can be used after an *EntryPoint* or a *Decision* in a guideline. It is modelled by means of the set of concepts and roles shown in Figure 4.

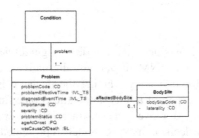

Fig. 4. Concepts and roles for encoding conditions

An instance of *Condition* is associated to one or more instances of the concept *Problem,* which indicates a single clinical concern affecting the patient that needs to be treated. A set of concrete roles is defined to express, for instance, the code identifying the problem, the time when a patient experienced the problem and when a clinician assessed its presence, the body site affected, its importance, severity and status.

The concepts *Split* and *Merge* enables to direct the guideline flow to multiple parallel tasks. In particular, the concept *Split* allows branching to multiple tasks, whereas the concept *Merge* allows synchronizing parallel tasks by making them converging into a single point. Instances of *Split* and *Merge* can have a direct connection only to/from an instance of *Task*, and each set of parallel tasks must start and terminate with exactly one instance of *Split* and *Merge*. These constraints, which must be granted also in the case of nested sequences of parallel tasks, require the navigability of the TNM in order to explicitly recognize the number of sequences of parallel tasks starting from one instance of *Split* or terminating into an instance of *Merge*. This navigability has been realized by means of a set of rules built on the top of ontology concepts and roles according to the abstract syntax described in the next-subsection.

Table 4. Ontology axioms and rules for the concepts *Condition*, *Split* and *Merge*

Concept	Axioms and Rules
Condition	*Condition* ⊑ *Task* ⊓ ¬ (*Decision* ⊔ *Split* ⊔ *Action* ⊔ *Merge*) ⊓ ≥1 *problem.Problem* ⊓ ≥1 *connectionFrom.(Decision* ⊔ *EntryPoint)* ⊓ ≤1 *connectionFrom.(Decision* ⊔ *EntryPoint)*
Split	*Split* ≡ *Task* ⊓ ¬ (*Decision* ⊔ *Condition* ⊔ *Action* ⊔ *Merge*) ⊓ ¬ (∃*connectionTo.Merge*) ⊓ ≥1*connectionTo.Task* ⊓ ≥1 *indirectConnectionTo.Merge* ⊓ ≤1 *indirectConnectionTo.Merge* *IF (Split(?x) connectionTo(?x,?y) connectionTo(?y,?z) Merge(?y))* *THEN indirectConnectionTo (?x,?z)* *IF (Split(?x) indirectConnectionTo (?x,?y) connectionTo(?y,?z) Merge(?y))* *THEN indirectConnectionTo (?x,?z)*
Merge	*Merge* ≡ *Task* ⊓ ¬(*Decision*⊔*Condition*⊔*Action*⊔*Split*)⊓ ¬(∃*connectionFrom.Split*) ⊓ ≥1*connectionFrom.Task* ⊓ ≥1*indirectConnectionFrom.Split* ⊓ ≤1*indirectConnectionFrom.Split* *IF (Merge(?x) connectionFrom(?x,?y) connectionFrom(?y,?z) Split(?y))* *THEN indirectConnectionFrom (?x,?z)* *IF (Merge(?x) indirectConnectionFrom (?x,?y) connectionFrom(?y,?z) Split(?y))* *THEN indirectConnectionFrom (?x,?z)*

Ontology axioms related to the concept *Condition*, and axioms and rules associated to the concepts *Split* and *Merge* are formally reported in Table 4.

3.5   Decision

The concept *Decision* models decision criteria in a guideline and directs the control-flow from a point into the TNM to various alternatives. The concrete role *automaticMode* is defined for indicating whether the decision is a proposal requiring a further evaluation of an expert or a fully automatic choice finalized without requiring any further intervention. Moreover, the abstract role *decisionModel* is specified to associate to *Decision* a decision-making model, represented by the generic concept *Decision Model*, aimed at generating preferences among alternatives.

To date, existing languages for encoding decision criteria are either proprietary solutions or based on GELLO [20], which is an expression language recently accepted as a standard by HL7 and ANSI. However, it is widely considered as complex for someone without technical training, and, plus, does not yet have a non-proprietary compiler for its use [7]. Thus, a simpler and more intuitive rule model has been here proposed as decision model It consists in one or more weighted rules in the form "*if antecedent then consequent*", where the weight indicates the strength of each rule. Its antecedent part is made of a conjunction of one or more statements to be verified, whereas its consequent part is made of a conjunction of one or more statements representing the preference to be suggested. Disjunction can be realized via more rules with the same consequent, i.e. with the same preference. Different kinds of statement can be defined and combined conjunctly to build more complex expressions so as to support generality and flexibility: unary and binary predicates, and also their negated forms, to be verified or asserted, built-in statements for coding logical or arithmetical expressions, assessing the current time or verifying presence/absence of an element within a list. Such a model in the form of concepts and roles is reported in Figure 5.

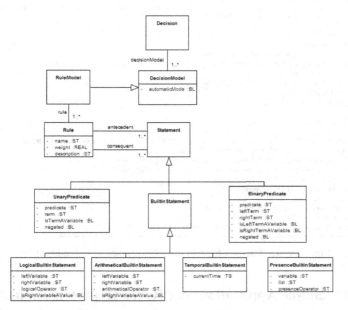

Fig. 5. Concepts and roles for encoding decisions

Unary and binary predicates involved in the rule's statements can be associated to ontology concepts *Action* (including all its sub-concepts), *Condition* and their roles defined in GLM-CDS. This rule model is very simple to be instantiated in terms of a rule language working on the elements of the GLM-CDS. In particular, since the GLM-CDS is encoded in terms of ontology concepts and roles, a hybrid knowledge language as described in [21] can be used, which integrates an ontology language belonging to Description Logic and a rule language belonging to First Order Logic. This enables the possibility of using existing rule engines, which, thanks to a reasoning scheme based on forward chaining, are able to assure the soundness and completeness of the decision-making process. Starting from this model, a more compact abstract syntax is formalized by means of the Extended BNF, as reported in Figure 6.

3.6   Standard Terminologies

Representation of information in GLM-CDS depends on existing standard terminological resources which can be used to populate the concrete roles with appropriate semantic content. The external terminological resources chosen for being utilized in GLM-CDS are Logical Observation Identifiers Names and Codes (hereafter, LOINC) [22] and Systematized NOmenclature of MEDicine (hereafter, SNOMED)[23]. Currently, at the simplest level, the value of a concrete role used in a CIG corresponds exactly to a pre-coordinated term in one of these specific standard terminologies.

```
Rule::= Weight "IF (" Antecedent ") THEN (" Consequent ")" ;
Weight ::= Value;
Antecedent::~ {Statement};
Consequent::= {Statement};
Statement::= UnaryPredicate | BinaryPredicate | BuiltinStatement;
UnaryPredicate::~ Negated UPredicate "(" Term ")";
UPredicate::~ OntologyConcept;
BinaryPredicate::= Negated Bpredicate "(" Term "," Term ")";
BPredicate::= OntologyRole;
Term::~ OntologyIndividual | Variable;
Negated::= not;
Variable::= "?"a | "?"b | ...... "?"z;
Value::= Real Number;
BuiltinStatement ::~ LogicalBuiltinStatement | Arithmetical BuiltinStatement | TemporalBuiltinStatement | PresenceBuiltinStatement;
LogicalBuiltinStatement::= LogicalOperator "(" Variable"," Variable Value")";
LogicalOperator::= equal | notEqual | lessEqual | lessThan | greaterThan | greaterEqual;
ArithmeticalBuiltinStatement::~ ArithmeticalOperator "(" Variable"," Variable|Value")";
ArithmeticalOperator ::= sum | difference | product | quotient;
TemporalBuiltinStatement::= TemporalOperator "(" Variable ")";
TemporalOperator::= now;
PresenceBuiltinStatement::~ PresenceOperator "(" Variable "," List ")";
PresenceOperator ::= isIn| isOut;
List::= {OntologyConcept | OntologyRole  OntologyIndividual };
```

Fig. 6. Abstract syntax for rule model expressed in Extended BNF

4   An Example Application: A CIG for Hypertension in Adults

This section reports, as an example, the application of GLM-CDS to the guideline for the "Clinical management of primary hypertension in adults", issued by the National Institute for Health and Care Excellence (hereafter, NICE) in August 2011. It offers evidence-based advice on the care and treatment of adults with primary hypertension in the National Health Service in England and Wales.

Such a guideline has been encoded according to the GLM-CDS as the TNM reported in Figure 7, containing recommendations on blood pressure measurement, the use of ambulatory/home blood pressure monitoring (hereafter, ABPM/HPBM), the management of hypertension and the antihypertensive drug treatment. For the sake of clarity, this TNM is represented on multiple levels of abstraction, i.e. sub-guidelines are used, for instance, to group lifestyle interventions and antihypertensive drug treatment. However, due to space limitations, their content is not further detailed.

In order to highlight the structure of the underlying data model, for example, the instance of the *Observation* named *"Check clinic blood pressure"* is here considered. This instance, which requires the measurement of systolic/diastolic blood pressure, is thus linked to two individuals of *ObservationItem*, named *SystolicBloodPressure* and *DiastolicBloodPressure*, whose roles *observationFocus* and *observationMethod* are valued according to the data type *CD* of the HL7 vMR-DAM as shown below:

```
ObservationItem: SystolicBloodPressure          ObservationItem: DiastolicBloodPressure
   observationFocus:                                observationFocus:
      code: 198081000000101                            code: 198091000000104
      codeSystemName: SNOMED-CT                         codeSystemName: SNOMED-CT
      displayName: Ambulatory systolic blood pressure   displayName: Ambulatory diastolic blood pressure
   observationMethod:                               observationMethod:
      code: 164783007                                  code: 164783007
      codeSystemName: SNOMED-CT                         codeSystemName: SNOMED-CT
      displayName: Ambulatory blood pressure recording  displayName: Ambulatory blood pressure recording
```

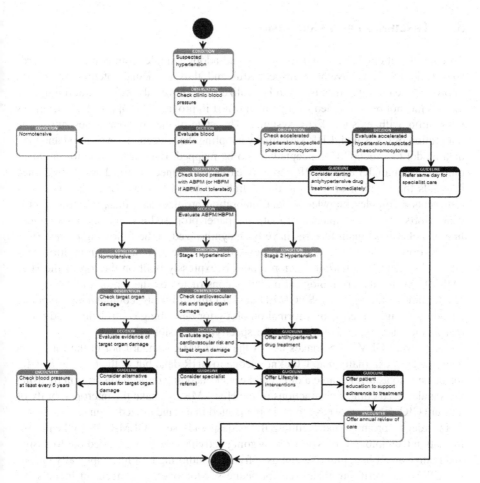

Fig. 7. The NICE guideline for primary hypertension in adults encoded in GLM-CDS

Finally, in order to show the decision model adopted, the instance of the *Decision* named *"Evaluate blood pressure"* is considered. This instance is aimed at evaluating three different situations, described in natural language as follows: i) clinic blood pressure < 140/90 mmHg, ii) 140/90 mmHg ≤ clinic blood pressure < 180/110 mmHg, iii) clinic blood pressure ≥ 180/110 mmHg. For the sake of brevity, only the decision model applied to the first situation is here reported, which assumes the form of one *if-then* rule encoded according to the above-defined syntax as reported below:

```
IF (Observation(?x) ObservationItem(?y1) observationItem(?x,?y1) observationFocus(?y1,?z1)
dysplayName(?z1,' Ambulatory systolic blood pressure') observationValue(?y1,?w1) lessEqual(?w1,140)
ObservationItem(?y2) observationItem(?x,?y2) observationFocus(?y2,?z2)
dysplayName(?z2,' Ambulatory diastolic blood pressure') observationValue(?y2,?w2) lessEqual(?w2,90)
Condition(?a) Problem(?b))
THEN(problem(?a,?b) problemCode(?b,?c) code(?c,' 2004005 ') codeSystemName(?c, 'Snomed-CT')
dysplayName(?c, 'Normal Blood Pressure'))
```

5   Discussion and Conclusions

To date, the attempts involved to specify and adopt a single, common and standard-ized model for CIGs have been unsuccessful, and, thus, the actual potential of CIGs in improving health outcomes is yet to be realized. Moreover, the effort in defining new models has not been coupled by a parallel effort in providing a support for a seamless integration with existing EHR systems. The state-of-the-art approaches allow the integration of CIGs with EHR systems by adopting the concept of vMR as a canonical data model to which CIG concepts have to be mapped. Even if this one-to-one map-ping between a CIG and a vMR certainly eases the connection to EHRs [9,18], since it avoids the creation of multiple direct links among CIGs and EHR data codes, it represents a complex knowledge-data integration problem and, thus, requires signifi-cant efforts. As a consequence of that, this paper proposed a standards-based guide-line model, whose main features have been synthesized in the following points: i) its control-flow model is a formal TNM devised to represent guidelines on multiple lev-els of abstraction; ii) its information model is expressly built on the top of the HL7 vMR-DAM; iii) its terminological model is constructed on the top of standard medi-cal terminologies such as SNOMED and LOINC; iv) its computer-interpretable encoding is built in terms of a formal ontology for describing control-flow and infor-mation models, and a rule formalism for specifying decision criteria.

As a result, GLM-CDS makes use of the HL7 vMR standard not in the form of a data model to externally map CIG knowledge to EHR data, but as the basis of its CIG formalism, so as to: i) enable a direct and easier encoding of decision criteria by using the standardized clinical abstractions of the HL7 vMR, ii) make the interoperability of a future CIG engine very easy to be implemented in a standardized manner.

In order to promote and facilitate the widespread use of GLM-CDS by health in-formation technology professionals, on-going activities are being carried out to design and realize an ad-hoc, intuitive and user-friendly authoring tool for graphically encod-ing CPGs and verifying their well-formedness. Moreover, new decision models are being integrated, such as fuzzy and case-based models. Finally, GLM-CDS will be further enhanced in order to offer more flexibility and adaptiveness and handle situa-tions characterized by exceptions and changes due, for instance, to a worsening of the patient's condition or to new advancements achieved in evidence-based medicine.

References

1. Institute of Medicine, Crossing the Quality Chasm: A New Health System for the 21st Century. National Academy Press, Washington (2001)
2. Field, M.J., Lohr, K.N.: Guidelines for Clinical Practice: From Development to Use. Insti-tute of Medicine, National Academy Press, Washington, DC (1992)
3. Sonnenberg, F.A., Hagerty, C.G.: Computer-interpretable clinical practice guidelines: Where are we and where are we going? In: Kulikowski, C., Haux, R. (eds.) IMIA Year-book of Medical Informatics (2006); Methods Inf. Med. 45(suppl. 1), 145–158 (2006).
4. De Clercq, P., Kaiser, K., Hasman, A.: Computer-Interpretable Guideline formalisms. Stud. Health. Technol. Inform. 139, 22–43 (2008)

5. Minutolo, A., Sannino, G., Esposito, M., De Pietro, G.: A rule-based mHealth system for cardiac monitoring. In: 2010 IEEE EMBS Conference on Biomedical Engineering and Sciences, pp. 144–149 (2010)
6. Mulyar, N., van der Aalst, W.M.P., Peleg, M.: A Pattern-based Analysis of Clinical Computer-interpretable Guideline Modeling Languages. J. Am. Med. Inform. Assoc. 14(6), 781–787 (2007)
7. Isern, D., Moreno, A.: Computer-based execution of clinical guidelines: a review. Int. J. Med. Inform. 77, 787–808 (2008)
8. Tu, S.W., Musen, M.A., Shankar, R., Campbell, J., Hrabak, K., McClay, J., Huff, S.M., McClure, R., Parker, C., Rocha, R., Abarbanel, R., Beard, N., Glasgow, J., Mansfield, G., Ram, P., Ye, Q., Mays, E., Weida, T., Chute, C.G., McDonald, K., Molu, D., Nyman, M.A., Scheitel, S., Solbrig, H., Zill, D.A., Goldstein, M.K.: Modeling guidelines for integration into clinical workflow. Stud. Health Technol. Inform. 107(pt. 1), 174–178 (2004)
9. Peleg, M., Keren, S., Denekamp, Y.: Mapping computerized clinical guidelines to electronic medical records: Knowledge-data ontological mapper (KDOM). Journal of Biomedical Informatics 41(1), 180–201 (2008)
10. Health Level 7. HL7 Virtual Medical Record Project Wiki (vMR),
    http://wiki.hl7.org/index.php?title=
    Virtual_Medical_Record_(vMR)
11. Tu, S.W., Campbell, J.R., Glasgow, J., Nyman, M.A., McClure, R., McClay, J., Parker, C., Hrabak, K.M., Berg, D., Weida, T., Mansfield, J.G., Musen, M.A., Abarbanel, R.M.: The SAGE Guideline Model: Achievements and Overview. J. Am. Med. Inform. Assoc. 14, 589–598 (2007)
12. Boxwala, A.A., Peleg, M., Tu, S., Ogunyemi, O., Zeng, Q.T., Wang, D., Patel, V.L., Greenes, R.A., Shortliffe, E.H.: GLIF3: a representation format for sharable computer-interpretable clinical practice guidelines. J. Biomed. Inform. 37(3), 147–161 (2004)
13. Seyfang, A., Miksch, S., Marcos, M.: Combining diagnosis and treatment using Asbru. Int. J. Med. Informat. 68(1-3), 49–57 (2002)
14. Tu, S.W., Musen, M.A.: Modeling data and knowledge in the EON guideline architecture. Stud. Health. Technol. Inform. 84(pt. 1), 280–284 (2001)
15. Fox, J., Johns, N., Rahmanzadeh, A.: Disseminating medical knowledge: the PROforma approach. Artif. Intell. Med. 14, 157–181 (1998)
16. Johnson, P.D., Tu, S.W., Musen, M.A., Purves, I.: A virtual medical record for guideline-based decision support. In: AMIA Annu. Symp. Proc., pp. 294–298 (2001)
17. Health Level 7. HL7 Reference Information Model, Version 3,
    http://www.hl7.org/implement/standards/rim.cfm
18. González-Ferrer, A., Peleg, M., Verhees, B., Verlinden, J.M., Marcos, C.: Data Integration for Clinical Decision Support Based on openEHR Archetypes and HL7 Virtual Medical Record. In: Process Support and Knowledge Represent. in Health Care, pp. 71–84 (2013)
19. Open Clinical Decision Support Tools and Resources, http://www.opencds.org
20. Health Level 7. HL7 Version 3 Standard: Gello: A Common Expression Language, Release 2, http://wiki.hl7.org/index.php?title=Product_GELLO
21. Colantonio, S., Esposito, M., Martinelli, M., De Pietro, G., Salvetti, O.: A Knowledge Editing Service for Multisource Data Management in Remote Health Monitoring. IEEE Trans. Inf. Technol. Biomed. 16(6), 1096–1104 (2012)
22. Regenstrief Institute, Inc. and the LOINC Committee. Logical Observation Identifiers Names and Codes (LOINC), http://loinc.org/
23. International Health Terminology Standards Development Organisation. Systematized Nomenclature of Medicine (SNOMED), http://www.ihtsdo.org/snomed-ct/

Author Index